History Meets Fiction

History Meets Fiction

BEVERLEY SOUTHGATE

Longman
is an imprint of

Harlow, England • London • New York • Boston • San Francisco • Toronto • Sydney • Singapore • Hong Kong
Tokyo • Seoul • Taipei • New Delhi • Cape Town • Madrid • Mexico City • Amsterdam • Munich • Paris • Milan

Pearson Education Limited

Edinburgh Gate
Harlow CM20 2JE
United Kingdom
Tel: +44 (0)1279 623623
Fax: +44 (0)1279 431059
Website: www.pearsoned.co.uk

First edition published in Great Britain in 2009

© Pearson Education Limited 2009

The right of Beverley Southgate to be identified as author
of this work has been asserted by him in accordance with the
Copyright, Designs and Patents Act 1988.

ISBN: 978-1-4082-2012-2

British Library Cataloguing in Publication Data
A CIP catalogue record for this book can be obtained from the British Library

Library of Congress Cataloging in Publication Data
Southgate, Beverley C.
  History meets fiction / Beverley Southgate. – 1st ed.
    p. cm. – (History: concepts, theories and practice)
  Includes bibliographical references and index.
  ISBN 978-1-4082-2012-2 (pbk.)
  1. Historiography–Philosophy. 2. History–Philosophy. 3. Fiction. I. Title.
  D13.S6234 2009
  907.2—dc22

                                                                2009015912

10 9 8 7 6 5 4 3 2 1
13 12 11 10 09

Set by 35 in 11/13pt Bulmer MT
Printed in Malaysia (CTP-VVP)

The Publisher's policy is to use paper manufactured from sustainable forests.

For Sheila, who makes it all possible, with my love.

Contents

Preface

Some few years ago, my friend the late Dennis Brown lent me a copy of Wyndham Lewis's novel *Self Condemned*. He thought that its representation of a Professor of History, so disaffected with his subject that he felt bound to resign his prestigious position, might be of interest; and so interesting did it in fact prove that I went on to read other works that revealed a similar concern with historical *theory* – a subject that initially seemed an unlikely topic for writers of fiction, but later came to appear as almost obsessive. And one thing that particularly struck me in the course of my reading was that fictional representations of historians, insofar as these were conventional practitioners of their subject, seemed to be almost uniformly negative – often depicted as nothing better than dry-as-dust, boring old pedants. And, as far as their subject was concerned, what emerged overall was an attitude highly critical towards traditional perceptions of both the nature and the assumed purposes of history.

This book, then, is in part a record of my own exploration of territory previously outside my own disciplinary purview – a study that impinges on both history and fiction (and no doubt invites criticism from both specialist camps), but that is, I hope, grounded in my continuing interest in historical theory, or philosophy of history.[1] It deals, as my title indicates, with a number of ways in which *history meets fiction*, and there encounters critiques of itself and of its practitioners, as well as indications of a subject that might be

---

[1] On presenting some preliminary findings to a research seminar at the Institute of Historical Research, London, in 2007, I was reminded by Keith Jenkins of Hayden White's earlier treatment of this subject in his 1966 essay, 'The Burden of History', reprinted in *Tropics of Discourse: Essays in Cultural Criticism*, Baltimore and London, Johns Hopkins, 1978, pp. 27–50. On reading (or re-reading) this, I realised that a part of my theme had indeed been anticipated; but I hope that my own discussion here is rather fuller.

described (in the words of F. H. Bradley) as 'a weary labyrinth of *truth and tangled falsehood*'.[2]

A particular feature here is the use of case studies – or the examination of a number of specific novels at some length – in order to show how writers of fiction have treated issues relating to history and historical theory and have frequently introduced and illustrated these in a helpfully accessible way. I hope that what is thus an essentially cross-disciplinary study will prove of interest to students and readers of both history and literature, as well as those concerned more generally with intellectual and cultural studies.

The relationship between history and fiction has always been contentious and sometimes turbulent, not least because the two have traditionally been seen as mutually exclusive opposites. From the earliest times, historians have defined their subject by direct reference to its absolute distinction from fiction: history is history precisely because it is *not* fiction, but aspires rather to supplant fiction with *fact*. Writers of fiction may make use of historical backgrounds and contexts for their imaginative creations, but they remain outside the pale of proper history: a clear frontier marks them off from what, at least from the nineteenth century, has developed as an autonomous and professional *discipline*.

Recent trends, however, both in popular historical practice and in historical theorising (or in philosophy of history) have been challenging the propriety of that long assumed absolute distinction: from the one side, 'fact' and 'fiction' have become inextricably intertwined, or increasingly indistinguishable, in such hybrid forms of entertainment as 'docudramas', 'historical fiction', 'non-fiction novels', 'novelised' biographies, and the more dauntingly labelled 'historiographical metafiction'; while from the more theoretical side, critiques of history and the nature of narrative have culminated in the assimilation of the 'factual' and 'fictional' – or, to put it more bluntly, the claim that history itself is nothing more than an alternative form of fiction. At the very least, then, boundaries between the two have been eroding; so that their respective territories now are in a state, if not of downright warfare, then at least of interesting flux.

This book, then, is an intervention in what is something of an intellectual maelstrom, and aims to provide not merely (it is hoped) illumination but, more importantly, provocation to further thought and research. It is concerned with areas where history and fiction meet – initially, with some aspects of the general relationship between history and fiction, and then, more

[2] F. H. Bradley, *The Presuppositions of Critical History* [1874], ed. Lionel Rubinoff, Chicago, Quadrangle Books, 1968, p. 86.

particularly, with some of the ways that history and historians themselves have been represented in works of fiction. And a recurring theme throughout – with references here to specific examples – is the expression within fictional works of some critical attitudes towards historiography; one argument running through the whole is that novelists and dramatists have managed, far better than theorists themselves, to 'popularise', or make more widely accessible, such key issues in historical theory as those concerning truth, relativism, memory, ethics, and identity.

The first two chapters provide an overview of debates concerning the relationship between history and fiction generally. After an introductory historical survey, the first focuses on the use of fiction as historical evidence, and on narrative, whether in history or fiction, and the construction of meaning. The second chapter turns to claims for the strictly non-fictional nature of history, and to corresponding challenges to that position; and a case study provides specific exemplification of these introductory matters in a contemporary work of fiction (Penelope Lively's *Cleopatra's Sister*). The focus of Chapter 3 is on the representation of historians in fiction, and particularly the 'dryasdust' model cited already in the early nineteenth century. This is put into the context of nineteenth-century scientist aspirations and responses to that scientific emphasis; and implications are drawn for education in terms of both fiction (Charles Dickens' Thomas Gradgrind) and history (John Stuart Mill). Further important contributions made by writers of fiction to questions relating to the nature of history (historical theory) are discussed in Chapters 4–6: such central matters as memory, ethics, and identity, and their connections with history, are shown to have been discussed by novelists including Daphne du Maurier, Virginia Woolf, Penelope Lively, Leo Tolstoy, André Gide, and Tim O'Brien – whose work (together with that of other writers) provides the basis for further specific case studies. Chapter 7 turns to a consideration of history's functions as discussed in fiction: here particular attention is given to the political messages assumed in Thomas Pynchon's *V* and Don DeLillo's *Libra*, and to related issues discussed in Graham Swift's *Waterland*. In the final chapter we return to more general questions of history's meeting points with fiction – including especially the nature of the current boundaries, or perhaps more appositely borderlands, between them. Here illumination is provided by a final case study – Daniel Mendelsohn's *The Lost: A Search for Six of Six Million*. This account of a practical investigation reveals much about the ways that history meets fiction; and it leads to my own conclusions – or confessions – in a Postscript, concerning the problematic mix, by which all of us are confronted daily, of '*truth and tangled falsehood*'.

List of Plates

Author's Acknowledgements

Once again I should like to thank those who contrive to keep the post-retirement intellect alive, and in particular members of Robert Burns's Philosophy of History Seminar at the Institute of Historical Research, London. I am especially grateful for their continuing encouragement to Keith Jenkins, Mark Mason, and Alexander Macfie; and, for his enthusiastic response to my proposal, to Series Editor, Alun Munslow. Pearson readers of my drafts – some still anonymous, but importantly including Martin Davies and Robert Rosenstone – have been meticulous, and positive even where critical. Had I followed all their suggestions, I would still be writing; but I have benefited from their constructive appraisals. Final revisions on hard copy have been made possible by Jayne Bloye, of the University of Hertfordshire; and Lindsey Brake has been a wonderfully tactful and meticulous copy-editor. I am extremely grateful for enthusiastic encouragement and practical advice from commissioning editor Christina Wipf-Perry. Finally, and most especially, I thank my wife Sheila, who continues to give the physical, intellectual, and emotional support that makes everything possible.

Publisher's Acknowledgements

The publisher would like to thank the following for their kind permission to reproduce images:

Plate 1, Plate 3, Plate 4 and Plate 7 akg-images Ltd;
Plate 2 National Portrait Gallery, London/Mark Gersion;
Plate 5 akg-images Ltd/RIA Novosti;
Plate 6 National Portrait Gallery, London/Wyndham Lewis and the estate of the late Mrs GA Wyndham Lewis by kind permission of the Wyndham Lewis Memorial Trust (a registered charity);
Plate 8 National Portrait Gallery, London;
Plate 9 akg-images Ltd/ullstein bild.

Every effort has been made to trace the copyright holders and we apologise in advance for any unintentional omissions. We would be pleased to insert the appropriate acknowledgement in any subsequent edition of this publication.

Chapter 1

History and fiction

*Before addressing specific issues of fiction and historical theory, two intro-
ductory chapters are concerned with a historical and philosophical examination of the relationship more generally between history and fiction. Topics in
this first chapter include the original Aristotelian distinction between history
and imaginative literature, with a sketch of its subsequent development; historians' own use of fiction for evidence, and the use of the past in drama and
historical fiction; and the construction, through narrative, of meaning in
both history and fiction.*

The relationship between history and fiction has always been close but
problematic: as in any relationship, it has sometimes proved difficult to
strike a mutually acceptable balance between interdependence and autonomy,
and any equilibrium achieved has always proved temporary. In an ongoing
attempt at stabilisation, a fence has long since been erected between the two,
and has been claimed to mark one of the most fundamental of disciplinary
boundaries – one that has, especially from the historical side, been most
fiercely, passionately, and even desperately, defended.

For historians have long prided themselves on producing works that
specifically *contrast* with fiction – that are 'historical' works precisely by virtue
of *not* being fictional, that are verifiably 'true' in a way that fiction does not
aspire to be. It may be the case that, as Carlyle claimed, 'the Epic poems of old
time [the historically orientated works of Homer, for example] . . . were
Histories, and understood to be narratives of *facts*'.[1] But already by the time of

---

[1] Thomas Carlyle, *English and Other Critical Essays*, London, J. M. Dent, 1915, p. 70
(original emphasis).

classical antiquity a deliberate attempt was made to distinguish between those two genres.

So history, in Aristotle's early formulation, described reality 'as it was' or as it had been, whereas poetry – which we can include here within the category of 'fiction' – could roam more imaginatively over what 'might be' or might have been. 'The main object of . . . [history]', as the Roman Cicero explained later, but within the same classical tradition, 'is *truth*', while that of poetry is 'delight and *pleasure*'.[2] There might be some overlap and confusion between the two inasmuch as both are ultimately concerned with the recital and representation of 'facts' of one sort or another, and they may sometimes appear as complementary; as Voltaire puts it, 'History is the recital of facts represented as true. Fable, on the other hand, is the recital of facts represented as fiction.'[3] But the crucial point has generally been maintained that different knowledge claims are to be made about their respective representations – that, in contradistinction to 'fiction', history has to do with 'fact', with what is 'true'; and 'truth' is the only appropriate goal for any historian. As the great Dutch historian Johan Huizinga wrote: 'If the deeply sincere desire to find out how a certain thing "really happened" is lacking as such, he [the writer] is *not pursuing history*.'[4]

That most important distinction, which had been implied in Aristotle's theoretical formulation, was early confirmed by the professed practice of his near contemporary Thucydides: with his pretensions to a 'scientific' treatment of the past, he took care to distance himself from more 'romantic' predecessors, who had (as he alleged) been less constrained by the evidential and procedural requirements of proper historians. But despite such self-affirming protestations, the distinction was never as clear as Thucydides claimed. Even his own resort to direct speech – where he puts words into the mouths of his characters that could at best represent what he thought they might have said – laid him open to the charge of embellishing his work in order to make it more attractive (something better left to those pleasure-giving poets). And such confusions, between supposedly 'factual' narrative and evidently 'fictional' intrusions, were, perhaps inevitably, perpetuated in the case of later writers who dealt with past people and events.

---

[2] Cicero, *Treatise on the Laws*, Book I, in *The Political Works of Marcus Tullius Cicero*, trans. Francis Barham, 2 vols; London, Edmund Spettique, 1841, vol. II, p. 27 (my emphases).

[3] Voltaire, *Philosophical Dictionary*, quoted by Ronald Britton, *Belief and Imagination: Explorations in Psychoanalysis*, London, Routledge, 1998, p. 109.

[4] Johan Huizinga, 'The Task of Cultural History' (1926), in *Men and Ideas: History, the Middle Ages, the Renaissance*, Princeton, Princeton University Press, 1959, p. 43 (my emphasis).

The fourteenth-century English poet Geoffrey Chaucer, for example, can be seen to mingle the two traditions in his *Monk's Tale*, where he includes figures variously derived, not only from supposedly factual histories (Julius Caesar, Claudius, and Nero), but also from the Bible (Samson and Delilah) and even pagan mythology (Hercules and Anataeus)[5] – with these all thrown haphazardly together in a way that foreshadows the more obviously contrived postmodern 'metafiction' of the twentieth century. More immediately, though, within the context of English poetry, the use of historical material is shown most obviously in the so-called 'history plays' of William Shakespeare. In these the dramatist uses mainly the second edition (1587) of Raphael Holinshed's *Chronicles* – themselves a source of questionable reliability – as the basis for his own treatment of mediaeval power struggles, focusing on the Kings Henry IV, V, and VI, John, and Richard II and III. The genealogies presented by Shakespeare are generally accepted as reasonably accurate (or in line with the historical record), but he takes imaginative liberties in such matters as chronology, the ages of his characters, and the anachronistic presence of such items as clocks and games of billiards. Historically derived 'fact', then, is once again mixed in with poetic 'fiction', all in this case for dramatic (or, once again, pleasurable) effect.

For what Shakespeare does is (as we shall see below) akin to what Hayden White has more recently claimed of historians generally: that is, he contrives to impose an appropriate (in his case, theatrically appropriate) narrative on earlier chronicles. And as Thomas Heywood noted in the early seventeenth century, by doing that, and with the help of skilful actors, he succeeds in bringing the dead back to life – eroding the distinctions between past and present and providing instruction in such virtues as patriotism and obedience. So the audience at Shakespeare's play entitled *The Famous History of the Life of King Henry the Eighth* (1612–13) is instructed by the Prologue to 'think ye see/ The very persons of our noble story/ As they were living'. That is, the *poetical* drama is designed to bring *history* – the past – *back to life*, and so produce a kind of historical truth. And according to Heywood, that has sometimes, even in the distant past, been achieved to good effect: he describes how, as tutor to Alexander (later The Great), Aristotle arranged for a dramatic representation of an important historical event to be performed, in order to provide an example for him to emulate – to provide, as we might say, a 'role model' from the past. So he 'caused the destruction of Troy to be acted before his pupil'; and

---

[5] I am indebted for this point to Leo Braudy, *Narrative Form in History and Fiction*, Princeton, Princeton University Press, 1970, p. 4.

Alexander was indeed so impressed by the portrayal of valour shown by Achilles that he modelled himself upon that character; and as Heywood concludes, 'it may be imagined had *Achilles* never lived, *Alexander* had never conquered the whole world'.[6] Such is the power of historically orientated drama.

If Shakespeare's 'History Plays' mark a meeting and confluence of 'history' and 'fiction', with their deliberate use of the historical past for dramatic and poetic (as well as political and patriotic) purposes, historians of mediaeval historiography have noted, conversely, an early divergence between those two genres. For an interest in the individual lives of heroic figures, who were themselves perceived as liberated from any 'historical' constraints, developed into a type of imaginative romantic fiction that ran alongside the development of the severer discipline of history itself.[7] And in the later theorising of such Renaissance writers as Sir Philip Sidney there are indications that historians specifically were expected to ascertain 'the truth', in order the more persuasively to present their examples for moral instruction. George Puttenham likewise distinguishes between, on the one hand, the poet who was free 'to fashion [his material] at his pleasure', and, on the other hand, historians ('th'other sort'), who 'must go according to their *veritie*' [truth], if they were to avoid incurring 'great blame'.[8]

Even through the eighteenth century, though, and as late as the nineteenth, distinctions in practice between fact and fiction were sometimes far from clear or finally resolved. For, as Leo Braudy explains, 'Both novelists and historians sought to form time, to discover its plot, and to give a compelling and convincing narrative shape to the fact of human life';[9] so that, for example, Daniel Defoe insisted that his novel *Robinson Crusoe* (1719) was not a 'romance'

---

[6] For material in this paragraph I am indebted to Graham Holderness, *Shakespeare: The Histories*, Basingstoke, Macmillan, 2000; for the quotations from Thomas Heywood's *Apology for Actors* (1612), see p. 56. Another interesting essay on this subject is Michael Hattaway, 'The Shakespearean History Play', in Michael Hattaway (ed.), *The Cambridge Companion to Shakespeare's History Plays*, Cambridge, Cambridge University Press, 2002, pp. 3–24. (Shakespeare, of course, also uses earlier figures – including Pericles and Julius Caesar – as the subjects of other dramas.)

[7] See e.g. Robert W. Hanning, *The Vision of History in Early Britain*, New York and London, Columbia University Press, 1966.

[8] George Puttenham, quoted by Herschel Baker, *The Race of Time*, [Toronto], University of Toronto, 1967, p. 81 (my emphasis).

[9] Braudy, *Narrative Form*, p. 3.

but 'all historical and true in Fact'.[10] Henry Fielding, similarly, as a novelist considered himself to be also an historian – a point revealed in some of his titles, such as *The History of Pendennis* (1845–50), and *The History of Henry Esmond* (1852), works in which Fielding believed that he was dealing with the sort of personal material that other historians should, but did not, include in their own studies; for he, no less than Hume and Gibbon, was interested in such central human concerns as character, chance, providence, and the meaning of the past.

With their reclaimed emphasis on science as an appropriate model, modern historians (as we shall see below) have often taken care to re-confirm the distinction of their craft from that of novelists, or writers of mere fiction. But it is a distinction that has sometimes (and of late with increasing insistence) been questioned from at least two directions. First, some writers of fiction have always chosen to base their work in 'historical' times and on 'real' historical events; and sometimes they have deliberately chosen to depict aspects of the past (or embellish them) in less than 'scientific', but rather more imaginative ways. That tendency culminates in full-blown 'historical novels', such as are exemplified by the enormously popular works of Sir Walter Scott in the nineteenth century, and more recently by popular writers such as Rose Tremaine, Sebastian Faulkes, and Sarah Dunant.

Scott is particularly important here, and is becoming a subject of increasing interest to historical theorists. Claimed by Geörg Lukács (in 1937)[11] as the inventor of the historical novel, Scott in *Waverley* (1814), as David Harlan has recently described, 'broke new ground', by including 'not only the determining conditions of a historical era but how those conditions shaped the mental and emotional lives of the people who lived through them'.[12] In works such as this, the attempts of characters to understand themselves include consideration of how they perceive themselves in time – understand themselves, that is, as historically situated. The author is concerned to retrieve and represent the 'inner lives' of such characters – their singular 'voices' (which are, again, partly a function of the time in which they lived); and that involves the inclusion of material that had often been previously neglected in conventional histories –

---

[10] Defoe, quoted in Mark C. Carnes (ed.), *Novel History: Historians and Novelists Confront America's Past (and Each Other)*, London, Simon & Schuster, 2001, p. 15.

[11] Geörg Lukács, *The Historical Novel* [1937], trans. Hannah and Stanley Mithell, Harmondsworth, Penguin, 1969.

[12] David Harlan, 'Historical Fiction and Academic History', in Keith Jenkins, Sue Morgan and Alun Munslow (eds), *Manifestos for History*, London, Routledge, 2007, p. 112.

the inclusion, as one contemporary reviewer put it, of 'the blood and tears of thousands . . . [that had long been] passed over with a yawn'.[13]

It is, then, the 'inner' lives of people, in all their complexity, that writers such as Scott seek to represent, and it is the 'human' interest of historical fiction that still draws a popular response; for it can reveal alternative subjects and perspectives, and invite an enjoyable (as it seems) 'empathy' with people from the past. Herbert Butterfield is a comparatively rare example of a twentieth-century historian who appreciated what he called 'the peculiar virtue of fiction as the gateway to the past'; for it is, he believed, in historical novels that 'we find the *sentiment* of history, the *feeling* for the past'. So Scott in particular 'does something for history that the historian by himself cannot do, or can seldom do; he recaptures the *life* of an age' – that '*atmosphere* [which] eludes the analyst'. Professional historians may provide 'a chart of the facts' that governed people's lives in the past, but such history 'withholds the closest *human* things, the touches of *direct experience*' – and it is precisely those that are the domain of the historical novelist.[14]

Other historians have been less impressed by such an approach, and historical novelists have often been the butt of academic contempt. As Macaulay, despite his own interest in such matters, ironically noted, the material conditions of everyday life in the past have customarily been accounted 'too trivial for the majesty of history'.[15] But there seems little doubt that through its success – and Scott himself enjoyed immediate popularity – historical fiction has opened up and extended the range of what has been, at any given time, considered 'proper' history; and historical novelists from Scott on have (at least for the non-professional historian) served to blur once again any supposed sharp distinction between 'history' and 'fiction'.

A second challenge, though, to the conventional categorisation has been gaining strength from quite another direction: historical theorists, or philosophers of history, have, especially over the last half century, questioned historians' own claims to be able to represent the '*truth*' about the past; and at their most extreme, these critics have likened histories to fictions, and implied that

---

[13] *British Lady's Magazine*, quoted by Ann Rigney, *Imperfect Histories: The Elusive Past and the Legacy of Romantic Historicism*, Ithaca and London, Cornell University Press, 2001, p. 37. This book provides a detailed discussion of Scott and his historical novels, together with contemporary and subsequent reactions to his work. See also James Kerr, *Fiction against History: Scott as Storyteller*, Cambridge, Cambridge University Press, 1989, and Harry E. Shaw, *Narrating Reality: Austen, Scott, Eliot*, Ithaca, Cornell University Press, 1999.

[14] Herbert Butterfield, *The Historical Novel: An Essay*, Cambridge, Cambridge University Press, 1924, Preface, pp. 3, 29, 97, 112 (my emphases).

[15] Macaulay, quoted by Rigney, *Imperfect Histories*, p. 164, n. 36.

the two genres, the two types of narrative, are effectively indistinguishable. In practical terms this erosion or blurring of distinctions between the two has been manifested in such works as Truman Capote's *In Cold Blood* (1966), described as the first non-fiction novel[16] (and to be further discussed in Chapter 2); and other post-modern era (and often popular) genres include 'historiographical metafiction' (in the terminology used by Linda Hutcheon and others), so-called 'docudramas' (as seen on television and in the cinema), and even some biographies (such as Edmund Morris's *Dutch: A Memoir of Ronald Reagan* (1999), described as 'a literary hybrid of fiction and fact', or Robert Rosenstone's *King of Odessa* (2003), a 'fictional biography . . . based on the known historical facts').[17] In such works, history meets fiction in ways that confirm the theorists' contention of their inextricable entanglement.

We shall need later to discuss some of these matters at greater length, but first let's consider briefly another aspect of the relationship between history and fiction: the use made of fiction as historical evidence.

Fiction as historical evidence

One of the most obvious points of contact between history and fiction lies in the use made of fiction as historical evidence: as one cultural artefact among many, fiction has always provided useful material, especially for social and cultural historians. That procedure is, however, by no means universally approved; for, it might be asked, what use can history, with all its pretensions to *factuality*, possibly make of evidence derived from an admittedly *fictional* source? 'Evidence', after all, is supposed to be reliable – to be derived from witnesses who can be trusted and who themselves depend upon properly empirical procedures. Yet writers of fiction avowedly resort to their own imaginative faculties and trade in feelings – hardly the stuff of proper history. So

---

[16] Arthur C. Danto, *The Transfiguration of the Commonplace: A Philosophy of Art*, Cambridge, Mass., Harvard University Press, 1981, p. 144.

[17] Edmund Morris, letter to *New York Review of Books*, 12 April 2007, p. 83; Robert Rosenstone, email from author. Other recent examples of 'fictional biographies', or 'novelised lives', include Colm Tóibín, *The Master* (2004) and David Lodge, *Author, Author* (2004) – both of them about Henry James, and A. N. Wilson, *Winnie and Wolf* (2007), the main characters in which are Winifred Wagner and Adolf Hitler. Since writing this, the term 'non-fiction non-novel' has been applied to Gordon Burn's *Born Yesterday: The News as a Novel* (2008) by Theo Tait, *London Review of Books*, 5 June 2008, p. 16.

Richard Evans, for example, has criticised the approach of G. M. Trevelyan in his best-selling *English Social History*, in that 'it relied too heavily on imaginative literature for source material, *and so was often led astray*'.[18]

Yet it would be hard to conceive of a historian of, say, classical Athens who did not resort to 'fictional' writings of the time – the work of poetic dramatists or 'romantically' inclined writers of philosophy and even history. With evidence at a premium, it is small wonder that cultural historians should cite some comedies of Aristophanes (say, *Lysistrata* and *Women in Parliament*) as sources for their theories on the social position of women at the time; or that intellectual historians should mine the works of Plato (with his imaginative reconstructions of contemporary events) and Euripides (with his own retelling in tragedy of poetic myths). And even in the twentieth century, when historical evidence is abundant (or actually over-abundant), it would be a strangely narrow-minded historian of certain aspects of the Great War who declined to use evidence (where relevant to his or her theme) provided by a novelist such as Erich Maria Remarque (author of *All Quiet on the Western Front*) and the 'war poets', including Wilfred Owen and Siegfried Sassoon. Even in less obviously dramatic times, fiction can prove a useful source of evidence – as for historians of post-war Britain and their use of the 'kitchen-sink' dramas of the 1950s and 1960s to illuminate some social attitudes of the time.

For fiction represents and actually embodies some of the widely accepted social mores and intellectual presuppositions of its age; and so it often provides evidence, not so much for historical periods in which its stories may be set, but for the time in which it was actually written (though, as in the last example, these may sometimes coincide). So historians are unlikely to use Dickens, for example, in their researches on the French Revolution (about which he wrote in *A Tale of Two Cities*, 1859), since the novelist's imaginative input here is relevant, not to the period about which he was writing but rather to the time in which he himself wrote; he constitutes a source, not for the Revolution itself, but for mid-nineteenth-century British attitudes towards it.

But Dickens' fiction does become a more direct source of historical evidence when he writes about contemporary events, adopting as he does the role of social commentator and critic. So that, as we shall see in Chapter 3, a fictional work such as *Hard Times* (1854, about which the critic F. R. Leavis remarks of Dickens that 'he writes with a poetic force of evocation'[19]) does appear to provide evidence for life in industrialised England, and more particularly for educational theory and practice at the time.

---

[18]   Richard J. Evans, *In Defence of History*, London, Granta, 1997, p. 166 (my emphasis).
[19]   F. R. Leavis, *The Great Tradition*, Harmondsworth, Penguin, 1972, p. 267.

Similar examples come readily to mind, with such novelists as Elizabeth Gaskell and her descriptions in *North and South* (1854–5) of the contrasts between rich and poor, employers and 'hands', southern countryside and northern cities; or Charles Kingsley, himself a Professor of History at Cambridge, and influenced by Carlyle, with his social commentary in *Alton Locke* (1850); or even (more unexpectedly, perhaps) Proust's comments on wartime Paris and Parisians at the time of German air-raids in 1916. For the United States, F. Scott Fitzgerald's novel *The Great Gatsby* (1925) has been described as 'an international source for American social history', or, as the critic John Lukacs writes, 'a gem, a historical cameo not of American thinking but of American feeling . . . suffused with the atmosphere and with some of the actual evidences and effects of the early 1920s'; and for mid-twentieth-century Britain, 'social realist' novels such as Alan Sillitoe's *Saturday Night and Sunday Morning* (1958) present a recognisable picture of the time – more recognisable than some of the reconstructions presented by younger historians. It is clear that, as Lukacs claims, 'certain novels tell us more about a certain time and about certain people than even the best of histories'.[20]

Despite their strictly speaking 'fictional' status, then, and despite possible anxieties about some circularity of argument (for which is the chicken here, and which the egg? Do we not get our impressions of a period 'atmosphere' and 'feeling' from precisely those artefacts – books, paintings, music, and so on – which we then retrospectively claim as supporting evidence?), such obvious (or less than obvious) quarries of evidence for their respective times would be hard for historians to ignore; and this then argues further *against* any such rigid distinction between history and fiction as is often maintained by orthodox historians. The boundaries between the two are obviously fluid, with two-way traffic and meetings, whether intentional or inadvertent, not infrequent.

An interesting new dimension to that traffic flow was revealed in September 2007, when a story deliberately presented as fictional was shown to represent an actual historical event, and it was reported that the Polish author Krystian Bala had been convicted of the murder of Dariusz Janiszewski in 2000, and jailed for twenty-five years. In his novel *Amok*, published in 2003, Bala had described how a victim was humiliated, starved, tortured, strangled, and thrown into a river – in ways that corresponded exactly with a case that had been (up to that point unsuccessfully) investigated by police. The novelist had sent emails in which he boasted of the 'perfect crime' – but, in the real case,

---

[20] John Lukacs in Carnes (ed.), *Novel History*, pp. 235, 237–8. The specialist cited on Scott Fitzgerald is Matthew J. Bruccoli.

there were no leads for the police to follow until, some five years on, the detective in charge received an anonymous phone call suggesting that he read Bala's book. He realised that it included details of the crime that had never been revealed to the public, and that only the actual perpetrator could know; so that fiction in this case finally provided the evidence for the actual historical event with which the author – the perpetrator – and the police were concerned.[21]

Such illumination in criminal cases is likely to be rare, but that is not to say that light cannot be shed by novelists in other ways that might prove useful to historians; for as Ann Rigney has written, 'The fascinating thing about imaginative literature is that it provides a laboratory where historically variable ways of seeing the world are expressed through the prism of poetical forms in such a way that they are made uniquely observable both for contemporaries and later historians.' That is to say, novelists, unconstrained by any pressures to disciplinary consensus, might be more free than historians to look at the past in fresh ways – and so, as individual observers, catch sight of alternative people and events from alternative perspectives. Such writers can also foreground topics that have otherwise been ignored or sidelined, and so can act as catalysts in relation to other historical practices. Imaginative 'artists', suggests Ann Rigney, thus 'help keep historical horizons open'.[22]

This, then, is to turn on its head the conventional wisdom that fiction somehow contaminates history, introducing blemishes upon the pure face of factuality: it suggests, rather, that fiction can help to keep history creatively alive; not bound by the disciplinary rules of its more 'rigorous' partner, it can continue to extend the parameters of history's interests and concerns, by proposing and providing fresh evidence for what the subject might consist of.

Such intertwining of our two protagonists is further revealed through consideration of their shared objective – the construction of *meaning*.

Narrative and the construction of meaning in history and fiction

There are times when we have to disentangle history from fairy-tale. There are times (they come round really quite often) when good dry textbook history takes a plunge into the old swamps of myth and has to be retrieved with

---

[21] Reported in *The Independent*, 6 September 2007.
[22] Ann Rigney, 'Being an Improper Historian', in Jenkins et al. (eds), *Manifestos*, pp. 151, 155. See further Rigney, *Imperfect Histories*.

empirical fishing lines. History, being an accredited sub-science, only wants to know the facts. History, if it is to keep on constructing its road into the future, must do so on solid ground. At all costs let us avoid mystery-making and speculation, secrets and idle gossip. And, for God's sake, nothing supernatural. And above all, let us not tell *stories*.[23]

That extract from Graham Swift's novel *Waterland* (1983) refers us back to the orthodox distinction between history and fiction, and then goes on conveniently to introduce a number of related issues. So in the first sentence we have a reassertion of the need to retain the disciplinary distinction – the need to keep the two disentangled – while the second goes on to acknowledge that they do, even often, meet and become entwined. In an effort, then, to keep the two distinct, history is claimed to be established on a firm grounding of empirical evidence, whereas fiction has more to do with imagination; history is to be classified as a 'science', which can then lay claim to 'facts', whereas fiction may resort to speculation and such mysteries as cannot be empirically verified; history above all, in order to provide a reliable foundation – a base from which we can orientate ourselves in relation to our future – is to eschew *stories*, or *narrative*.

We shall need to examine a number of presuppositions in that paragraph, and may find (indeed, have already found) reasons to question the claimed sharp distinctiveness between history and fiction; but let us look first at Graham Swift's exclusion (or proposed exclusion) from history of 'stories'. For that is consistent with orthodox historiography, as represented by, for example, Arthur Marwick: as an influential writer on the nature of history in the latter half of the twentieth century, Marwick comments on the popular historian A. J. P. Taylor, that he 'was simply being ridiculous when he said that historians "should not be ashamed to admit that history is at the bottom simply a form of story-telling"'.[24] In other words, we are asked to believe either that Taylor was wrong about history being a form of story-telling, or that he was wrong not to feel ashamed to admit that: stories, according to Marwick (as to Graham Swift's character), are to be excised from history and consigned to their proper place in the realm of fiction.

---

[23] Graham Swift, *Waterland* [1983], London, Picador, 1992, p. 86 (original emphasis). For an interesting analysis of *Waterland* in relation to history and fiction, see John Ibbett, 'The Significance of a Past', in T. Bela and Z. Mazur (eds), *The Legacy of History: English and American Studies and the Significance of the Past*, Krakow, Jagiellonian University Press, 2003, vol. 1, pp. 33–50.

[24] Arthur Marwick, *The New Nature of History: Knowledge, Evidence, Language*, Basingstoke, Palgrave, 2001, p. 15.

Yet Swift's own professed exclusion from history of narratives – of stories – has, in the context of his novel, a paradoxical and even ironic ring; for it is precisely stories that are to be unfolded – stories of individual lives within the context of stories about local enterprises, activities and industries, and all within the wider narrative of world events; and such stories are seen to be essential, not only to fiction but also and no less to history. It is stories that make both literary forms *of interest* to people generally; so it is to stories that the history teacher, Tom Crick, resorts in his classes. Disillusioned with conventionally spooning out yet more facts, and providing 'a rag-bag of pointless information', Crick, in his 'new-fangled lessons', tells stories instead – stories, the truth of which is admittedly not always clear; for they are, he concedes, 'crazy yarns (true? made up?)'.[25] And in that recognition of their uncertain or ambiguous status, he exemplifies in fiction an intractable problem relating to historical theory.

For one reason for the enduring and close relationship between history and fiction – one reason for their fluctuating conjunctions and disjunctions – is that both are concerned essentially with the same task: with the construction of *meaning*, with making some sense out of what otherwise appears as the chaotic jumble of data that makes up human lives. Both, that is to say, need to tell stories – construct *narratives*. To revert to Graham Swift: 'Man . . . is the story-telling animal. Wherever he goes he wants to leave behind not a chaotic wake, not an empty space, but the comforting marker-buoys and trail-signs of stories';[26] and it is the function of both historians and novelists to provide just such stories, just such markers and signs, by which one thing leads on to another in what appears to be a comprehensible and meaningful way.

The claim to be *constructing* such meaning, however, is already contentious inasmuch as it applies to history;[27] and the contention goes to the root of the relationship we are exploring here. For while writers of fiction, on the one hand, would be happy to accept that their business is indeed imaginatively to construct meaningful narratives, usually (though not of course always) within an easily read chronological framework that boasts a beginning, a middle, and an end, many (if not most) historians, on the other hand, would deny that their function is to *construct* anything at all: rather, they would argue, what they do is endeavour to *reconstruct* a story that is already there – a story that is inherent in the past, awaiting their retrieval. So that historians act, not as

---

[25] Swift, *Waterland*, pp. 23, 6.
[26] Swift, *Waterland*, pp. 62–3.
[27] See Alun Munslow, *Deconstructing History*, London, Routledge, 1997; and on narrative, see the same author's *Narrative and History*, Basingstoke, Palgrave Macmillan, 2007.

imaginative creators, but as mediums who contrive on others' behalf to stand between the past and present, and through their own professional techniques and expertise to reveal what had become obscured (but had always nonetheless been there).

Claims of that kind have been made by historians especially after the 'professionalisation' of their discipline in the nineteenth century, and the attempted assimilation of their procedures to those used in the 'hard' sciences. Since that time they have often seen themselves as intermediaries, speaking, as it were, not with their own voices, but that of a personalised 'History' itself. Just as 'Nature' reveals itself to the physicist who speaks the appropriate language (of mathematics), so too with 'the past'. So it is, wrote Fustel de Coulanges (1830–89), 'not I who speak, but history which speaks through me'.[28] More recently (1976), the British historian E. P. Thompson, in response to a question concerning what one should do 'to learn to be a proper historian', has reaffirmed the belief that 'The material itself has got to speak to him [the historian]', and that 'If he listens, then *the material will begin to speak through him*.'[29] Part of that passage is quoted in turn by Richard Evans, who seems to agree, with his further claim that '*history* [sic] . . . can identify, or posit with a high degree of plausibility, *patterns, trends and structures in the human past*'; which is what justifies its claims to 'scientific' status.[30]

As priest-like figures, whose (literal) self-sacrifice enables them to see further and more clearly through the mists of the past to what actually occurred, historians merely report back, and re-present, as accurately and clearly as possible, what they find. Thus, as a contemporary example, David Carr writes of 'a continuity . . . between historical reality and historical narrative'. He is concerned to defend history against those sceptical attacks which question the validity of knowledge claims, whether made in science or elsewhere; or which, as he puts it, question the objectivity and truthfulness of any 'claims to know'. So he reaffirms the view that 'the very reality of history' – those past actions, events, experiences that constitute its subject matter – actually and intrinsically 'has the narrative form' in which it is later to be written up; so that 'far from differing in structure from historical reality, *historical narrative shares*

---

[28] Fustel de Coulanges, quoted in Fritz Stern (ed.), *The Varieties of History from Voltaire to the Present*, New York, Meridian Books, 1956, p. 25.

[29] E. P. Thompson, quoted in Henry Abelove et al. (eds), *Visions of History*, Manchester, Manchester University Press, 1983, p. 14 (my emphases).

[30] Evans, *Defence*, pp. 116; 60–61 (my emphases).

the form of its object;[31] or as Barbara Hardy had earlier claimed, narrative is 'a primary act of mind transferred *to art from life*'.

That last quotation is taken from an essay by Louis O. Mink, who argues against Hardy that the qualities of narrative are, conversely, transferred the other way, *to life from art*: 'Stories are not lived but told', asserts Mink; and in obvious agreement, one biographer has recently written of turning 'the bracing *storylessness* of human life into the flaccid narrativity of biography'.[32] Despite the obvious limits of birth and death, life has no inherent narrative form: meaningful stories are imposed upon it only retrospectively. So as Mink explains:

> Life has no beginnings, middles, or ends; there are meetings, but the start of an affair belongs to the story we tell ourselves later, and there are partings, but final partings only in the story. There are hopes, plans, battles, and ideas, but only in retrospective stories are hopes unfulfilled, plans miscarried, battles decisive, and ideas seminal . . . Narrative qualities are transferred *from art to life*.[33]

That notion, by implication insisted upon by Louis Mink, of the need for historians to take responsibility for the manner of their own *emplotment* of events – for how they re-present the succession (or rather *a*, selected, succession) of events within a narrative – is generally associated with the cultural critique of Hayden White. For White is likewise adamant that 'We do not *live* stories, even if we give our lives meaning by retrospectively casting them in the form of stories.' He noted a generation ago how reluctant historians were in fact to accept that responsibility for their narrative constructions: they preferred, as we have just seen above, to think of themselves as mere mouthpieces of a history that somehow told its own story to those equipped to hear it. But going on to assimilate historical and fictional narratives in a way that still offends many, White insists that the former, no less than the latter, are quite manifestly 'verbal fictions, the contents of which are as much *invented* as *found*'.[34]

---

[31]   David Carr, 'The Reality of History', in Jörn Rüsen (ed.), *Meaning and Representation in History*, Oxford, Berghahn, 2006, p. 124 (my emphases). See also Carr's *Time, Narrative, and History*, Bloomington, Indiana University Press, 1986.

[32]   Janet Malcolm, quoted by Terry Castle in her review of *Two Lives: Gertrude and Alice*, *London Review of Books*, 13 December 2007, p. 16.

[33]   Louis O. Mink, 'History and Fiction as Modes of Comprehension', in Brian Fay, Eugene O. Golob, and Richard T. Vann (eds), *Historical Understanding*, Ithaca and London, Cornell University Press, 1987, pp. 59–60 (my emphases).

[34]   Hayden White, 'The Historical Text as Literary Artifact' [1974], in *Tropics of Discourse:*

So, as he explains, a bare chronicle of events through time has no inherent meaning: events are not necessarily connected with one another in a single way; their interrelationships can be viewed and described in accordance with a huge variety of possibilities. The job of historians then becomes to fit them into the literary structure that they themselves consider most appropriate, viewing them as components of a story that might be tragic or comic, romantic or ironic, or any mixture of the four. And just how the events are then 'encoded' or 'emplotted' will obviously depend, not only on the personal approaches of historians – reflecting or defining their own attitudes and interpretations – but also on the intellectual and literary forms that are currently available within their cultures.

David Carr is not unaware of such contrary arguments concerning historical narratives, but insists that, despite sporadic upsets (attributable to variations in our perception of passing time, for example), we do nonetheless live our lives in narrative form: that elusive 'plot' is not something belatedly discovered at our graves in the burial ground, but, as revealed in narrative, 'is the practical and "existential" form of human time'. So narrative becomes, in short, 'the structure of our very being'; and as such, it constitutes 'the very "reality" of history'.[35]

David Carr's position, then, together with that of Hayden White, reveals that there is a fundamental question to be confronted, of whether our lives – and the lives of our societies and states – are actually lived in a narrative form, which it is the historian's function to ascertain, recover, reconstitute, and relate; or whether any orderly structure perceived in our lives (and histories) is a retrospective construction – that is, a story that we (and/or others) contrive to impose upon our lives only after the event. And that has clear implications for whether we perceive such narratives as *factual*, in the sense of being recovered from what 'really' happened, or *fictional*, inasmuch as they are (however much derived from 'real' events) at least in part imaginative constructions.

The answer that we individually give to that question seems to me to be dependent on our own personalities and outlooks, our own experience and way of relating to the world; it is something that cannot ever be definitively proved one way or the other, but seems to be a matter of faith. Whether guided by religion or some other belief in a super-human teleological power (nature, evolution, destiny), some people subscribe to the view that human life is intrinsically meaningful, purposeful, and appropriately structured; while

Essays in Cultural Criticism, Baltimore and London, Johns Hopkins, 1978, pp. 90, 82 (original emphases). See also 'The Fiction of Factual Representation', in ibid., pp. 121–34.
[35] Carr, 'Reality', p. 126.

others see it, rather, as essentially dis-ordered, chaotic, and needing to have some meaning and form imposed upon it by humans themselves.

There is of course a trivial sense in which a human life has a clearly structured inbuilt narrative: birth and death make obvious end points, which a biographer might be expected to take as introduction and conclusion. Yet even there, certainties soon dissolve: for to provide any meaningful account of our subject's life, we would surely need to go back before his birth – to consider his family and antecedents; and how far back would that take us? And we would also surely need to look beyond his death, to examine any memories of him that may linger, and any posthumous influence that he possibly continues to exert (perhaps as a parent or friend or teacher or writer); and how far forward would we need to go?

Such questions and problems become yet more acute when we look at what lies between the beginning and the end, for the middle is as difficult to define and describe in individual human lives as it is in more general historiography, with references to periods of 'middle age' or 'middle ages'. Such ages, as lying between two decisive events (birth/death; antiquity/renaissance) are comparatively long and almost infinitely malleable, with historical renaissances identified ever earlier and personal antiquity indefinitely postponed; so they often require further chronological stratification – require, that is, to be broken up into shorter periods, or manageable chapters (whether of lives or histories).

Such structuring can sometimes seem quite obvious, even seemingly self-evident, when for instance at an individual level we experience some epiphanic instant – some moment of illumination – which changes the course of our lives, and in literary terms conveniently opens a new chapter. We may, for example, suddenly, as it appears to us, fall in love, or conclude that we can no longer sustain a relationship with our partner. But even with such abrupt transition points, we are, if we seek some explanation, carried back into the past indefinitely: how and when did it come about that we fell for that particular person at that particular time? What led up to that decision to separate? These momentous personal occurrences, insights, decisions, may seem to be sudden and inexplicable – but they too have their antecedents, their causal chains, which we may variously claim to descry amidst the chaos, leading back into the recesses of the past and also, no less, leading forwards into the future.

But even granted the validity of claiming a few 'decisive' moments, is there any justification for claiming an overall direction – a forward trajectory through linear time – that contains within itself some meaning for us to attribute to our lives (for meaning is what narrative is ultimately about)? Or is it not rather the case that we constantly review and revise that narrative thread (which is apparently required for our identity formation and retention) – appropriately readjusting our life stories in the interest of our changing hopes and fears, and of our own self-respect and self-preservation?

For we would all presumably agree that our own present sense of identity is somehow dependent upon our pasts. But it is not those pasts per se that determine what we are: different people respond to situations and events in very different ways; and, most importantly, we ourselves (as individuals and thence as communities) can come to modify our responses – completely change the way we look at the past and so are influenced by it. That, after all, underpins any belief in the efficacy of psychotherapy; and David Carr himself concedes that 'it is through the implicit construction (and constant revision) of a life story that the individual achieves or acquires an identity'.[36]

So it is just not true, as Carr goes on to conclude, that 'our story-telling must come to terms with the world as it is, not as we wish it were'. We interpret a world (including our own past) that offers a quarry of potentialities; the past is 'real' enough (it happened), but what we make of that past – what narrative we adopt to 'emplot' and describe and explain it – is up to us; to assert that 'history has *its own story to tell*' might then appear as nothing short of an abnegation of responsibility on the part of historians (or of us as individuals).[37]

Still, regardless of whether they be seen as inherent or imposed, we do need narratives: whether provided by what we label as 'history' or 'fiction', we do need (most of us) some meaning, however contrived. 'Men', as George Eliot recognised, 'can do nothing without the make-believe of a beginning' – even if we are dimly aware that 'no retrospect will take us to the *true* beginning'.[38] 'Cut us off from Narrative', as Carlyle wrote, and 'how would the stream of conversation' – and, we might add, the stream of life itself – 'even among the wisest, languish into detached handfuls'. Those 'detached handfuls' of our conversations and our lives do need to be somehow integrated, in the service of our identity formation – made into a coherent story whose plot we can more or less follow. That is why 'in a certain sense all men are historians',[39] and it is why the function of novelists and of historians (acting often in conjunction with, if not in the service of, politicians and theologians) has always been to help provide the narratives we need.

---

[36] Carr, 'Reality', p. 126.

[37] Carr, 'Reality', pp. 135, 134 (my emphasis).

[38] George Eliot, *Daniel Deronda* [1876], ed. Terence Cave, London, Penguin, 1995, p. 1 (epigraph to chapter 1).

[39] Carlyle, 'On History' [1830], in *Essays*, pp. 81, 80.

Those narratives clearly need in some sense to be 'tidy': their function is to tidy up the chaos of experience (whether in the past or present); and it is in their relative ability to do that – or in their claims to be doing so – that writers of fiction and of history can sometimes be seen to differ. For, as Dominick LaCapra has pointed out, 'narrativisation is closest to fictionalisation . . . when it conveys relatively unproblematic closure'.[40] That is to say, despite the fact noted by Frank Ankersmit, that 'the (great) novel is endlessly reinterpretable' in resembling life itself, while the historian 'always aims for explicitness and wishes the text to be as unambiguous and as resistant to multiple interpretations as possible',[41] it seems that novelists actually have a better chance of producing a complete and rounded story than historians can ever hope to have. For 'truth', as the American writer Herman Melville notes, when 'uncompromisingly told, will always have its ragged edges';[42] histories, of however great a length, will always be unfinished. So as Fernand Braudel explains, historians might like ideally to emulate novelists, and keep their 'subject under control', but 'Fortunately or unfortunately, the historian has not the novelist's freedom',[43] so that, despite their best efforts, they will inevitably end up with a compromise and an awareness that much remains unsaid and still outside the narrative, untidy and with 'ragged edges'.

That is by no means to say that novelists themselves have been unaware of the contingency of their own narratives. Virginia Woolf writes of biographies – or in her case accounts of fictional characters – as requiring writers 'to tack together torn bits of stuff, stuff with raw edges'; she is well aware of the tidiness being imposed upon such treatments as enable people, or even compel them, in real life as well as in novels, 'to fit in with others' even 'compel us to walk in step like civilised people'.But the main character in her novel *The Waves*, Bernard, professes to be frustrated by such attempts to provide meaningful (and conventional) order for lives that must nonetheless remain essentially messy and disordered: 'How tired I am of stories, how tired I am of phrases that come down beautifully with all their feet on the ground! Also, how I distrust neat designs of life that are drawn upon half-sheets of note-paper.' Reality, he realises, is not like that: 'Life is not susceptible perhaps to the treatment we give it when we try to tell it.'[44]

---

[40] Dominick LaCapra, 'Resisting Apocalypse and Rethinking History' in Jenkins et al. (eds), *Manifestos*, p. 166.

[41] Frank Ankersmit, 'Manifesto for an Analytical Political History', in Jenkins et al. (eds), *Manifestos*, p. 195, n. 3.

[42] Herman Melville, *Billy Budd*, quoted by Rigney, *Imperfect Histories*, p. 43.

[43] Fernand Braudel, *The Mediterranean and the Mediterranean World in the Age of Philip II* [1949], 2 vols; London, Fontana, 1975, Preface to the First Edition, p. 17.

For one thing any narrative will be defective, if only as a result of our linguistic deficiencies: language always fails to express completely what we *feel*; the perfect description, towards which we strive – when words will exactly correspond to our experience – forever eludes us, and there always remains a shadow between our words and the external reality to which they are meant to apply. So as Virginia Woolf wrote in a letter in 1930, 'One's sentences are only an approximation, a net one flings over some sea pearl which may vanish; and if one brings it up it won't be anything like what it was when I saw it.'[45] Returning to *The Waves*, then, Bernard is 'eternally engaged' in the process 'of finding some perfect phrase that fits this very moment exactly', but has to concede his ultimate failure: 'I am astonished, as I draw the veil off things with words, how much, how infinitely more than I can say, I have observed.' His verbal descriptions can only ever represent a minute part of the totality to which they refer: 'Whatever sentence I extract whole and entire from this cauldron is only a string of little fish that let themselves be caught while a million others leap and sizzle, making the cauldron bubble like boiling silver, and slip through my fingers.'[46]

But however problematic, their shared concern with the construction of meaning through narrative is one important reason for history's close and enduring relationship with fiction. In both fields, the writer's job is to reduce the chaos of potential data – the virtually infinite subject matter potentially available – to some sort of order within a narrative that, by its coherence and consistency, compels (or at least persuades towards) belief and acceptance as valid (or in some sense 'truthful') by the reader. We talk of fictional characters and their stories as being 'believable' or 'credible' or 'true to life', when they are presented in a consistent and coherent way; and similarly with histories, a test for truth has often been, in Ernst Renan's formulation, 'a logically probable narrative, harmonious throughout'.[47]

In the case of both history and fiction, too, any appearance of an intrusive personal authorship has regularly been made to disappear, with narratives laying claim to a narrator who somehow narrates 'from nowhere'. That is to say, in the interest of persuasiveness, personal and involved narrators have conventionally been absent, but have appeared rather to speak from outside

---

[44] Virginia Woolf, *The Waves* [1931], Harmondsworth, Penguin, 1951, pp. 222–3, 204, 229.

[45] Virginia Woolf (1930), quoted by Julia Briggs, *Virginia Woolf: An Inner Life*, London, Harcourt, 2005, p. 238.

[46] Woolf, *Waves*, pp. 59, 71, 220.

[47] Ernst Renan, *The Life of Jesus* (1865), p. 32; quoted by Rhodri Hayward, *Resisting History: Religious Transcendence and the Invention of the Unconscious*, Manchester, Manchester University Press, 2007, p. 13.

the stories that they are telling. In that way their function is marked by its impersonality and 'objectivity' – and they are presumed not to speak from their own necessarily limited perspective, but to tell it 'how it was'. And they thus contrive to embellish their tales with what Sande Cohen has described as 'the *patina of necessity*',[48] and endow them with the semblance of truth.

In that respect, historians can be seen as resembling spiritualist mediums, who disclaim any involvement in their own productions. The Welsh preacher Evan Roberts explained in 1905 how he was sometimes tempted 'to speak *my own words*';[49] but that devilish temptation was overcome with the help of God, who then provided the 'words and ideas to answer to the needs of the crowd'. We have there, as historian Rhodri Hayward describes, 'a situation in which the narrative of another runs through the body'; and the narrator, whether prophet, novelist, or historian, is inspired, and all the more persuasive, for having devolved responsibility to some higher power – whether God, or Muse, or mere archival evidence.

Conclusion

What I hope is already clear is that history and fiction are inseparably twinned. They have always made use of each other – with historians drawing on evidence derived from fictional sources, and writers of fiction setting their stories in earlier periods about which they need historical support. Further, as we have just seen, the two subjects share certain aims and procedures, inasmuch as both are concerned to present coherent narratives by means of which a plethora of data is reduced to some sort of order. Both in short aim to provide a story that is meaningful, or (again in some sense) true.

To some extent, then, they may be seen to be in competition, and it may be that that has provoked practitioners on both sides (but particularly historians) to distinguish themselves clearly from one another – seeking some exclusivity and no doubt superiority in the disciplinary hierarchy. So while the overall direction of our argument here will be to indicate, not so much the separateness and distinctiveness of history and fiction and the boundaries between them, but rather their interrelatedness and interdependence and the borderlands they share, let us look first, in the following chapter, at claims made for

---

[48] Sande Cohen at the Institute of Historical Research, London, 8 November 2007.
[49] Evan Roberts, quoted by Hayward, *Resisting History*, p. 112. The following quotation is from Hayward, p. 113.

the factuality – *non-fictionality* – of history, before going on to see how the claimed fact/fiction distinction has been and is being eroded.

Further reading

Braudy, Leo, *Narrative Form in History and Fiction*, Princeton, Princeton University Press, 1970.

Carnes, Mark C. (ed.), *Novel History: Historians and Novelists Confront America's Past (and Each Other)*, London, Simon & Schuster, 2001.

Carr, David, *Time, Narrative and History*, Bloomington, Indiana University Press, 1986.

Curthoys, Ann and Docker, John, *Is History Fiction?*, Sydney, University of New South Wales, 2006.

Jenkins, Keith, Morgan, Sue, and Munslow, Alun (eds), *Manifestos for History*, London, Routledge, 2007.

Kelley, Donald (ed.), *Versions of History from Antiquity to the Enlightenment*, New Haven and London, Yale University Press, 1991.

Mink, Louis O., 'History and Fiction as Modes of Comprehension', in Brian Fay, Eugene O. Golob, and Richard T. Vann (eds), *Historical Understanding*, Ithaca and London, Cornell University Press, 1987.

Munslow, Alun, *Narrative and History*, Basingstoke, Palgrave Macmillan, 2007.

Stern, Fritz (ed.), *The Varieties of History from Voltaire to the Present*, New York, Meridian Books, 1956.

White, Hayden, *Metahistory: The Historical Imagination in Nineteenth-Century Europe*, Baltimore, Johns Hopkins, 1973.

White, Hayden, *Tropics of Discourse: Essays in Cultural Criticism*, Baltimore and London, Johns Hopkins, 1978.

History: fact or fiction?

In this second introductory chapter, we are concerned first with claims for the 'scientific' nature of history, implying its factual – strictly non-fictional – status. We then examine the parallel tradition of sceptical critiques associated particularly with Romanticism, which culminates in postmodernist claims for the actual identification of history with fiction. The chapter concludes with a case study which shows a novelist – a writer of fiction – addressing some of the historiographical issues introduced here.

We have seen in the previous chapter that, as in many pairings, history and fiction at once benefit and suffer from their cohabitation: aspiring to inhabit at least some of the same territory, they have a relationship characterised by periods of tranquillity interspersed with more aggressive competitiveness. For the most part, each has been prepared to accept an early territorial dispensation, in terms of which specific allocations were made with clearly demarked disciplinary boundaries; but periodic temptations to stray into each other's patrimony have not always been resisted, so that tensions between the two have inevitably erupted, often accompanied by strident cries for the establishment of independent and autonomous domains.

In this chapter, then, we shall look, first, at claims for the strict *non-fictionality* of history – claims that it is a 'scientific' study that has to do with 'facts' and 'truth' – and so is the diametric opposite of fiction; and, second, at challenges to such claims, and the attempted erosion of their clear distinctiveness. These two intellectual strands often run, at any given time, in parallel; but a conventional narrative points to the dominance of the former as historians sought status for their subject through emulating proponents of nineteenth-century sciences, and the ascendancy of the latter as one aspect of a reactionary 'Romanticism' that has more recently resurfaced in the guise of 'postmodernism'. They might, then, be seen as representing or exemplifying two intellectual fashions or cultural emphases; and it may be that the strength of each indicates the need to view them, not so much as mutually exclusive, but rather as complementary. Their relationship, at the very least, might (like any human relationship) best be perceived, not as definitive and static, but as a process that remains ongoing, with each partner open to redefinition and renegotiation.

History as non-fiction

Historians, as Simon Schama acknowledged at a discussion in 2007, may be seen as party-poopers, inasmuch as they tend to spoil the fun of other people's fantasies. But for such seemingly negative behaviour, there is of course a positively virtuous justification: that *'we tell the truth!*'[1] Greg Dening similarly, while conceding that he is a storyteller, insists that, as an historian, he is 'a teller of *true* stories. I *do not write fiction.*'[2] So although he also insists that 'making history', or 'historying' as he calls it, is an endlessly ongoing process, it seems that, as with any science, there is expected to be a steady erosion of 'myth' by the advancing force of 'truth'. As Peter Gay has written, '[T]he objects of the historian's inquiry are precisely that, objects, out there in a *real and a single past*';[3] and, as with the objects of external nature, the professed aim is ultimately to reach 'the truth' about them. It is not without some justification, then, that the eminent American historian William H. McNeill has recently entitled his autobiographical 'Historian's Memoir' *The Pursuit of Truth*.[4] So while we have seen in the preceding chapter that there are good

---

[1] Simon Schama, speaking as a contributor to the discussion, 'America: the view from here', British Museum, London, 7 June 2007.

[2] Greg Dening, 'Performing Cross-culturally', in Keith Jenkins, Sue Morgan and Alun Munslow (eds), *Manifestos for History*, London, Routledge, 2007, p. 101 (my emphases). Note, however, that while this may seem to imply the inclusion of Greg Dening amongst the more conservative historians, he is far from being that, as any reader of his imaginative and moving Manifesto will confirm.

[3] Peter Gay, *Style in History*, London, Jonathan Cape, 1974, p. 210.

[4] William H. McNeill (Professor Emeritus of History, University of Chicago), *The Pursuit of Truth: A Historian's Memoir*, Lexington, University Press of Kentucky, 2005.

reasons for history's close relationship with fiction, it has long been a major concern of historians nonetheless to keep their distance. History's essential incompatibility with fiction is to be emphatically maintained: as against imaginative literature, its singularity as an autonomous discipline is marked by its concern with *truth*.

The status of history as specifically *non*-fiction – as positively excluding fiction, and seeing any fictional intrusions as defilements – was proclaimed even in antiquity. As early as the second century, Lucian of Samosata, for example, in an essay on the writing of history, insisted that it 'abhors the intrusion of any least scruple of falsehood'. For its primary purpose is to be useful, by enabling us to learn from past mistakes and by giving indications for the future; and that purpose can be fulfilled only from accounts of the past that are *true*. History's proper business, then, is 'the establishment of truth'; and the historian 'must sacrifice to no God but Truth' as he endeavours 'to make of his brain a mirror' that can reflect past events with perfect accuracy, and so 'tell the thing *as it happened*'. Admittedly, historians need to superimpose upon the past an orderly narrative, in which the various parts will be seen as constituting links in a single chain – or, to switch metaphors, 'parallel threads' will be woven together with 'their extremities intermingling' – but that is far from implying the need for any fictional or poetic intrusions. Indeed it has to be kept in mind that 'poetry and history offer different wares, and have their separate rules . . . It is surely a great, a superlative weakness, this inability to distinguish history from poetry.'[5]

That distinction, initiated in antiquity, became yet more firmly established as an orthodoxy in the nineteenth century, when historians decisively assumed their mantle of 'scientists'. At a time when scientific procedures attained a degree of popularity, with public demonstrations and experiments, and debates featuring such enthusiastic proponents as Thomas Huxley, historians quite naturally sought to align themselves with the cultural zeitgeist. History, then, no less than geology or biology, was to be seen as a science: just as physical scientists revealed the truth about nature, so historians revealed the truth about the past; in both cases, earlier myths (or fictions) were to be replaced by fact. Historians could thus feel justified in claiming as their special prerogative the transmission of the *truth* about the past; so that when (as we previously saw) Thackeray, as a mere novelist, entitled his work '*The* History *of Henry Esmond*', one early reviewer took care to distinguish such writing from the sort

---

[5] Lucian of Samosata, *The Works*, trans. H. W. Fowler and F. G. Fowler, 4 vols; Oxford, Clarendon Press, 1905, vol. II, pp. 112–14, 128–9 (my emphasis), 132–3.

of *proper* history that 'requires absolute adherence to the truth and nothing but the truth'.[6]

That emphatic distinction, as insisted upon by earlier historians, has recently become more nuanced, though some continued to write in that vein through the twentieth century. Geoffrey Elton, for instance, is well known for his belief that the proper use of primary evidence 'should make possible a history that is *indisputably true, not* the historian's *invention*'.[7] Arthur Marwick, too, was emphatic: 'A work of history', he writes, '*differs totally* from a novel or poem'; for historians, unlike writers of fiction, make 'special efforts . . . to separate out *unambiguously* what is *securely established* from what is basically *speculation*'.[8]

The secure establishment of history's subject matter is provided – if it can ever be provided – by empirical evidence, just as in science; and confidence is further boosted by cohesiveness – by the way things fit (or appear to fit, or are made to fit) together. So historians famously derive their theories and descriptions from archival sources – those remnants that survive from the time about which history is being written. Those sources are the equivalent of external nature for the physical scientist: it is they that, as in any science, act as (supposedly) firm foundations for the theoretical constructions built upon them. And the further test of coherence is applied by 'peer review' and 'professional consensus': historians, it is claimed, just like scientists in other fields, have the training and the tools to enable them to make judgements in these matters; they know what fits in tidily with the existing body of work relevant to the particular issues involved. That body of historical knowledge (again, like that of science) is continually building, and each new block must make its contribution to the whole. The truth of history is such that it not only *corresponds* with 'the reality' of the past, but also *coheres* with a whole existing body of research relating to that past.

That gives the body of 'historical knowledge' the evident virtue of great strength, and just as in the case of scientific knowledge, it seems immune to challenges from sceptics and cranks from outside the discipline. That saves a lot of time and energy which might otherwise need to be spent in confronting spurious alternatives, and it also leaves little room for dissent: one model, or paradigm of explanation, is generally accepted as the framework within which

---

[6] Goldwin Smith (1859), quoted by Christina Crosby, *The Ends of History: Victorians and 'The Woman Question'*, London, Routledge, 1991, p. 45.

[7] So Patrick Collinson in *London Review of Books*, 29 November 2007, p. 33 (my emphases).

[8] Arthur Marwick, *The New Nature of History: Knowledge, Evidence, Language*, Basingstoke, Palgrave, 2001, pp. 215 (my emphases), 82.

new research is required to fit; and that model persists until challenged by 'revisionists' who have the power (with new evidence, or enhanced analytic techniques, or simply the ability to look 'with new eyes') to supplant the old with a whole new explanatory framework. Which is fine: that is how any science works and progresses.[9]

So history, as a science, is progressive, and is not infrequently viewed as superior to the fiction with which it is so unambiguously contrasted. Certainly Arthur Marwick implied that 'speculation' is less reputable than what is claimed as 'indisputably true'. Even Ann Rigney, as a theorist, suggests that one of the virtues of historical fiction is that, through its own attractiveness, it might serve as a 'stepping stone' and motivation to further *historical* enquiry;[10] and, as an historical novelist, Sarah Dunant, while confessing to some 'conscious manipulation of history', laments that 'extensive research and a deep love of the period cannot, *alas*, turn a writer of fiction into an historian' – where not only is the distinction between fiction and history stoutly maintained, but the 'alas' seems to indicate some deficiency in the novelist's inability to become anything so exalted as 'an historian'.[11] Finally, to revert to the opening of this section, it has to be said that historian Simon Schama seemed (at least to this member of his audience) to be far from apologetic or defensive in his admission to being a party-pooper: historians, he implied, were engaged in something far more serious and more important than mere partying in their telling of 'the truth'. History, after all, is something more than fiction.

The fact/fiction distinction eroded

Yet it has never been as easy as historians might wish to distinguish clearly between fact and fiction; a periodic blurring is apparent in both genres. We have already seen how a writer of 'historical novels' such as Walter Scott, although sometimes disclaiming any intent to 'intrude upon the province of history',[12] nonetheless challenged the narrow definition of 'history' on which

---

[9] For the classic analysis, see T. S. Kuhn, *The Structure of Scientific Revolutions*, Chicago and London, University of Chicago, 1962.

[10] Ann Rigney, 'Being an Improper Historian', in Jenkins et al. (eds), *Manifestos*, p. 155.

[11] Sarah Dunant, *In the Company of the Courtesan*, London, Virago, 2007, p. 403 (my emphasis).

[12] So the narrator in *Waverley*, quoted by Diane Elam, *Romancing the Postmodern*, London, Routledge, 1992, p. 54.

nineteenth-century academics were insisting; and the dividing water was further muddied by another novelist a generation later. For William Makepiece Thackeray, while claiming the status of historian for himself, can sound like a forerunner of contemporary theorist Hayden White: thus, providing us with an early example of a fiction-writer's critique of history, he insists that, with events following one another, as they do, without any necessary connections, 'Blunders there must be in the best of narratives' – and the best of narratives include those presented by historians, in which too 'more [is] asserted than they can possibly know or vouch for'. For historians, no less than novelists, rely on questionable evidence; so that 'the public must once for all be warned that the author's individual fancy very likely supplies much of the narrative; and that he forms it as best he may, out of stray papers, conversations reported to him, and his knowledge, right or wrong, of the characters of the persons engaged'. And if that is a personal confession by a man who only *claims* to be an historian while writing what is better described as *fiction*, Thackeray quite justifiably likens his own work to that of such accepted historians as Sallust or Livy (and he might have added Thucydides), whose orations are similarly sourced, and no more nor less 'authentic'. Indeed, when Thackeray describes elsewhere how 'I have drawn the figures as I fancied they were; set down conversations as I think I might have heard them', he could virtually be translating from Thucydides' account of his own historiographical procedures.[13]

A similar erosion of the fiction/history distinction is provided, again from a literary standpoint, by Henry James who, like Thackeray, and just as contentiously, claims that '*the novel is history*'. For as he goes on to argue in his essay on 'The Art of Fiction': 'To represent and illustrate the past, the actions of men, is the task of either writer'; though it is the novelist who has the harder task, since the evidence that he collects is 'far from being purely literary'. The novelist, that is, needs to penetrate more deeply into the psychological aspects of human beings, with which the historian, working on a broader canvas, may not be concerned. But a novelist like Trollope, James believes, who admits to 'making believe' with a narrative that can go in any direction the reader might wish, is perpetrating nothing less than 'a terrible crime'; such an attitude constitutes (just as would be asserted of an historian who wrote similarly) 'a betrayal of a sacred office'.[14]

[13] William Makepiece Thackeray, quotations from *The Newcomes* (1853–55), ch. XXIV, and *The Virginians* (1857–59), ch. 1; in Geoffrey Tillotson, *Thackeray the Novelist* [1954], London, Methuen, 1974, pp. 76–8. Cf. Thucydides, *History of the Peloponnesian War*, trans. R. Crawley, London, J. M. Dent and Sons, 1910, p. 11.
[14] Henry James, 'The Art of Fiction', in *The Art of Fiction and Other Essays*, ed. M. Roberts, New York, Oxford University Press, 1948, pp. 5–6.

From the other side of the disciplinary divide, historians themselves have also periodically blurred the orthodox distinction. Even Thucydides, who aspired to scientific accuracy, included his notorious speeches that are deliberately rendered in such a way as to give the impression of being verbatim reports of what was said by given individuals at particular times; yet they are of course (in the absence of tape-recorders or conveniently located writers of shorthand, and as Thucydides himself clarifies) imaginative reconstructions based on personal knowledge of the speaker, reports from others, and an assessment of what was likely to be said in the circumstances. They may constitute an extremely good estimate of what actually took place, but strictly speaking they qualify more as imaginative fiction than as factual history.

And as the 'father' of scientific history, Thucydides had many descendents, not all of whom were as open as he was concerning their own methodologies; so that fiction has often been inextricably bound into history – unacknowledged, and accepted as factual until later exposed. Thus, for example, Geoffrey of Monmouth – writing in the twelfth century and an important source for Britain's early history – describes King Arthur's battle with Lucius Tiberius in great detail: he gives, as his modern editor describes, 'precise information about the positioning of the divisions on each side, the number of men engaged and the names of divisional commanders'; and in Thucydidean style he quotes directly (or purports to do so) the words of Arthur's and his opponent's speeches to their troops. 'One is', as Lewis Thorpe (Geoffrey's editor) writes, 'tempted to say that this is *romanticised history* with a vengeance, until one remembers that *the battle never took place* and that it is merely *romantic fiction*'; and yet, as he continues, 'history keeps peeping through the fiction'.[15]

The two, though, are not always easily distinguished; and such reciprocal 'peepings through' between fact and fiction become more widely accepted and acceptable in times when the singular status of science generally is brought into question – in periods that will be characterised here as 'Romantic'.

Romanticism

'I see little difference', confesses Rousseau, 'between . . . romances and your histories.' And with that challenge to the conventional distinction between fiction and history, he goes on explicitly to devalue the latter: for while 'the novelist draws more on his own imagination', the historian meanwhile

---

[15] Lewis Thorpe, Introduction to Geoffrey of Monmouth, *The History of the Kings of Britain*, Harmondsworth, Penguin, 1966, pp. 18–19 (my emphases).

'slavishly copies what *another* has imagined'.[16] Fictional romances, then, at least have the virtue of being first-hand accounts of their author's own imagination, whereas histories are relegated to being mere copies of someone else's; and the whole claimed superiority of historical narratives, as being (unlike fiction) actually *true*, is demolished.

Rousseau – well known for his early challenges to contemporary intellectual orthodoxies derived from 'the Enlightenment' – justifies his virtual assimilation of the two genres by explaining that, with their shared origin in the imagination, they are equally unreliable as descriptions of the past. So as far as history is concerned, 'It is inevitable that the facts described in history should *not* give an exact picture of what really happened; [for] they are transformed in the brain of the historian, they are moulded by his interests and coloured by his prejudices.' No less than with fictional romances, subjectivity intrudes, so that 'Ignorance or partiality disguises everything'.[17]

In that questioning (or denial) of the 'factual' and 'objective' nature of history, Rousseau lies in what can be identified as a whole tradition of thinkers whom we can (for the sake of our own narrative) conveniently label as 'Romantics'. That label implies opposition to the more 'scientific' mainstream – where 'mainstream' indicates what has proved to be the prevalent and most influential approach to nature and the past through modern times. So Rousseau can be seen as exemplifying a minority tradition wherein, by the eighteenth century, a number of philosophers had already applied the techniques of ancient scepticism to historical study – as a result of which some extremists felt justified in concluding that, in the words of one English commentator, 'all history is fabulous [i.e. fictional]'. Indeed, as Lord Bolingbroke goes on to explain, some sceptical critics of orthodox historiography had gone so far as to assert that, 'the very best is nothing better than a probable tale, artfully contrived, and plausibly told, wherein *truth and falsehood are indistinguishably blended together*'.[18]

That emphatic obliteration of the history/fiction distinction, as described by Bolingbroke, was reiterated in the following century by another influential figure – indeed, a veritable cultural guru of his time: Thomas Carlyle, whose fame rested not least on his own vivid historical study of the French Revolution, was also the author of a number of essays on the nature of history

---

[16] Jean Jacques Rousseau, *Émile* [1762], trans. Barbara Foxley, London, J. M. Dent, 1911, p. 200 (my emphasis).

[17] Rousseau, *Émile*, p. 200 (my emphasis).

[18] Bolingbroke, Lord Henry St. John, *Letters on the Study and Use of History* [1752], London, Alexander Murray, 1870, p. 27 (my emphases).

itself. In these we have already seen him insisting on the *human need* for narrative; but he is also deeply sceptical about any associated claims for truth. For there are, he realises, problems first in relation to the very building blocks of facts: 'What', he asks through his mouthpiece in another well known work, *Sartor Resartus* (1836), 'What if many a so-called *Fact* were little better than a *Fiction?*' And as one purporting here to be the editor of some highly important philosophical works, he feels bound to go on to ask the fundamental question: '*What are your historical Facts?*'[19]

Further, whatever 'historical facts' are, do they really reveal what we need to know in order to understand an individual man or humanity more generally: 'Wilt thou know a Man, above all, a Mankind, by stringing together beadrolls of what thou namest Facts?' That humanist questioning of the validity and the value of 'facts' themselves will be picked up notably by Charles Dickens, as we shall see in Chapter 3. But we can already note Carlyle's awareness of the further problem that arises in 'stringing together' facts in a narrative; for he reminds us that any supposedly '*authentic* fragments' of history are bound to be 'mingled with *Fabulous* [i.e. fictitious] chimeras'.[20]

In that recognition of the inevitable mingling of fact and fiction, Carlyle is aligned more with Hayden White than David Carr (whom we saw in the previous chapter disagreeing about there being narrative form inherent in human life). And in similar vein, he refers in his essay 'On History' to the 'unfathomable' chaos – the 'Chaos of Being' – which it is the function of historians to depict: 'By its very nature', as he writes elsewhere, 'it is a labyrinth and chaos, this thing we call Human History.'[21] It is no wonder, then, that he goes on to highlight the inevitable inadequacy of historians, and their inability ever satisfactorily to draw a single line through that chaotic totality. For 'all Narrative is, by its nature, of only one dimension; only travels forward towards one, or towards successive points: Narrative is *linear*' – whereas what requires representation, on the other hand, is by its nature multi-dimensional; 'Action is *solid.*' So historians work in defiance of the utter complexity of the interconnected whole of the past – a past that is, as an additional complication, connected also to the future, so that 'only by the combination of both is the meaning of either completed', and history necessarily becomes 'a looking both before and after'.[22]

---

[19]   Thomas Carlyle, *Sartor Resartus* [1836], London, Ward, Lock, n.d., p. 134 (my emphases).

[20]   *Sartor Resartus*, pp. 134, 76 (my emphases).

[21]   Thomas Carlyle, *The Letters and Speeches of Oliver Cromwell*, ed. S. C. Lomas, 3 vols; London, Methuen, 1904, p. 6.

[22]   Thomas Carlyle, *English and Other Critical Essays*, London, J. M. Dent, 1915, pp. 84–5 (original emphases), 80.

Historians are thus, as Carlyle concludes, reduced to offering oversimplified explanations, not least of that central concept, causation: they 'assiduously track' a chain 'or chainlets, of "causes and effects" . . . when the whole is a broad, deep Immensity, and each atom is "chained" and complected with all!' – when 'every single event is the offspring not of one, but of all other events, prior or contemporaneous'. So that overall it becomes clear that any historical narrative can 'at best' never be more than 'a poor approximation' to what actually happened, 'running path after path, through the Impassable'; it can never be more than an oversimplified way through the palimpsest of the past – 'that complex Manuscript, covered over with formless inextricably-entangled unknown characters', which, it surely has to be conceded, 'can be fully interpreted *by no man*'.[23] So where then is history's defining characteristic of 'truth'?

History's inevitable deficiency – the fact that scientific history could deal only with a *part* of the totality of human experience – left open a door through which others in the nineteenth century soon strode, claiming for themselves those parts of the past which, as they quickly saw, would be otherwise lost. Those more subjectively experienced pasts became the preserve of writers labelled novelists, but novelists who saw themselves as, no less than historians, purveying not fiction but another form of truth.[24] As Tolstoy claims, or aspires: 'the hero of my story, whom I love with all my heart and soul, whom I have attempted to portray in all his beauty and who has always been, is now and always will be supremely magnificent, is *truth*.'[25]

Once again, then, the two genres have become blurred and tangled, in an intellectual and cultural tradition that has become particularly prominent in our own postmodern times.

Postmodernism

There is a sense in which postmodernism can be seen as a contemporary extension of Romanticism, as described above: in the context of our present concerns, it lies in a continuing tradition of sceptical questioning of any absolute distinction between history and fiction. But postmodernist theorists have

---

[23] *Essays*, pp. 84–6 (my emphasis), 90.
[24] See e.g., as we have already indicated, Thackeray, *The History of Henry Esmond*, which has been described as 'a counter-text to history proper'; 'in Thackeray's text, fiction is not separate from history, but rather is all that history proper must not admit: the instability of identity, of subject and object, of time itself' (Crosby, *Ends of History*, pp. 8, 47).
[25] Tolstoy, 'Sebastopol Sketch' (1855), quoted by Orlando Figes, *New York Review of Books*, 22 November 2007, p. 6.

raised the stakes by producing more sophisticated arguments, derived not only from philosophical scepticism but also from linguistics. These come together particularly to focus on their treatment of narrative, and in this context (as we have seen in Chapter 1) the work of Hayden White is crucial. For what White does is utterly to erode the supposed distinction between historical and fictional narratives: 'stories', he insists, 'are not true or false, but rather more or less intelligible, coherent, consistent and persuasive, and so on. And this is true of historical, no less than fictional stories'; for as his commentator Keith Jenkins goes on to clarify, '*Anyone* who writes a narrative is fictionalising.'[26] In other words, there can be no distinction upheld between the knowledge claims of historians and of novelists: the stories produced by both are just that – stories, derived from their imaginative ordering of data, ideally expressed in an attractive form and presented in a cogent manner.

For the content of any narrative about the past, as we have seen White insisting, is not just found – is not just there, lying around, as it were, awaiting rediscovery and re-presentation by historians. The data that constitute historical evidence have to be imaginatively welded together into a coherent form; they have to be emplotted in one of a number of possible frameworks (that is, the frameworks that are provided and available within any given culture), made to fit into a linguistic structure, so that a plausible and persuasive story can be told. Quite contrary to their frequent claims, therefore, historians are themselves responsible for translating what might be claimed as 'factual' data into fiction; for it is they who transform the data (their evidence) by selecting certain elements (and necessarily ignoring others), and then emplotting them within their own choice of narrative form – whether comic, tragic, ironic, or whatever. They 'may not like to think of their works as translations of fact into fictions; but this is one of the effects of their works'.[27] So as the novelist E. L. Doctorow agreed: 'There is no fiction or nonfiction as we commonly understand the distinction: there is only narrative.'[28]

That last intervention by a novelist indicates the interest in postmodernist theorising shown by practising writers of fiction – and that will be a major theme running through this book. The similarity (if not identity) of fictional and historical narrative construction is a conclusion that recurs, for example, in the theorising to be found in the novels of Penelope Lively. We shall be

---

[26] Hayden White, quoted in Keith Jenkins, *Why History? Ethics and Postmodernity*, London, Routledge, 1999, p. 120; cf. p. 124 (my emphasis).

[27] Hayden White, *Tropics of Discourse: Essays in Cultural Criticism*, Baltimore and London, Johns Hopkins, 1978, p. 92.

[28] E. L. Doctorow (1977), quoted by Barbara Foley, *Telling the Truth: The Theory and Practice of Documentary Fiction*, Ithaca and London, Cornell University Press, 1986, p. 9.

considering her work further in the following section and in Chapter 4, but refer now to her novel *According to Mark* (1984). The central character, Mark Lamming, is a biographer who is researching the life of an earlier writer, Gilbert Strong. Strong himself is represented as having written of how a biographer is a sort of historian, so could not be expected to reveal any final truth; for 'we all know that history can give no final truth'. So perhaps, he suggested – in direct contradiction to orthodox opinion – while historians inevitably fail in their objective, 'novelists are the only people who do tell the truth'. The reason is that they, faced (just like historians) with an infinity of choices, deliberately and consciously choose 'what is to happen, to whom it happens, and in what way [they] will relate what happens'. A narrative, as constructed by the novelist, can thus at least claim the virtue of being 'complete in its own terms. When he says, "This is the story and the whole story", we must accept it.' So its 'truth' lies in some internal coherence that has been deliberately carved out of, or imposed upon, an infinity of alternative possibilities.[29]

But real life, and history, are of course quite different; for 'Life like history is one and indivisible'. So although it is, for the sake of analysis and description, necessary 'to chop it up into more manageable segments', the manner of our dissections and classifications and narrative constructions remains contingent, just as Hayden White argues. We may like to think of the past as the fictional Mark viewed its relics in a museum – as providing a wealth of information, with 'all this evidence of the past, labelled and pinned down and marshalled into glass cases'. But the reality, again, whether for biographer, or historian, or ourselves, is much more problematic, for nothing remains stable in that way: on the contrary, just 'give the kaleidoscope a shake and a different picture forms' – and any final picture or narrative continues to elude us. The historian's truth, then, just like that of the novelist, consists in nothing more than the internal coherence and aesthetic quality of a narrative that could have been quite different.[30]

That fusion of historical and fictional narrative construction can be seen in another 'fictional' work that, in certain respects, anticipates disciplinary discussions later provoked by postmodern theorists – a good example of an imaginative writer beating historical theorists to the draw.[31] For even some

[29] Penelope Lively, *According to Mark*, Harmondsworth, Penguin, 1985, pp. 41, 15.

[30] Lively, *Mark*, pp. 51, 97, 212.

[31] Further American examples are discussed in a book published too late for my consideration here: Timothy Parrish, *From the Civil War to the Apocalypse: Postmodern History and American Fiction*, Amherst, University of Massachusetts Press, 2008, where it is argued that 'fiction in the postmodern era has become the primary medium for arguing about what history is' (p. 34).

seven years before Hayden White's theoretical challenge in *Metahistory*, Truman Capote had provided a practical example of blurred distinctions in *In Cold Blood*[32] – a work we have already seen described as 'the first non-fiction novel'.

That seemingly self-contradictory definition invites further thought about just what we mean by 'non-fiction' (including 'history') and 'novel' (i.e. 'fiction'). For *In Cold Blood* is regularly characterised as *fiction* – a story centred on the brutal murder of a farmer, with his wife and two of their children, on a remote farm in Kansas. But as a novel it has some unusual features, including not least the fact that the author's subject matter, and his own research and writing techniques, are virtually indistinguishable from those more usually ascribed to *history*. For, first, the central event – the murders – actually did take place, on a November night in 1959; and Capote goes to great trouble to unravel what really happened – interviewing, most importantly, the perpetrators, and then everyone else who had any involvement (whether as friends, relations, neighbours, criminal investigators, etc.). 'All the material in this book not derived from my own observation', writes the author in his Acknowledgements, 'is either taken from official records or is the result of interviews with the persons directly concerned' – those interviews being numerous and 'conducted over a considerable period of time'. One could hardly better that as a statement of correct procedures for a contemporary historian – corresponding closely as they do, once again, to those proclaimed by Thucydides: writing of how he had not even trusted his own first impressions, the Greek historian explains that his narrative (just like that of Capote) 'rests partly on what I saw myself, partly on what others saw for me, the accuracy of the report being always tried by the most severe and detailed tests possible'.[33]

Capote's own narrative construction is complex: there is no straightforward story, progressing from beginning, through middle, to concluding dénouement, but rather intimations and projections, with hints of what is to come, as well as flashbacks and cuts between the stories of the various protagonists. The carefully constructed whole is presented in such a way as to maintain the interest of the reader, in a manner that, conventionally speaking, befits a novelist who aspires to keep the pages turning rather than a detached historian-recorder of the truth.

But that attractive mode of presentation would surely not disgrace a less conventional (perhaps more 'popular') historian; and nor would the author's constant resort to so-called 'primary' evidence – including direct speech

---

[32]   Truman Capote, *In Cold Blood* [1966], London, Penguin, 1967.
[33]   Thucydides, *History*, p. 11.

(again in the manner of Thucydides) and quotation from contemporary documents, such as private letters and reports. At one point (on p. 132), I began to
doubt the veracity of one of these transcriptions, when Perry, one of the two
young murderers, was portrayed as using the word 'ostensibly'; for this
seemed to hint at a somewhat unlikely sophistication of vocabulary. But a few
pages later, in a letter from his sister Barbara, we read of how his 'vocabulary is
excellent'; and we also learn that Perry kept a thick notebook, 'which constituted his personal dictionary, a non-alphabetically listed miscellany of words
he believed "beautiful" or "useful", or at least "worth memorising" ' – in which
were included such abstruse examples as 'facinorous', 'hagiophobia', and
'thanatoid'. That last was later actually used in direct speech by Perry as he
describes an old man being propped up at a restaurant table, providing some
justification for his friend Dick's criticism that he 'was always using hundred-
dollar words he doesn't half know the meaning of'.[34]

So *In Cold Blood* is a novel – *fiction* – inasmuch as it is an imaginative construction written to hold the attention of its readers, and make them want to
keep on reading. It is *history* inasmuch as the author's endeavour is (yes, again
imaginatively) to *re*construct – to reconstruct a past event within a context
sufficiently wide as to enable him to understand, on the basis of reliable
evidence, how it came to pass. Truman Capote used the long period – nearly
two thousand days – of the murderers' incarceration on Death Row, before
their execution in April 1965, to carry out the most detailed investigation into
what had taken place – and in particular into the psychopathological states of
the perpetrators. That psychological investigation of its agents' motivations
includes an assessment in relation to contemporary theories of psychological
trauma and 'personality disorganisation'; and it is possibly here that the
author can be seen to *sympathise* with the objects of his study, rather than
keeping them at arm's length in the manner of a properly '*detached*' historian.[35]
Yet without his own closeness, without his ability to *sympathise*, it is arguable
that Capote would never have established the sort of relationship with the
murderers – the objects of his study – that made their more intimate revela-
tions possible; and it is indeed difficult to see how otherwise an 'historian'
with the intention of writing up the same story as 'recent' or 'contemporary'
history could have acted.

So which is it – history or fiction? And does it really matter? The answer
must depend on our own definitions, our own characterisations and

---

[34] Capote, *Cold Blood*, pp. 137, 142, 204, 326.
[35] Thus, for example, he records what one Dr Jones *would have* testified in Court, had his
nuanced psychological findings been permitted as evidence: Capote, *Cold Blood*, pp. 286f.

descriptions of the author's various aims and procedures in relation to the two disciplines. And those disciplines are to be defined by us: we can apply our definitions as we think fit; so they will no doubt vary over time, in line with fluctuations in disciplinary parameters and developments in academic expectations and requirements. The overall point, though, surely, is that Truman Capote's book once again challenges the sharp distinctions that are often made between two closely overlapping genres; and in this it anticipates, or (depending on our chronologies) is an early exemplification of, historiographical trends in postmodernity.

So too, in another way, is Wallace Stegner's novel *Angle of Repose*, which appeared in the following decade. Of that work, an historian has written that 'He is still unsure what to call it. Fiction? Of course. History? Why not. And then he wonders: Does it really matter?'[36] Like *In Cold Blood*, the book transgresses conventionally accepted boundaries: described unequivocally by its author as 'a novel' and 'in no sense a family history', it has been praised nonetheless as 'a first-rate fictional representation of the *historical* development of the West' and 'a deeper, more powerful evocation of "family *history*" than anything done by scholars'.[37]

The seeming contradictions there – the ambiguities and critical ambivalence – arise because Stegner based his work on actual historical documents. His narrator, a retired historian named Lyman Ward, is portrayed as researching the lives of his grandparents, Susan and Oliver; but the evidence with which he works – the actual material that forms the basis for the grandparents' 'fictional' biographies – is a cache of (actual) 'historical' data. Stegner, through his mouthpiece Ward, uses the notes, correspondence, maps, and illustrations of a little known nineteenth-century writer and illustrator, Mary Hallock Foote – a Quaker from New York, who married a mining engineer and followed him in his work to the American West and Mexico, and who conveniently left literary and pictorial records of her experiences.[38] So Stegner concedes that in

[36] John Demos, 'Real Lives and Other Fictions: Reconsidering Wallace Stegner's *Angle of Repose*', in Mark C. Carnes (ed.), *Novel History: Historians and Novelists Confront America's Past (and Each Other)*, London, Simon & Schuster, 2001, p. 144. I am indebted to John Demos's essay for alerting me to Stegner's fascinating work.

[37] Richard W. Etulain, 'Western Fiction and History: A Reconsideration', in Anthony Arthur (ed.), *Critical Essays on Wallace Stegner*, Boston, G. K. Hall, 1982, p. 148; John Demos, quoted at: www.grandpoohbah.net/Grandpoohbah/BookReviews/angle.htm (my emphases).

[38] This original material was independently (and fortuitously) published only one year later, in 1972, as *A Victorian Gentlewoman in the Far West*, edited by Rodman W. Paul. Stegner himself was well qualified to make use of such material, since he had personal experience of the terrain described and had previously written the biography of another western explorer – John

his fictional work he 'utilizes selected facts from . . . real lives': his historical fiction is based on, derived from, 'real' characters and real scenes; and extracts from the source material, including especially informative letters, are incorporated within the novel, sometimes at some length, either verbatim or with minimal editing (much as an historian might illustrate his work with extracts from 'primary sources').

Wallace Stegner did thank Mary Hallock Foote's granddaughters 'for the loan of their ancestors'; but he has been accused of 'unethical borrowing' and plagiarism for proceeding in what was (for a novelist) an unorthodox way – for using another person's writings at length, for his own purposes and without due public acknowledgement. Mary Ellen Williams Walsh, in particular, enumerated his borrowings in some detail, and was concerned that he had attributed questionable and downright wrong, *fictional*, characteristics to a recognisable and identifiable *historical* figure; which, she clearly felt, was tantamount to posthumous character assassination.[39] But Stegner, made 'irritable' by such charges, maintained his right to use Foote's archive as 'raw material, broken rocks out of which I could make any kind of wall I wanted to'. Remaining insistent that his work was a novel, he described his method as being unapologetically 'to *mix history and fiction*': 'I see nothing wrong', as he insisted, some ten years later, 'with letting reminiscence or fiction serve the purpose of history, and vice versa.'[40]

The ethics of the case is not clear-cut, and some of the issues raised remain matters of contention in relation to other works that blend and blur hitherto distinctive genres. But the outcome in *Angle of Repose*, at all events, is a moving account of people at a pivotal time in American westward expansion, which has all the appearance of being a vivid evocation of their experiences and their responses to them. It also draws distinctions and parallels between the generations: throughout the novel Lyman Ward self-consciously inserts his own thoughts – including his thoughts on history itself and historical theory. And, like Stegner himself, the fictional historian is insistent that he is not (within the novel) writing history: 'I've written enough history books', he remarks, 'to know that this isn't one.'[41]

Wesley Powell, the first man to explore the Colorado River through the Grand Canyon. See *Beyond the Hundredth Meridian: John Wesley Powell and the Second Opening of the West* (1954).

[39] See Mary Ellen Walsh, '*Angle of Repose* and the Writings of Mary Hallock Foote: A Source Study', in Arthur (ed.), *Critical Essays*, pp. 184–209.

[40] Wallace Stegner, in Wallace Stegner and Richard W. Etulain, *Conversations with Wallace Stegner on Western History and Literature*, Salt Lake City, University of Utah, 1983, pp. 86–7.

[41] Wallace Stegner, *Angle of Repose* [1971], New York, Fawcett Crest, 1972, p. 186.

And yet some ambivalence does remain even within the pages of the book; for although, as Ward himself says, 'I may look to you like a novelist . . . [yet] I'm still a historian under the crust . . . I stick with the actual.' Which implies that, despite being obviously 'a biographer . . . with a personal motive', he remains aware that *qua* historian he is expected to remain detached from his object of study; so that when he catches himself smiling in complicity with his grandmother, he interjects that, 'It does not become a historian to smile' – or not in that way, which indicates too much sympathetic involvement. Nor must he let his imagination carry him too far beyond the evidence: responding to criticism that, despite writing only a novel, he won't allow himself to speculate about his grandmother's sex life, he explains that the investigation of such personal matters appears to him as beyond his remit, 'exceeding my licence as a historian'. A novelist, admittedly, is permitted freely to 'invent within the logic of a situation'; but as an historian he is constrained 'to invent within a body of inhibiting facts that I wish were otherwise'.[42]

Despite such professional constraints and expectations, Ward is portrayed as of necessity using his imagination at times – as when, for instance, he speculates about his grandmother's feelings in relation to her husband (and it is in their marriage that he is particularly interested). But when he does so, he does so openly: 'She felt, *I imagine*, both trapped with him and abjectly dependent on him.' He also, on other occasions, confesses his own total inability to imagine in that way or to recover certain aspects of a past relationship: 'What did he say? I am utterly unable to guess.' And at other times, when he does guess, he admits that that is what he is doing: 'Maybe he wanted to keep before her some aspect of himself that he did not want her to forget, though that is my guess, not hers'; and the trouble is, of course, that he can, as an historian, 'only guess backward from the consequences'. 'The fact is', as he admits about his grandfather, 'I don't know'; for unlike his wife, 'he left no novels, stories, drawings, or reminiscences to speak for him'. So: 'What went on? *I don't know*.'[43]

Ward relates that ignorance of the past to his inability even in the present to know what was going on between himself and his own wife (who suddenly and unexpectedly left him). How much more difficult – impossible even – it is to know what happened to the relationships of others in the past. 'So I don't know what happened' – that, in the end, is his inevitable conclusion. He had been trying to understand his grandmother, but ultimately failed, as one must in any attempt to understand another person: 'instead of my reward, a living woman, there is a skeleton with a riddle between its ribs'.[44]

[42] *Angle*, pp. 236, 468, 79, 237.
[43] *Angle*, pp. 88 (my emphasis), 102, 245, 208, 453 (my emphasis).
[44] *Angle*, pp. 454, 468.

Wallace Stegner, being an historian as well as a novelist, is well aware of such inevitable deficiencies in any history – aware, too (as he shows through Ward's son Rodman), of current accusations of the subject's 'irrelevance', and of it being mere escapism; but he remains convinced of the subject's importance, and shows in *Angle of Repose* how, melded with fiction, it might be enlarged to embrace what his protagonist describes as 'a kind of investigation into . . . life'.[45]

That prospective enlargement of what is considered 'history' – and not least through its overlapping with 'fiction' – has been increasingly explored by postmodernist theorists since the 1960s and 1970s when Truman Capote and Wallace Stegner were writing; and any remaining frontiers between the two genres are coming under ever more insistent attack. More recently, for example, postcolonial developments have indicated that alternative modes of historical representation may be desirable or even requisite: traditional forms may not suffice for the expression of certain experiences and memories that now need to be related. So Dipesh Chakrabarty has cited an Aboriginal intellectual, Tony Birch, who has indicated that, for him, 'The past is sometimes represented equally, or at times, more accurately through a range of textual forms, including story-telling and poetry.'[46] The Australian historian Greg Dening has similarly defined history, somewhat unconventionally as is his way, as 'the past transformed into words *or paint or dance or music or play*';[47] David Harlan has quoted John Demos regarding the possible conveyance of 'the inner feel, the specific textures of experience' in historical films and novels;[48] and Frank Ankersmit is decisive in asserting that, 'How we *feel* about the past is no less important than what we *know* about it – and probably even more so.'[49]

Unsurprisingly Frank Ankersmit, as a leading postmodern theorist, sees his own position, with its renewed emphasis on *feelings*, as 'a rehabilitation of the *romanticist's* world';[50] and that position (now far from unusual in the first

---

[45] *Angle*, p. 503.

[46] Dipesh Chakrabarty, 'History and the Politics of Recognition', in Jenkins et al. (eds), *Manifestos*, p. 80.

[47] Greg Dening, 'Performing Cross-culturally', in Jenkins et al. (eds), *Manifestos*, p. 102 (my emphases).

[48] John Demos, quoted by David Harlan, 'Historical Fiction and Academic History', in Jenkins et al. (eds), *Manifestos*, p. 110.

[49] Frank Ankersmit, *Sublime Historical Experience*, Stanford, Stanford University Press, 2005, p. 10 (my emphasis).

[50] Ankersmit, *Sublime*, p. 10 (my emphasis).

decade of the twenty-first century[51]) implies once more a need to re-examine the ways in which history meets fiction – their boundaries and borderlands, and their mutually entangled definitions.

History meets fiction – a case study: Penelope Lively, **Cleopatra's Sister**

As indicated above, one contemporary novelist whose works provide a rich quarry for those interested in the nature and purpose of history is Penelope Lively; and it will be convenient to use one of her books now as a case study in order to show further the interaction of fiction and history, and, more particularly, how fiction can serve to bring to popular notice some important issues in historical theory. For her stories introduce and illustrate a wide range of questions under current debate – and incidentally serve to make them widely accessible to the 'general reader'. These problematic questions, often otherwise consigned to the jargon-laden pages of specialist academic journals, relate to such subjects as truth, relativism, interpretation, contingency, chronology, and memory; and it is clearly shown that these are subjects which are not properly confined to erudite scholarly discussion, but impinge far more widely, and inevitably, on the everyday lives of all.

We shall have occasion to look later at other novels by Penelope Lively, but will here consider *Cleopatra's Sister* (published in 1993), where we find a quite explicit treatment of history and historiography. For the author presents us with an imagined history of a fictional Middle Eastern country, Callimbia, which is described as lying somewhere between Egypt and Libya. This imaginary history she interleaves with her main narrative centred on the palae-ontologist Howard Beamish, so that we are provided with some 'historical background' to his incarceration in Callimbia, and his embryonic love affair with Lucy. The history itself, covering as it does well over two millennia, is necessarily much (and wittily) abbreviated; indeed, it may be seen as a parody of the ways in which histories are often constructed. But my focus here is on the serious historiographical points that arise in relation to it, and on the ways that these interrelate with the stories of the novel's individual characters.

Most obvious, in the context of an openly invented history, is the indication that other 'real' histories are not so very different in kind. While history may

---

[51] See e.g. Ramsay MacMullen, *Feelings in History*, Claremont, Regina Books, 2003, which includes a bibliography.

seem to provide a coherent and truthful account of the past, based on reliable evidence and accurately transmitted through the centuries, in reality its whole 'edifice is itself a chimera, a construct of the human intellect'. No less than the fictional history of Callimbia presented here, narrative history is to be seen as an imaginative, largely foundationless, literary construction: 'It has no bricks or stones – it is *words, words, words.*' It may purport to distinguish fact from fiction, but any history's content is nonetheless highly problematic and contentious, highlighting as it necessarily does just a few colourful but unreliable relics from a long and often colourless past: 'The events are myths and fables, distortions and elaborations of something that *may or may not* have happened; they are the rainbow survivors of some vanished grey moment of reality.'[52]

That highly sceptical view of history is derived partly from a recognition and acceptance of the high degree of contingency always present, in the course of both individual lives and history as a whole. Lives may appear to consist of tidy and purposeful progressions – to be entities that can be readily captured within coherent narratives: 'A lifetime is so conveniently structured: it begins and ends. It can be seen as a whole.' But a life can also be 'dismantled and analysed', and shown to be not so straightforward after all, but rather 'an uneasy balance between the operation of contingency and decision, with the subject tottering precariously between the two from the cradle to the grave'. And that precarious balancing act is not only shown in individual lives, but no less 'is the stuff of history itself' (15–16).

Contingency, and the place of chance in natural (as well as human) developments, is particularly well illustrated in Howard Beamish's academic interest – palaeontology. In his researches, he is struck by the 'strange conjunction of likelihood and contingency which is the root of life, in every sense'; and he wonders about hypothetical alternative outcomes – 'if the contingent events of evolution had proceeded differently' (44). Such speculations are fuelled further by the recognition of contingencies in his personal life. By chance he sees an estate agent's 'For Sale' sign outside a flat, and buys it, and thence becomes involved in various related problems – and this 'all because, on a particular morning, he walked down one street rather than another'. He concludes that 'The course of an individual life has to be seen as a dizzying maze', and it is often a matter of chance, rather than deliberate choice, as to which path through that maze one takes (55–6).

It was sheer chance, again, that led to his meeting with the woman whom he later married. They met in hospital after each had had an accident: 'Howard

---

[52] Penelope Lively, *Cleopatra's Sister*, London, Quality Paperbacks Direct, 1993, p. 17 (my emphases). Further page references will be given in the text.

met Vivien because he fell from a borrowed step-ladder and broke his kneecap . . . [and Vivien] had incurred a similar injury after pitching down a flight of stairs' (83). It is chance that in such ways determines whom, out of literally millions of possibilities, we are to meet – and chance then that, as Howard concludes, determines our subsequent happiness, or unhappiness: 'The world teems with people; a minute number of these, fished from a hat as it were, would determine the quality of your existence' (94). 'Choice and contingency', as we are reminded early in the book, 'form a delicate partnership' (4) – a partnership whose essential instability points to the potential chaos in both personal and public histories, and makes the orderly representation of each highly problematic.

That recognition of contingency runs (as we shall see also in Tolstoy's historical theorising in *War and Peace*, to be discussed in Chapter 5) in parallel with a belief in some sort of destiny – some sort of unfolding plan, of which we may lack cognisance but by which our lives are in fact mapped out. So Howard, through his professional studies of nature through time, becomes preoccupied by the extent to which not only nature but individual lives are somehow pre-ordained – by whether they may even be 'implicit in the scheme of things, as though a silent refrain from the future were woven into the narrative, if only you knew how to pick up the frequency' (7).

That is a theme which recurs in another quite different professional context, when Lucy, as a journalist, becomes acutely aware of the rapid succession of events – 'most of it unpredictable, a continuing unfurling of surprise'. Yet in her childhood, she had had moments of illumination, when she had seemed to foresee herself as she would later become – 'when a fusion of emotion and opinion sent a shaft of light towards another time and another place' (in the future) (28). And she now, in the hurly-burly of everyday events, begins to wonder whether there was not 'behind it all some invisible unstoppable force, charging ahead' (105).

Some such relentless process through time seems to be implied by much historical writing. Yet it is clear too (as will be confirmed in other novels, including Penelope Lively's own *Moon Tiger*) that time, whether in personal lives or public histories, appears to move at different speeds. Lucy experiences that subjective temporal distortion, when she is imprisoned and in a state of great anxiety about Howard: she 'lay on her bed. She lay on her bed for a *long time*, but when she stood up again, checked her watch, it had been *twelve minutes only*' (245, my emphasis). And a similar sort of mistake about time's passage can be actually encouraged by historians themselves: the ambitious history of Callimbia, though fictional, serves to highlight that general problem. So we are told that, 'The first century gave way to the second, the third, the fourth. Time was slowing up.' Or it appeared to be, and for a very good reason: 'because of its ever-expanding freight of information'. The more evidence that survives about a period, the more historians will have to say; and so, in line with their descriptions of it, the longer time itself appears to get. And the freight of information expands particularly when languages develop and evidence gets written down, until finally, 'It would get to a point when time could barely creep ahead at all for the weight of its cargo of information' (59). Penelope Lively is of course describing here the situation as it had already evolved by the early twentieth century, when Lytton Strachey came to realise that the history of the Victorian Age could never be written because 'we know too much about it'.[53]

The cargo of information has been further weighted down from an acceptance of newly legitimised evidence from alternative sources. As a child, the fictional Howard had early learnt 'that an interpretation of the world cannot be had from any single person' (6); and the implied relativism is picked up in relation to the History of Callimbia, where it is noted that 'definition is in the eye of the beholder' (59). Thus, for example, 'One man's Christian is another man's infidel'; and both geographical and temporal categories, long unthinkingly accepted in historical writing, may need to be re-assessed: 'The Middle East? East of what? And the Middle Ages? Middle of when? That frozen, egocentric vision of history once more. Everything depends on the point of view' (79). That is of course something that has been repeatedly hammered home in the closing decades of the twentieth century by postcolonial writers concerned and dismayed (even angered) by the Eurocentric emphasis of conventional histories – histories in which the 'Middle East' lies between Europe and what is to 'the far East' of Europe, and the 'Middle Ages' lie between the two essentially European eras of classical antiquity and its subsequent rebirth. But remove that focus and introduce innumerable alternatives, and the cargo of available 'facts', and their potential for narrativisation from an infinite number of perspectives, seems liable to sink the practice of history altogether.

One further point is worth noting: that, although some of Penelope Lively's fictional history is written in a way that wittily parodies the writing of conventional history, and so seems almost flippant, there is an underlying seriousness – an appreciation of the real power that historians wield. So she writes of early Callimbia that 'The painters and the poets will arrive, and along with them, *far more dangerously*, the historians' (20, my emphases). Historians and historiography, then, are to be taken very seriously; and Penelope Lively here, although by no means focusing on these matters, succeeds in showing how

---

[53] Lytton Strachey, *Eminent Victorians* [1918], London, Chatto and Windus, 1928, p. vii.

and why that is indeed the case, by relating relevant issues not exclusively to history itself but also to individual lives. She thus provides an introductory example of how writers of fiction can themselves be of importance for raising matters of historical theory in interesting and accessible ways.

Conclusion

This preliminary look at the wider relationship of history and fiction may lead us to doubt the fundamental distinction between the two subjects that has long been conventionally claimed for them – claimed in particular by historians, who have since antiquity set themselves apart from practitioners of other literary genres. For while dramatists, poets, and later on novelists have all been content to be thought of, from time to time, as historians of a sort – using historical subjects and events as grist for their own literary mills – historians themselves have generally wished to be seen as aligned more with 'scientists', and have claimed for their discipline the scientific virtues of 'objectivity' and 'detachment' – virtues that necessarily involve a distancing from such subjective emotions and feelings as are associated with imaginative literature, or fiction.

There are of course good historical reasons for history's disciplinary rejection of 'feeling'; for had not Hegel, in his own discussion of the subject, contemptuously defined it as 'the lowest form in which any mental content can exist' – something that humans have 'in common with the animal', something therefore that is there to be transcended? For as he explained, there was, in the context of contemporary scientistic aspirations, a fundamental problem with feeling: it was, by definition, a subjective experience that could never be verified; its very assertion constituted a retreat from 'the common soil of understanding' and so authorised the reduction of everything to a merely 'subjective point of view' – a hazardous move indeed, that 'actually gets rid of truth as it is in and for itself'. That, then, is no way for history to proceed – no way for any 'scientific' subject that demands to be taken seriously as aiming at truth.[54]

With fiction dealing unashamedly with subjectivity, we have seen how a rigid differentiation between that and history was asserted especially after

---

[54] G. W. F. Hegel, *Reason in History: A General Introduction to the Philosophy of History* [1837], trans. Robert S. Hartman, New York, Bobbs-Merrill, 1953, pp. 17–18.

the professionalisation of historical study in the nineteenth century; and that disciplinary apartheid continued with scarcely decreasing fervour through much of the twentieth. But we have also seen how in parallel there has always run an alternative tradition that might be characterised as 'Romantic' – a tradition that reasserts the centrality of such non-scientific (non-quantifiable) characteristics as feeling and emotion, and that therefore doubts the ability of any scientifically orientated study to comprehend the totality of human experience (including the past). Within that tradition there have been, and continue to be, doubts as to the ability of scientific history to be as 'definitive' or conclusive, or even persuasive, as is sometimes claimed.

Furthermore, the 'factuality' of history – precisely what supposedly distinguishes it from 'fiction' – has itself come into question. To what extent can 'facts' be relied upon to serve as a firm base for historical knowledge? As soon as 'what happened' is described for use as historical evidence, it is subject to differing interpretations from different perspectives, and is prone to all the difficulties that any use of language inevitably entails – that shadow which falls between any word and its referent, that inadequacy, inexactitude, incompleteness of which we are aware in any attempted description. And how anyway are 'facts' established? How and why have they, and not others, been chosen – selected (on what basis and by whom?) from an infinity of alternative possibilities? And then, further to complicate matters, by what process have those facts been incorporated into a narrative (for it is the construction of such meaning-giving narratives with which history is ultimately concerned)? How does the 'emplotment' of those facts into an *historical* narrative differ from their use in an alternative narrative that is admittedly *fictitious*?

In the end, 'factual' history is revealed as subjectively chosen, subjectively interpreted, subjectively constructed and incorporated within a narrative, in a language which has a questionable relation to the external world and must always be less than 'perfect', and in a form that is inevitably subject to cultural constraints and limitations. So history and fiction appear to come ever closer to each other – even, in some analyses, to become assimilated with one another; and the competition between them therefore becomes ever more intense. For theirs is a competition for academic and cultural centrality (and so for institutional support): both are concerned with the construction of narratives that give, or aspire to give, meaning to human life – and as religion (at least for many) declines, that task of giving meaning becomes ever more important.

Finally, our introductory case study has shown how the debates in which historical theorists are engaged can be expressed in 'popular' terms – in a way that is attractive and accessible to the wider reading public, and in a way that shows the practical relevance of these seemingly abstruse and highly 'theoretical' matters. Following on from the definition-challenging works of Truman Capote and Wallace Stegner, Penelope Lively's novel provides an actual example of the fictional embodiment of historical theory; and that will be an important focus through much of what follows, before we return, in a concluding chapter, to more general questions relating to what seems to be the increasingly problematic – or, perhaps better, *exciting* – ways in which history meets fiction.

Further reading

Ankersmit, Frank, *Sublime Historical Experience*, Stanford, Stanford University Press, 2005.

Bentley, Michael, *Modern Historiography: An Introduction*, London, Routledge, 1999.

Capote, Truman, *In Cold Blood* [1966], London, Penguin, 1967.

Elias, Amy J., *Sublime Desire: History and Post-1960s Fiction*, Baltimore and London, Johns Hopkins, 2001.

Evans, Richard J., *In Defence of History*, London, Granta, 1997.

Hutcheon, Linda, *A Poetics of Postmodernism: History, Theory, Fiction*, London, Routledge, 1988.

Jenkins, Keith, *On 'What is History?': From Carr and Elton to Rorty and White*, London, Routledge 1995.

Jenkins, Keith, *Refiguring History: New Thoughts on an Old Discipline*, London, Routledge, 2003.

Lively, Penelope, *Cleopatra's Sister*, London, Quality Paperbacks Direct, 1993.

Novick, Peter, *That Noble Dream: The 'Objectivity Question' and the American Historical Profession*, Cambridge, Cambridge University Press, 1988.

Parrish, Timothy, *From the Civil War to the Apocalypse: Postmodern History and American Fiction*, Amherst, University of Massachusetts Press, 2008.

Rigney, Ann, *Imperfect Histories: The Elusive Past and the Legacy of Romantic Historicism*, Ithaca and London, Cornell University Press, 2001.

Stegner, Wallace, *Angle of Repose* [1971], New York, Fawcett Crest, 1972.

Dryasdust and Co.: some fictional representations of historians

In this chapter we encounter some nineteenth- and twentieth-century fictional representations of historians and associated educators. In an attempt to account for their characteristically negative nature, we consider some implications of history's scientistic aspirations, and in particular the emphasis on 'facts' and mechanistic explanation at the expense of feeling and imagination. In the context of a resultant backlash, and as another exemplary meeting of history with fiction, we examine Charles Dickens' fictional Thomas Gradgrind in Hard Times *and his historical equivalent, James Mill.*

No one need be surprised that 'Dryasdust' – the deeply unappealing man whose personality appears to be quite literally as dry as dust – typifies the literary representations of historians in fiction. For since the 'professionalisation' of their subject in the nineteenth century, and their subsequent emphasis on the supposed scientific virtues of rationality, empiricism, objectivity, and detachment, historians have inevitably exposed themselves to something of a 'romantic' reaction from those concerned to reinstate as virtues the very qualities that they have self-consciously abandoned. Leaders in such reactionary movements are more or less bound to be those who put greater emphasis on imagination, subjectivity, emotional involvement – just those characteristics that are regularly associated with creative artists, including writers of poetry and other fiction.

Dryasdust was an imaginary, tediously thorough and pedantic authority cited by Sir Walter Scott – himself a writer (historian as well as novelist) who was of course aware of his own critics amongst more 'academic' historians. So the Dedicatory Epistle of his famous historical novel *Ivanhoe* (1819) is addressed to The Rev. Dr. Dryasdust, F.A.S., who is there quoted as having observed that in England, which had a long-established civilisation, 'our ideas of our ancestors are only to be gleaned from *musty records* and chronicles, the authors of which seem perversely to have conspired to suppress in their narratives all interesting details'; in which depressing situation an English author, deprived of any direct contact with the actual life of the past (as might still be found in Scotland), can 'only have the liberty of selecting his subject amidst the *dust of antiquity*, where nothing was to be found but dry, sapless, mouldering, and disjointed bones'. Scott is obviously concerned to distance himself from any such dry and dusty endeavour, and to defend himself against orthodox historians, or 'the severer antiquary', who might (and did) accuse him of '*mingling fiction with truth*' and thus 'polluting the well of history'. So while he concedes 'that I neither can nor do pretend to the observation of complete accuracy', he claims more importantly to have brought back the past, in an attractive and exciting manner, by showing its likeness and relevance to the present. Through that more direct contact with the life and colour and emotion of the past, he hopes that the modern reader 'will not find himself . . . much trammelled by the *repulsive dryness* of *mere antiquity*' – that hallmark of the 'dryasdust' approach.[1]

Scott's success in that respect is indicated by his adoption as representative of the *anti-dryasdust* style: his own approach, as an imaginative writer of romantic fiction was specifically differentiated from that of Henry Hallam, as a practitioner of 'critical and argumentative history', by Macaulay in his review of the latter's *Constitutional History of England* in 1828. History, as Macaulay described, consisted of two strands: it was ideally a compound of poetry and philosophy, representing respectively imagination and reason. But those two had become 'completely and professionally separated'; so that while Hallam had obtained 'almost complete mastery' over his feelings (associated with imagination), and displayed throughout his book that 'unsparing impartiality which is his most distinguishing virtue', the second strand of history, incorporating the particularities and 'reality of human flesh and blood' (though still indeed the proper concern of historians), had been 'appropriated by the historical novelist' (exemplified by Scott).[2]

---

[1] Walter Scott, *Ivanhoe. A Romance, with the Author's Last Notes and Additions*, Paris, Baudry's Foreign Library, 1831, pp. xxii, xxiv–xxvi (my emphases).

[2] Thomas Babington Macaulay, Review of Hallam's *Constitutional History of England* in *The Edinburgh Review*, 1828; in *Critical and Historical Essays*, ed. A. J. Grieve, 2 vols; London, Dent, 1907, vol. 1, pp. 1–4, 55.

It was thus in a context of professional divisiveness and mutual antagonism (not to say, competition) that Dryasdust becomes a derisory term for anyone who presents historical 'facts' in a dry and detached way, without a hint of any emotional involvement or feeling for the personalities involved. And the name is taken up importantly by Thomas Carlyle, who can himself be seen here as an exemplar of the more 'romantic' approach to history and historical writing. His *French Revolution* (1837) best illustrates his own historical practice, a work that was praised by John Stuart Mill for its combination of fact and feeling – and its consequent ability to create 'the history of the French Revolution, *and* the poetry of it, both in one'.[3] Indeed, Mill concluded, 'This is not so much a history, as an epic poem; and notwithstanding, or even in consequence of this, the truest of histories.'[4]

Carlyle's own attitude to his contemporaries' surrender to the 'scientific' model is further demonstrated in a specifically theoretical interjection in the introductory chapter of his *Oliver Cromwell's Letters and Speeches* (1845), where 'Dryasdust' himself re-appears in a chapter actually entitled 'Anti-Dryasdust'. There he refers to the 'dreary old records', which convey no living voice, but rather 'a widespread inarticulate slumberous mumblement, issuing as if from the lake of Eternal Sleep'. So it is, he explains, small wonder that 'to the English mind at this hour, the past History of England is little other than a dull dismal labyrinth'.[5] For 'Alas', as he laments elsewhere, 'what mountains of dead ashes, wreck and burnt bones, does assiduous Pedantry dig up from the Past Time, and name it History!'[6] In similar vein, through his mouthpiece Teufelsdröckh, he refers to his teachers more specifically as 'hide-bound Pedants': 'I learned what others learn; and kept it stored by in a corner of my head, seeing as yet no manner of use in it. My Schoolmaster, a downbent, broken-hearted, under-foot martyr . . . did little for me, except discover that he could do little.'[7]

We shall look further at Carlyle's oppositional stance below, but can note here that his influence in this context extended through the nineteenth and

---

[3] Mill quoted by F. Parvin Sharpless, *The Literary Criticism of John Stuart Mill*, The Hague and Paris, Mouton, 1967, p. 189.

[4] John Stuart Mill, 'Carlyle's French Revolution', in *Mill's Essays on Literature and Society*, ed. J. B. Schneewind, London, Collier-Macmillan, 1965, p. 184.

[5] Thomas Carlyle, Elucidations, in *The Letters and Speeches of Oliver Cromwell*, ed. S. C. Lomas, 3 vols; London, Methuen, 1904, vol. 1, pp. 2–3, 5. On Carlyle's historical theorising, see Ann Rigney, *Imperfect Histories*, Ithaca and London, Cornell University Press, 2001, ch. 3: 'Sublimity: Thomas Carlyle and the Aesthetics of Historical Ignorance'.

[6] Thomas Carlyle, *Past and Present*, [1843], London, Ward, Lock, n.d., p. 36.

[7] Thomas Carlyle, *Sartor Resartus* [1836], London, Ward, Lock, n.d., pp. 75–6.

twentieth centuries to advance some extremely negative fictional representations of historians. In this he was no doubt assisted by others, importantly including Nietzsche and Herbert Spencer. The former writes scathingly of a degenerate form of history consisting of little more than 'a restless raking together of everything that has ever existed', and characterised by a 'habit of scholarliness [which] rotates in egoistic self-satisfaction around its own axis';[8] while the latter similarly repudiates a useless form of history concerned only with 'dead unmeaning events', such as 'the births, deaths, and marriages of kings, and other like trivialities'.[9]

Both Nietzsche and Spencer were writing in the 1870s – a decade that saw the appearance of one of the best-known fictional representations of a 'dryasdust' historian, George Eliot's Mr Casaubon in *Middlemarch*. Casaubon is portrayed as a meticulous scholar, who burrows away in the archives for many years making notes, but who finds it hard ever to draw his researches to any sort of conclusion or to offer any practical justification for them. His empirical procedures, as he endlessly collects his data, may be impeccable, but they come at the cost of any imaginative input – either into his work or into his personal life. So he appears as a sad figure who, on honeymoon in Rome, abandons his younger wife Dorothea for days on end, while continuing his (to him) essential research in the Vatican archives. It is small wonder, then, that he is described by Will Ladislaw, the romantic young artist with whom he is contrasted, as a 'dried up pedant . . . [an] elaborator of small explanations about as important as the surplus stock of false antiquities kept in a vendor's back chamber', and that he is presented by George Eliot herself as 'a lifeless embalmment of knowledge'. It may be a more general occupational hazard for historians, but even Casaubon himself comes to recognise that he lives 'too much with the dead'.[10]

[8] Nietzsche, *Untimely Meditations*, ed. Daniel Breazeale, Cambridge, Cambridge University Press, 1997, p. 75.

[9] Herbert Spencer, *Education*, London, Williams and Norgate, 1910, p. 14.

[10] George Eliot, *Middlemarch* [1871–2], London, Oxford University Press, 1947, pp. 218–19, 210, 213, 12. It has been claimed (most recently by Peter Thonemann in *London Review of Books*, 7 February 2008, pp. 23–4) that the 'fictional' Casaubon was modelled on the 'historical' nineteenth-century scholar Mark Pattison. On both Casaubon and Pattison, see A. D. Nuttall, *Dead from the Waist Down: Scholars and Scholarship in Literature and the Popular Imagination*, New Haven and London, Yale University Press, 2003; and for another relevant study, see Dominick LaCapra, 'In Quest of Casaubon: George Eliot's *Middlemarch*', in *History, Politics, and the Novel*, Ithaca and London, Cornell University Press, 1987, pp. 56–82.

A near contemporary of George Eliot's Casaubon, and another deeply unflattering representation of an academic historian, is Ibsen's character Jörgen Tesman in *Hedda Gabler* (1890). Tesman is described as 'an indefatigable researcher', 'a scholar engaged in research in the history of civilisation'; and he is shown as having just returned from his honeymoon, which had been, for him, 'a kind of research tour . . . – with all those old records I had to hunt through. And then, you know, the enormous number of books I had to read.' He had not, as his sister observes, wasted his time, since he has a suitcase crammed full of notes which he had made 'going through the archives'; and when his sister hints that there might soon be a good use for the empty rooms in his new house, he misunderstands the implication but agrees – for, nurseries apart, he might indeed need a bigger library. There is, after all, no end to the number of learned publications he needs: 'one can never have too many of them. One has to keep up with everything that's written and printed.' And 'rummaging in libraries is the most entrancing occupation he knows', explains his glamorous wife Hedda, as she gives her own description of their honeymoon, with him 'sitting and copying out old parchments, or whatever they are'.[11]

Hedda herself, meanwhile, had been 'excruciatingly bored', and she makes some generalisations with which other less fortunate academics' spouses might concur: 'learned men are not entertaining as travelling companions . . . Well, you just try it yourself! Listening to someone talking about the history of civilisation', and more particularly about his own specific research topic, 'domestic crafts in Brabant in the Middle Ages'.[12]

In these fictional cases there is some consolation: as with Casaubon, there is a rival for Hedda's affections – another historian, but a far less conventional figure, both personally and professionally. Previously dissolute and disgraced, Ejlert Lövborg returns from the past as a reformed character: he has managed to stop drinking (before he succumbs again at Hedda's instigation) and has just succeeded in actually publishing 'a big new book on the history of civilisation'. But more significantly, he is working on a sequel that 'deals with the future' – 'the factors that will control civilisation in the future . . . [and] . . . the probable direction civilisation will take'. That, as Tesman can see, is 'Amazing! It would never occur to me to write about a thing like that': the future, after all, is hardly the concern of the orthodox historian; and he realises that he lacks the necessary imagination to make such speculations. So after

[11] Henrik Ibsen, *Hedda Gabler* [1890], in *Three Plays*, trans. Una Ellis-Fermor, Harmondsworth, Penguin, 1950, pp. 300, 267–8, 270, 302.
[12] *Hedda Gabler*, pp. 298–9.

Lövborg's death and the destruction of his manuscript, the best that Tesman can do is to devote his life to piecing together the other man's notes and rewriting his book – never aspiring to be original, but content with 'getting another man's papers in order'.[13]

Tesman's mediaeval research topic is not so dissimilar to that of Jim Dixon over half a century later. The historian in Kingsley Amis's novel *Lucky Jim* (1954), Dixon had published an essay entitled 'The Economic Influence of the Developments in Shipbuilding Techniques, 1450–1485' – 'a perfect title', we are told, 'in that it – crystallised the article's niggling mindlessness, its funereal parade of yawning enforcing facts, the pseudo-light it threw upon non-problems'. As a lecturer still on probation, Dixon had of necessity read, or tried to read, dozens of similar publications by embryonic academics, but even to him 'his own seemed worse than most in its air of being convinced of its own usefulness and significance'. Such history, as he tacitly conceded, is appropriately described as something of a '*racket*'.[14]

That same disparaging term, 'racket', was applied to the subject by Wyndham Lewis, whose main character Professor Harding in his novel *Self Condemned* (coincidentally published in the same year, 1954), is – as we shall see in Chapter 5 – so disillusioned with history as then taught that, for the sake of his own integrity, he feels bound to resign his position. And two later twentieth-century representations show similarly unorthodox historians playing central roles. Graham Swift's Tom Crick in *Waterland* (1983) – introduced in Chapter 1, but to be considered in more detail in Chapter 7 – accused by his Headmaster of purveying 'a rag-bag of pointless information', and himself bored with mere 'spooned-down doses of the past', abandons conventional history teaching altogether and takes up telling stories (whether factual or fictional). And in Penelope Lively's *Moon Tiger* (1987) – a novel to be considered at greater length in Chapter 4 – the central character Claudia Hampton, although writing, as she diffidently explains, what 'I suppose you'd call . . . history', takes care to clarify that she has 'never been a *conventional* historian . . . never like that *dried up bone of a woman*' who had taught her mediaeval history at Oxford.[15]

So how did that image of an educational 'racket' of total irrelevance, taught by 'dried up' – 'dryasdust' – historians, take shape in the minds of novelists, and thence a wider public?

---

[13] *Hedda Gabler*, pp. 280, 310, 360.

[14] Kingsley Amis, *Lucky Jim* [1954], London, Penguin, 1961, pp. 14, 33 (my emphasis).

[15] Graham Swift, *Waterland*, London, Picador, 1992, pp. 23, 60; Penelope Lively, *Moon Tiger*, London, Penguin, 1988, pp. 103, 3 (my emphasis).

Science and the professionalisation of history in the nineteenth century

The attitude to history, and thence more generally to education, illustrated (as we shall see below, pp. 59–66) – or even parodied – in Charles Dickens' novel *Hard Times* can be seen (by the historically minded) to stem from the newly revived 'mechanical philosophy' of the seventeenth century. The approach to the natural world implied in that philosophy – an approach involving the need for detached study of an essentially material construct that operates in accordance with regular laws – had become well established, and indeed institutionalised so far as the natural sciences were concerned, by the end of the century; and the so-called 'Enlightenment' of the following decades consisted in part in an extension of that 'mechanistic' model to other areas of human experience.

So by 1774 Johann Gottfried Herder (1744–1803) felt justified in claiming that 'The new philosophy . . . is nothing but a *mechanism*' and that 'this mechanism is in fact the essential characteristic of the new spirit'. Though originating in the physical sciences, mechanism, or the mechanistic model of explanation, was now extending its territory far and wide: 'It has forced its way into the sciences, the arts, customs and ways of living, and is considered the sap and blossom of our century'; and one implication, of great importance for our theme here, was that '*The head and the heart are completely separated.*'[16]

That separation of head from heart was what led to the two quite different approaches to the past that were (as we have seen above) already evident by the early nineteenth century, when historians aspiring to scientific status wished to differentiate themselves from the imaginative treatments – the fictions – of historical novelists. So when Macaulay in 1828 indicated that, 'By judicious selection, rejection, and arrangement, he [the historian] gives to *truth* those attractions which have been *usurped by fiction*',[17] he was clearly on the defensive. History, it would seem, with its unique concern with 'truth', with its Rankean emphasis on 'facts' (for was not 'the father of history' even then insisting that 'the strict presentation of the *facts* . . . is undoubtedly the

---

[16] Johann Gottfried Herder, quoted in Robert M. Burns and Hugh Rayment-Pickard (eds), *Philosophies of History: From Enlightenment to Postmodernity*, Oxford, Blackwell, 2000, pp. 75–6 (my emphases).

[17] Thomas Babington Macaulay, quoted in Fritz Stern (ed.), *The Varieties of History*, New York, Meridian, 1956, p. 86 (my emphases).

supreme law'?[18]), was already starting to appear as a 'dryasdust' activity, lacking that *attractiveness* which people now looked for in 'fiction'. Macaulay himself was obviously denying that such an outcome was inevitable: history too, he believed, could be presented in such a way that it could, for all its primary idealistic objective, display its own more immediate 'attractions'. But there does already seem to be a perceived problem here.

Indeed, that problem is later made explicit, when Macaulay, conscious as he was of the enormous popularity of the novels of Walter Scott and others, suggested that, if historians read and used their sources with a real interest in human beings, then readers would no longer need to refer to such fiction as supplementary material for their understanding of the past: 'we should not then have to look for the wars and votes of the Puritans in [the historian] Clarendon, and for their phraseology in *Old Mortality* [Scott's novel of 1816]; for one half of King James in Hume [as historian again] and for the other half in *The Fortunes of Nigel*' (another novel by Scott, published in 1822).[19]

As Macaulay's contemporary, Thomas Carlyle was equally aware of those deficiencies in 'proper' histories, which were shown up by Scott's fictional treatment of the past. It seemed, he wrote, so obvious, but clearly needed spelling out again, that what made history (as the past), and what made history (as a record of that past) interesting, was human beings: that insight is what Scott, unlike professional historians, had realised and utilised. 'These historical novels have taught all men this truth, which looks like a truism, yet was unknown to writers of history and others, till so taught: that the bygone ages of the world were actually filled by *living men*, not by protocols, state papers, controversies and abstractions of men.'[20] (We shall look further at this more 'romantic' approach of Carlyle below.)

That observation about 'living men' may indeed have been a truism, but it was one that bore repetition as seeming to be inconsistent with what was then considered orthodox methodology. Thus, Count Yorck observed of Ranke in 1866, that 'His historical personages are properly speaking *personae*, performers of historical roles.' That implied *depersonalisation* inevitably resulted in something being left out: 'The *poet* remains hidden.' Or to put the point

---

[18]   Ranke, quoted in Stern (ed.), *Varieties*, p. 57 (my emphasis). It is, however, noteworthy that Ranke himself recounts his horror at his first experience of historical study at university, where students were expected to learn 'masses of unprocessed facts' that lacked any coherence – a point for which I am indebted to Daniel Braw: see his essay, 'Vision as Revision: Ranke and the Beginning of Modern History', *History and Theory* 46, 2007, pp. 45–60.

[19]   Macaulay, quoted in J. R. Hale (ed.), *The Evolution of British Historiography*, London, Macmillan, 1967, p. 36.

[20]   Carlyle, quoted in Hale (ed.), *Evolution*, p. 36 (my emphasis).

another way: 'As a historian Ranke is wholly an eye; *feelings and sensations*, being purely *personal* things, he keeps to himself; his history is history seen, *not history lived*.'[21] It seems that Ranke himself was aware of some deficiency in this respect, for, as Wolf Lepenies has written, he 'designated Scott's *Quentin Durward* as the true historiography', and more generally he person-ally acknowledged that 'the romantic historical works of Sir Walter Scott . . . played a principal part in awakening my sympathy for the actions and passions of past ages'.[22]

A century on, though, and the problem had been further exacerbated. For science through the nineteenth century had become, at least for the reading classes, almost a form of entertainment, with public demonstrations and experiments, and well publicised debates between the respective champions of science and theology. 'The great fairy Science', as Charles Kingsley wrote in 1863, seemed 'likely to be queen of all the fairies for many a year to come';[23] and so it proved. And not to be excluded from such exalted company, historians attempted, as a more 'romantically' inclined Lytton Strachey later described, 'to reconstruct the past solidly and patiently, with nothing but facts to assist them – pure facts, untwisted by . . . bias and uncoloured by romance'. The results, as Strachey claimed, could be dire: Samuel Gardiner, for example, whose professional detachment implied the lack of any 'point of view', contrived to write a 'book on the most exciting period of English history [which] resembles nothing so much as a very large heap of sawdust'; and in the work of Mandell Creighton, 'a perfectly grey light prevails everywhere . . . every suggestion of personal passion has been studiously removed'.[24] But that of course was deliberate: with his avowed aim of professional (if not personal) 'sobriety', Creighton himself, with his fellow founding-editor, wrote appro-priately in the first issue of the *English Historical Review* in 1886 of 'pursuing [history] for its own sake in a calm and *scientific* spirit'.[25]

J. B. Bury, then, was but reiterating a claim for intellectual respectability for his subject, when he entitled his 1902 Inaugural Lecture as Regius Professor in Cambridge, 'The Science of History'. And 'girded with new strength', his-tory as a science was (within Bury's prospective and my own retrospective chosen narratives) to assume even greater importance, and assert its own

[21] Count Yorck, Letter to Dilthey, quoted by Wolf Lepenies, *Between Literature and Science: The Rise of Sociology*, Cambridge, Cambridge University Press, 1988, pp. 253–4 (my emphases).

[22] Lepenies, *Between Literature*, p. 255; Ranke, quoted by Hale (ed.), *Evolution*, p. 36.

[23] Charles Kingsley, *The Water Babies* [1863], London and Glasgow, Blackie, n.d., p. 54.

[24] Lytton Strachey, *Portraits in Miniature and Other Essays*, London, Chatto & Windus, 1933, pp. 170, 208–9.

[25] *English Historical Review* 1, 1886, p. 5 (my emphasis).

autonomy, with new disciplinary allegiances: it was time to renounce outdated ties with such 'old associates [as] moral philosophy and rhetoric', and 'to enter into closer relations with the *sciences* which deal *objectively* with the *facts* of the universe'. History too, after all, had to be '*true*; and that can be attained only through the discovery, collection, classification, and interpretation of *facts* – through *scientific* research'.[26] Dryasdust was well and truly back in fashion, and set the tone for much of the century. Writing in 1968 a new Foreword to his *The Scientific Attitude* (1941), C. H. Waddington asserts 'that science has very wide implications on the *whole conduct of life*'; and he reproaches those who feel that they 'cannot reach the real depth of the *meaning of human life* without taking off for a flight into the nebulous realm of the mystical and transcendental'.[27] It is hardly surprising, then, that twentieth-century representations of orthodox historians in fiction – historians aspiring to be scientists – should embody characteristics seen as negative by those for whom 'the meaning of life' defied earthbound and 'factual' constraints.

In order, though, to gain further insight into why Dickens in *Hard Times* expressed the views that he did on history and education, it may be helpful to look at some 'romantic' responses to historians' own scientific emphasis, and in particular at the attitude expressed by Thomas Carlyle, as the man to whom Dickens dedicated his work.

'Romantic' response to the scientific emphasis

Walter Scott, who was himself a scholarly historian responsible for two 'standard' histories – *The Life of Napoleon* (1827), and a *History of Scotland* (1830) – deliberately advocated the use, as historical source material, of such 'works of fancy' as poetic romances. These, he insisted, are far more likely to provide the 'intimate knowledge' of human 'sentiments, manners and habits' in earlier times than all the 'dull and dreary monastic annals' that comprise appropriate evidence for orthodox historians. From such romances, we can learn not just what people did, but '*what they were*'; and it is that that is most interesting.[28] And it is that, too, that indicates Scott's own approach in his historical novels, which, for all their factual inaccuracies, convey imaginative and colourful evocations of the times in which they are set.

---

[26] J. B. Bury, quoted in Stern (ed.), *Varieties*, pp. 215–17 (my emphases).

[27] C. H. Waddington, *The Scientific Attitude* [1941], London, Hutchinson, 1968, p. xviii.

[28] Walter Scott, Review of Ellis's *Specimens of Early English Metrical Romances*, quoted by Hale (ed.), *Evolution*, p. 37 (my emphasis).

The approval of Scott expressed by Carlyle has been noted above, and it will be convenient here to consider further his approach to history and education as an influence on Dickens in *Hard Times*. That influence derived largely from *Sartor Resartus*, in which Carlyle expressed his dissatisfaction with some of the fashionable ideas of his time, and in particular with what he saw as an over-emphasis on reason and logic, together with an over-reliance on 'mechanism' as an explanatory tool, whether in science or the arts. That mechanistic approach, derived from the scientific methodologies of the time, became widely pervasive in the field of education, so that, as one of its advocates, T. H. Huxley could write approvingly of an educated person being someone whose body can work 'as a mechanism' and 'whose intellect is a clear, cold, logic engine'.[29] But that coldly logical, mechanistic attitude detracted, so Carlyle believed, from the importance to be assigned to *wonder* and *imagination*, and thence more generally to spirituality; and that in turn (as Dickens himself was to show so clearly in the case of Thomas Gradgrind) did go on to have important implications for education.

Sartor Resartus was written in 1831, and published in serial form in *Fraser's Magazine* from November 1833 to August 1834. It was first published as a single volume in Boston in 1836, with a Preface by Ralph Waldo Emerson, to whom Carlyle was personally introduced by John Stuart Mill. The book purports to be an edition of 'The Life and Opinions' of a German Professor, Diogenes Teufelsdröckh, and it presents his so-called 'Philosophy of Clothes'.[30] Significantly, it was described in the original Preface as 'A Criticism upon the Spirit of the Age', and we are not surprised therefore to find Carlyle pointing to the inadequacy of logic in attempts to define 'man' (or human beings): 'To the eye of vulgar Logic', says he, 'what is man? An omnivorous Biped that wears Breeches.' But that is obviously far too narrow a definition; it is far from telling the whole story. So considering the matter from another angle: 'To the eye of Pure Reason what is he? A soul, a Spirit, and Divine Apparition.'[31] This recognition of the limitations of logic in attempts to grapple with the totality of human experience is a theme of which we see a replay in *Hard Times*, where Gradgrind extracts from his star pupil Bitzer an appropriately 'factual' definition of a horse, as a quadruped with hard hoofs, forty teeth, and so on, but leaves Sissy Jupe, with her greater sensitivities and

[29] T. H. Huxley, 'A Liberal Education; and Where to find it' [1868], in *Collected Essays*, 9 vols; London, Macmillan, vol. III, 1893, p. 86. My thanks to Martin Davies for this reference.

[30] Note that in the quotations below, narrator-editor's comments have single commas, direct quotations from Teufelsdröckh, double; italics are in the original.

[31] *Sartor Resartus*, pp. xx, 51.

personal knowledge of such animals, floundering and embarrassed in her own attempts to come up with any such 'definitive' description.

'Logic-choppers', as Carlyle insists through his mouthpiece, are 'professed Enemies to Wonder';[32] and that sense of 'wonder', for which Dickens' character Sissy is later rebuked, is to be explicitly commended as an antidote to the prevailing 'mechanistic' attitude. So speaking of his supposed mentor Teufelsdröckh, Carlyle notes that 'he deals much in the feeling of Wonder; insists on the necessity and high worth of universal Wonder'. It is the 'progress of Science, which is to destroy Wonder, and in its stead substitute Mensuration [measurement] and Numeration [calculation]'; and that attempted substitution 'finds small favour with Teufelsdröckh', who is, as he later reiterates, 'a wonder-loving and wonder-seeking man', and someone who believes that 'The man who cannot wonder . . . is but a Pair of Spectacles behind which there is no Eye.' It is in the end 'not our Logical, Mensurative faculty, but our Imaginative one [that] is King over us'.[33]

That is presented by Carlyle as a minority and reactionary viewpoint at a time when the mechanistic model rules – when 'now the Genius of Mechanism smothers him [man] worse than any nightmare did: till the soul is nigh choked out of him, and only a kind of Digestive, Mechanic life remains'. As Dickens was to illustrate so vividly in his characterisation of Gradgrind and his like: 'In Earth and in Heaven he can see nothing but Mechanism; has fear for nothing else, hope in nothing else.' So it is hardly surprising to see this exemplified in the sphere of education, where (again describing the fictional but 'factually'-based Teufelsdröckh) Carlyle reports that 'his Greek and Latin were "mechanically" taught . . . "My Teachers", says he, "were hide-bound Pedants, without knowledge of man's nature or of boy's; or of aught save their lexicons and quarterly account-books."' In another anticipation of Dickens' account of Gradgrind, who 'seemed a kind of cannon loaded to the muzzle with facts', Carlyle describes how people 'discover, not without surprise, that fashioning the souls of a generation by Knowledge can rank on a level with blowing their bodies to pieces with Gunpowder'.[34]

Finally, the selfishness exemplified in Gradgrind's pupil Bitzer's unashamed self-interest, in proposing to betray his erstwhile friend Tom to the authorities, is foreshadowed in Carlyle's description of 'a Society . . .

---

[32] *Sartor Resartus*, p. 52; cf. Carlyle's Essay 'On History', where he refers to 'that class of cause-and-effect speculators, with whom no wonder would remain wonderful, but all things in Heaven and Earth must be computed and "accounted for"'. *English and Other Critical Essays*, London, Dent, 1915, p. 86.

[33] *Sartor Resartus*, pp. 52–3, 139, 148.

[34] *Sartor Resartus*, pp. 148, 77, 48, 78.

where there is no longer any social Idea extant . . . Where each, isolated, regardless of his neighbour, turned against his neighbour, clutches what he can get, and cries "Mine!"' In that sort of society, 'friendship' has become a thing of the past, and the ideal of laissez-faire is 'passionately proclaimed . . . Leave us alone of your guidance . . . eat your wages and sleep!' In this sort of 'wild desert', 'the highest of all possessions . . . [is] Self-help'.[35]

A number of the themes discussed above will be seen illustrated in the following case study, where historical (and more widely educational) theories are treated seriously in what is ostensibly a work of fiction.

Gradgrind in fiction: Charles Dickens, Hard Times

The novelist Charles Dickens is well known for his representation of 'the social realities' of his time (and, in parallel with that, for his advocacy of social reform): his writings – including such works as *Oliver Twist* (1837–8), *Dombey and Son* (1846–8), and *Bleak House* (1852–3) – constitute a veritable quarry of evidence for historians of Victorian Britain;[36] and here, in the context of fiction's meeting with history and historical theory, I want to concentrate attention on his critical treatment of Thomas Gradgrind, and the educational ideas expressed in *Hard Times*.[37]

That novel, published in 1854, although in one sense obviously 'fiction', has been described by F. R. Leavis as 'a moral fable';[38] and that description can easily be justified. For Dickens' work constitutes a damning critique of contemporary values as they are indicated in society and, more specifically, in educational philosophy. And it is noteworthy in this context that the author dedicates his work to that earlier great reformer Thomas Carlyle, who had discussed such matters in *Sartor Resartus* (as well as in his influential essay on 'Chartism', 1839), and who (as we have just seen) wrote specifically against the 'Dryasdust' approach to history.

---

[35] *Sartor Resartus*, pp. 154, 83.

[36] See also e.g. Elizabeth Gaskell, *Mary Barton* (1848) and *North and South* (1855); and Charles Kingsley, *Alton Locke* (1850) and *The Water Babies* (1863). Kingsley was influenced by Carlyle, and was for a time a Professor of History at Cambridge.

[37] Charles Dickens, *Hard Times* [1854], ed. David Craig, Harmondsworth, Penguin, 1969. References to page numbers in this edition will be given in the text.

[38] F. R. Leavis, *The Great Tradition*, Harmondsworth, Penguin, 1972, p. 258.

Hard Times itself famously opens with Thomas Gradgrind's openly proclaimed agenda for the classroom:

> Now, what I want is, Facts. Teach these boys and girls nothing but Facts. Facts alone are wanted in life. Plant nothing else, and root out everything else. You can only form the minds of reasoning animals upon Facts: nothing else will ever be of any service to them. This is the principle on which I bring up my own children, and this is the principle on which I bring up these children. Stick to Facts, sir!

That emphasis on 'facts', and the mindset implied by its acceptance lies at the centre of the author's concerns here. As one indication of the scientific – and indeed scientistic – emphasis then current in Victorian culture (described by Leavis as 'the aggressive formulation of an inhumane spirit'[39]), it is shown to have clear implications for morality and character formation, for interpersonal relations, and not least (as has been all too clear in the subject's subsequent development) for the teaching of History in particular.

Gradgrind's educational philosophy is initially put into context by Dickens with a description of the town he lives in. Coketown (modelled on the industrial town of Preston in Lancashire), we are told, 'contained several large streets all very like one another, and many small streets still more like one another, inhabited by people equally like one another, who all went in and out at the same hours, with the same sound upon the same pavements, to do the same work, and to whom every day was the same as yesterday and tomorrow, and every year the counterpart of the last and the next' (65). The barren physical uniformity of the town's architecture is emblematic of the inhabitants' lives[40] – their conformity and regularity and hopelessness, where the future is destined to be just the same as the present and the past. Deprived of any spiritual sustenance, the mill workers are barely accounted human, but are 'generically called "the Hands", – a race who would have found more favour

---

[39] Leavis, *Great Tradition*, p. 259.

[40] Cf. J. S. Mill, who similarly associates architecture with wider moral sensibilities: 'Nothing contributes more to nourish elevation of sentiments in a people, than the large and free character of their habitations'; and with 'the mean and cramped externals of English middle class life', he compares 'the spacious and lofty rooms' of his friend Jeremy Bentham's grand house in Somerset, which 'were to me a sort of poetic cultivation'. *Autobiography* [1873], London, Oxford University Press, 1924, pp. 46–7. See also Elizabeth Gaskell's account of the 'sameness' of the lives of workers confined in their 'pent-up houses' which themselves 'induce depression'. *North and South* [1855], London, Collins, n.d., pp. 181, 395.

with some people, if Providence had seen fit to make them only hands, or, like the lower creatures of the sea-shore, only hands and stomachs' (102–3).[41]

There is, furthermore, little sympathy for their condition, since they are held personally responsible for what and where they are. As the Social Darwinists were to teach, the fittest will prosper at the expense of those who must (by definition) be unfitted to survive. 'Any capitalist there [in Coketown], who had made sixty thousand pounds out of sixpence, always professed to wonder why the sixty thousand nearest Hands didn't each make sixty thousand pounds out of sixpence, and more or less reproached them every one for not accomplishing the little feat. What I did you can do. Why don't you go and do it?' (152).

So the very physical and emotional context of the town itself exemplified, and seemed to justify or naturalise, Gradgrind's educational fact-orientated philosophy: 'Fact, fact, fact, everywhere in the material aspect of the town; fact, fact, fact, everywhere in the immaterial' (66). What was necessary was to adapt oneself to that reality, to that truth – to the facts of life as they are given. So it is no doubt meant as an ironical compliment when Gradgrind is described as 'A man of realities', as well as a 'man of fact and calculation' (48). And it is altogether appropriate that he had married his wife for her mathematical abilities and lack of 'nonsense'; for 'By nonsense he meant fancy' (62) – or those imaginative faculties that are bound to lead people astray. For Gradgrind himself, 'two and two are four, and nothing over'; he could 'weigh and measure any parcel of human nature, and tell you exactly what it comes to'; and confronting children – and here we find most clearly revealed his likely approach to history[42] – 'He seemed a kind of cannon loaded to the muzzle with facts' (48). The teacher himself – the aptly named Mr M'Choakumchild (who had been recently trained in an academic institution resembling a 'factory'), significantly knew 'all the histories of all the peoples' (53); and children, he believed, could be viewed as 'little vessels . . . arranged in order, ready to have imperial gallons of facts poured into them until they were full to the brim' (47–8). Those absolute, unchanging 'facts' of course conveniently serve to confirm the unchanging 'reality' (intellectual, social, political) in which they live.

---

[41] The mill-owner Mr Hamper, in Mrs Gaskell's *North and South*, with a strike imminent, was 'comforted by the conviction that those who had brought it on were in a worse predicament than he himself – for he had head as well as hands, while they had only hands' (p. 193); but Mr Thornton, another industrialist, was aware that the heroine, Margaret Hale, 'does not like to hear men called "hands"' (p. 158).

[42] As a Benthamite Utilitarian, he had of course little use for the subject, Bentham himself having been particularly scathing about 'the wisdom of our ancestors'.

That description by Dickens of nineteenth-century education is not 'fictional' in the sense of being simply made up or a product of his own imagination: on the contrary, it exemplifies an actual educational philosophy of the time derived from (or illustrated by) the system of one Joseph Lancaster, who claimed to have 'invented, under the blessing of Divine Providence, a new and *mechanical* system of education'.[43] But what Dickens' fiction does here is to present very vividly that important aspect of intellectual and social history. And it shows clearly that the mechanical approach to education – which includes of course, and not least, education in *history* – implied, as we have just seen in the case of Mrs Gradgrind, a repudiation of 'fancy': an exclusive emphasis on 'facts' negates the need for (and desirability, or ultimately even possibility, of) imagination or wonder, which are to be seen as mere fanciful and self-indulgent distractions.

In *Hard Times*, then, despite her historical studies suffering from the fact that she remains '*extremely slow in the acquisition of dates*' (95, my emphases), the young girl Cecilia Jupe is indoctrinated as far as possible with Gradgrind's fact-orientated philosophy (though we later see her as having somehow, and against the odds, retained the capacity to transcend it); and she is warned correspondingly, 'never to fancy'. As one 'to be in all things regulated and governed . . . by fact', she is to 'discard the word Fancy altogether . . . [and] have nothing to do with it' (52). Forbidden ever to indulge in wonder, she is deprived of that childhood experience of seeing a face in the moon; and when caught by Gradgrind secretly peeping at a circus – the members of which and their acts defy the rules and regulations of conventional life – she incurs his wrath: "I should have soon as expected to find my children reading poetry" (61); where poetry of course notoriously exemplifies those anarchic imaginative faculties that have been contrasted with the more 'factual' characteristics of history since the time of classical antiquity.

---

[43] Joseph Lancaster quoted in his Introduction by David Craig (p. 23, my emphasis). Cf. Coleridge who had earlier referred to 'the philosophy of mechanism, which in everything which is most worthy of the human intellect, strikes *Death*, and cheats itself by making clear images for distinct conceptions'. Letter to Wordsworth, 30 May 1815, quoted by Raymond Williams, *Culture and Society, 1780–1950*, Harmondsworth, Penguin, 1961, p. 82. That is the philosophy in which, instead of seeing ourselves 'as one with the whole . . . we think of ourselves as separated beings, and place nature in antithesis to the mind, as object to subject, thing to thought, death to life' (*The Friend*, Section 2, Essay 11; quoted by Williams, *Culture and Society*, p. 82). And cf. Carlyle in *Signs of the Times* (1829), referring to 'the Mechanical Age . . . the Age of Machinery' (quoted in Laurence Lerner (ed.), *The Victorians*, London, Methuen, 1978, p. 49).

'Herein', explains Dickens as narrator, 'lay the spring of the mechanical art and mystery of educating the reason without stooping to the cultivation of the sentiments and affections. *Never wonder. By means of addition, subtraction, multiplication, and division, settle everything somehow, and never wonder*' (89, my emphases).

The educational assault on 'the tender young imaginations that were to be stormed away' (48) – the attempt to kill off the imaginative faculties with a strong dose of rationality – proved to have a particularly tragic outcome in the case of Gradgrind's own children. As a 'fictional' father, Gradgrind resembled (as we shall see further below) the 'factual' James Mill, who likewise professed 'the greatest contempt' for emotions of any sort, regarding them 'as a form of madness'.[44] Both sincerely tried to do the best for their respective children, by providing them with a good preparation for life; and that implied a thorough grounding in rationality. As Gradgrind puts it (and as James Mill might), "I have systematically devoted myself . . . to the education of the reason of my family. The reason is (as you know) the only faculty to which education should be addressed" (62). So as the narrating author himself (though not, again, without some irony) concedes: 'In gauging fathomless depths with his little mean excise-rod, and in staggering over the universe with his rusty stiff-legged compasses, he had meant to do great things' (244–5).

But tragically the results were far removed from those good intentions. Gradgrind's son Tom, 'whose imagination had been strangled in the cradle' (165), despite (no doubt for that very reason) being 'one of his model children' (300), went on to rob the bank where he worked, and was forced to flee the country. And before he went, he attempted to excuse himself to his father by playing some of his own theories back to him. His predicament, he claims, is after all only a matter of laws and statistics, so is hardly a matter of surprise or reproach: 'So many people are employed in situations of trust; so many people, out of so many, will be dishonest. I have heard you talk, a hundred times, of its being a law. How can I help laws?' (300)[45]

At that point in the story, Gradgrind suffers further disillusionment at the hands of his former pupil Bitzer, who, with self-interested motives, intends to inform the authorities of Tom's whereabouts and prevent his escape. Accused of being heartless, he claims most definitely to have a heart ('No man, sir, acquainted with the facts established by Harvey relating to the circulation of the blood, can doubt that I have a heart', 303); but he goes on to explain that

---

[44] Mill, *Autobiography*, p. 41.
[45] On Dickens' attitude to statistics, see I. Bernard Cohen, *The Triumph of Numbers: How Counting Shaped Modern Life*, New York and London, Norton, 2005.

(as a good pupil of a man who probably thought 'that the Good Samaritan was a Bad Economist', 238) his heart is naturally 'accessible to Reason . . . and to nothing else'. So of course he has no compassion for Tom, but intends to profit from his exposure as a criminal; for 'I am sure you know that the whole social system is a question of self-interest' (303). Was it not, after all,

> a fundamental principle of the Gradgrind philosophy, that everything was to be paid for. Nobody was ever on any account to give anybody anything, or render anybody help without purchase. Gratitude was to be abolished, and the virtues springing from it were not to be. Every inch of the existence of mankind, from birth to death, was to be a bargain across a counter. And if we didn't get to Heaven that way, it was not a politico-economical place, and we had no business there. (304)

Again, it is to his discomfiture that Gradgrind hears his own lessons played back to him, while being forced to confront the personal consequences of them.

A yet more explicit critique of his philosophy is provided by the important figure of his daughter Louisa – and once again a 'fictional' case resembles a 'factual' reality. Initially, the father seems to himself to have done a good job with her, and it is with some satisfaction that he claims: "You have been so well trained, and you do, I am happy to say, so much justice to the education you have received, that I have perfect confidence in your good sense. You are not impulsive, you are not romantic, you are accustomed to view everything from the strong dispassionate ground of reason and calculation" (132). Louisa might periodically have rebelled against her early upbringing, and did on one occasion confess to having, against her father's wishes, started to speculate and wonder about some apparently non-quantifiable aspects of human life: "looking at the red sparks dropping out of the fire, and whitening and dying", she had been provoked to ponder her own mortality – "how short my life would be, and how little I could hope to do in it". But the response to such self-indulgence was swift and unequivocal: "Nonsense!" said Mrs Gradgrind (94). And, "trained . . . so well, that I never dreamed a child's dream" (137), Louisa went on to do what was expected of her: reduced almost to an automaton, she accepts Josiah Bounderby's proposal of marriage, in deference to her father's well calculated wishes.

That marriage (to 'a man perfectly devoid of sentiment', 58) was clearly doomed from the start – or at least any hope of an emotional life for Louisa within the marriage was inconceivable. For, as we are told: 'The business was all Fact, from first to last', so there was no romantic nonsense. 'The Hours did not go through any of those rosy performances, which foolish poets have ascribed to them at such times; neither did the clocks go any faster, or any slower, than at other seasons. The deadly-statistical recorder in the Gradgrind observatory knocked every second on the head as it was born, and buried it with his accustomed regularity' (142). There was no more romance in the marriage than there was in Gradgrind's philosophy.

Louisa herself started openly to question the foundations of that marriage, and thence also of her own identity, through her association with another man, James Harthouse. Provoked by his pursuit of her towards some self-knowledge, she came to realise what had been done to her – the way that 'aspiration had been so laid waste in her youth'. Then she came to resent that loss, that deprivation: 'Her remembrances of home and childhood, were the remembrances of the drying up of every spring and fountain in her young heart as it gushed out' (223); she had simply become 'accustomed to self-suppression' (195). With that new realisation, Louisa goes back to her father, and is on the point of unburdening herself to him about her unhappy marriage to Bounderby and her growing relationship with Harthouse. But Gradgrind cannot cope – so cannot see (let alone answer) her need:

> to see it, he must have overleaped at a bound the artificial barriers he had for many years been erecting, between himself and all those subtle essences of humanity which will elude the utmost cunning of algebra until the last trumpet ever to be sounded shall blow even algebra to wreck. The barriers were too many and too high for such a leap. With his unbending, utilitarian, matter-of-fact face, he hardened her again; and the moment shot away into the plumbless depths of the past, to mingle with all the lost opportunities that are drowned there. (135)

That moving description of an emotionally crippled man is followed by another harrowing scene (239–42), where Louisa finally manages to confront her father and reproaches him with having ruined her life: "Oh father, what have you done . . . !" She has been trained 'from infancy to strive against every natural prompting that has arisen in my heart'; she has been robbed 'of the immaterial part of my life, the spring and summer of my belief, my refuge from what is sordid and bad in the *real* [my emphasis] things around me'; with her 'ardent impulse towards some region where rules, and figures, and definitions were not quite absolute', she has suffered from a hunger and thirst that has never been appeased; and she reveals 'the ordinary deadened state of my mind'.[46] At last, 'the feelings long suppressed broke loose'; and she fell to the ground, where Gradgrind 'saw the pride of his heart and the triumph of his system, lying, in an insensible heap, at his feet'.

Louisa's breakdown, like that of John Stuart Mill (to be considered below), constitutes what Leavis refers to as 'the confutation of Utilitarianism by life'.[47] And despite the widespread acceptance, and the dire effects, of Gradgrind's philosophy, Dickens does leave us in *Hard Times* with a positive message. For people are not so easily reduced to inhumanity: even the factory 'hands' of Coketown, in the face of all the odds, manage to resist all pressures and retain their sense of wonder. As the novelist ironically states: 'It was a disheartening circumstance, but a melancholy fact, that even these readers [in the Coketown library] persisted in wondering. They wondered about human nature, human passions, human hopes and fears, the struggles, triumphs and defeats, the cares and joys and sorrows, the lives and deaths, of common men and women!' (90).

Dickens' novel thus illustrates the meeting of fiction with history and historical theory in at least two important ways: first, it provides a wealth of evidence for historians relating to nineteenth-century intellectual and social developments; and second, it presents a critique of the then current historiographical (and more general educational) emphasis on 'facts' at the expense of the imagination. But there is a further way in which fiction meets history here, for the validity of Dickens' analysis in 'fiction' is – as we shall now go on to see – confirmed by the autobiographical record of an actual 'historical' figure.

Gradgrind in history: James Mill

Although not himself 'crammed with mere facts' like some of his contemporaries, John Stuart Mill came to realise that his education, which had been undertaken almost entirely by his father James, had greatly over-emphasised the development of his rational faculties, at the expense of his imagination and emotions. James Mill, like Dickens' Thomas Gradgrind, denigrated 'wonder': both educators appear to resemble those 'cause-and-effect speculators'

---

[46] The deliberate deadening of young minds is described also by Mrs Gaskell, who explains that northern manufacturers did not send their sons to university, but set them to work early at age 14 or 15 – 'unsparingly cutting away all off-shoots in the direction of literature or high mental cultivation, in hopes of throwing the whole strength and vigour of the plant into commerce'. *North and South*, p. 90.

[47] Leavis, *Great Tradition*, p. 269.

described (in his essay 'On History') by Thomas Carlyle, 'with whom no wonder would remain wonderful, but all things in Heaven and Earth must be computed and "accounted for"'. Carlyle goes on to pray that increasing specialisation does not 'aggravate our already strong Mechanical tendencies',[48] a prayer that, as we have just seen, remained unanswered in the case of Dickens' fictional characters Tom and Bitzer, and remained unanswered too in the factual case of J. S. Mill himself, who went on (in 1826–7) to suffer serious mental breakdown as a consequence.

As reported in his *Autobiography*,[49] Mill's education at the hands of his father resembles in important respects that described as a fashionable ideal in *Hard Times*; and the practical results in his case are particularly illuminating. He was of course hardly an average pupil, who studied Greek from the age of 3, and had read, amongst other works, the whole of Herodotus and six dialogues of Plato by the time he started learning Latin at the age of 7. More was always demanded of him intellectually than he was capable of – an educational strategy of which he later came to approve. But socially and culturally, he felt more deprived. His father made few concessions to childhood: 'Of children's books, anymore than of playthings, I had scarcely any' (7); and, significantly, his rigorous education necessitated him being 'carefully kept . . . from having any great amount of intercourse with other boys' – the aim being that he escape 'the contagion of vulgar modes of thought and feeling' (30).[50]

Therein lies the influence of Jeremy Bentham, whom James Mill met in 1808, and who has in our own time been described as 'a cold and sober accountant whose every step, in his own existence and in the existence of those he was able to influence, was scrupulously calculated'. Both Bentham and the older Mill, writes Wolf Lepenies, were 'fixated to the goal of *practical utility*'; and great emphasis was placed by them on logic – which in itself was something that the younger Mill never regretted. But there was a problematic corollary: that they were 'alienated from art and literature'; and for them the poet, whose 'business consists in stimulating our passions, and exciting our prejudices', must always, in Bentham's words, remain a mere 'dealer in *fictions*'.[51]

That is revealed as lying at the root of James Mill's limitations as an educator: his dismissal of emotions – of feelings, imagination, and a sense of wonder

[48] Carlyle, *Essays*, pp. 86, 90.

[49] Page references to the edition cited in n. 40 will be given in the text.

[50] Mill himself recognises the educational disadvantages suffered by those 'other boys' of his time: and as with Dickens and Coketown, he associates *architecture*, the physical environment, with wider moral sensibilities: see above, n. 40.

[51] Lepenies, *Between Literature and Science*, pp. 94, 99 (my emphases).

– is what immediately reminds us of Charles Dickens' Gradgrind. We have already noted how he expressed the utmost contempt for what he regarded as the insanity of passionate emotions: 'the great stress laid upon feeling' by some of his contemporaries (as it is by some of our own), he regarded as nothing other than an aberration (41).[52] So that it is not surprising that, as his son recalls in a delightful understatement, his 'teachings tended to the undervaluing of feeling' (93). And it was of course not only his teaching that was affected: that attitude had an obvious impact also upon his own personal relations; and Mill notes the circularity involved in the experience and expression of emotions: 'The element which was chiefly deficient in his moral relation to his children was that of tenderness . . . He resembled most Englishmen in being ashamed of the signs of feeling, and by the absence of demonstration, starving the feelings themselves' (43). So difficult did James Mill find personal communication, that it was, as his son touchingly reveals, only through others that he learnt what his father thought about his own first argumentative essay (60); and in his later emotional crisis, he 'was the last person to whom . . . I looked for help' (114–15).

J. S. Mill's emotional crisis is emblematic of the over-emphasis on science, on rationality and logic, on the attempted universalisation of a mechanistic model, on materialism and utilitarianism – and all at the expense of imagination and feeling, of the emotional and poetic, and of the mystical and any sense of wonder. His education had prepared him, like Dickens' Bitzer, to be an enthusiastic disciple of Bentham, and for two or three years, as he confesses, the description of a Benthamite 'as a mere reasoning machine' was 'not altogether untrue of me' (92). With a 'superabundance . . . of mere logic and analysis' (93), his intellect had come to resemble T. H. Huxley's ideal of 'a clear, cold, logic engine'; but as he himself later came to see, he lacked at that time the 'natural aliment' of *feeling*, or of any 'poetical culture'.

The practical result of this one-sidedness was his nervous breakdown. Like Gradgrind who, on learning from Louisa of his terrible failure in her upbringing, confesses, that 'The ground on which I stand has ceased to be solid under my feet' (244), so too did Mill face a challenge to his most fundamental beliefs, and an emotional crisis in which 'the whole foundation on which my life was constructed fell down' (113). It was during that period that he, like the ultimately redeemed Gradgrind, came to see the deficiencies in himself. Just as the fictional character came to realise that 'there is a wisdom of the Heart' as

[52] Wolf Lepenies describes him as being 'filled with an imperturbable faith in the revelatory power of facts', p. 94; and he goes on to make the obvious connection: 'It is not hard to recognise the elder Mill in the figure of Mr. Gradgrind', p. 112.

well as 'a wisdom of the Head' (245–6), and finally developed into 'a wiser man, and a better man, than in the days when in this life he wanted nothing but Facts' (293), so too did Mill come to realise 'that the habit of analysis has a tendency to wear away the feelings' (116), and that 'From this neglect both in theory and practice of the cultivation of feeling, naturally resulted . . . an undervaluing of poetry, and of Imagination generally (94) . . . I was wholly blind to its place in human culture' (95).

That denial of the poetic came, then, to be recognised by Mill, in his deep depression and desperation, as nothing less than a form of blindness; and his sight was restored in a Damascene conversion that resulted from reading the poetry of Wordsworth. Such poetry, he appreciated, 'expressed . . . states of *feeling*, and of thought coloured by feeling' (125, my emphasis); and thenceforth 'The cultivation of the feeling became one of the cardinal points in my ethical and philosophical creed' (122). That new-found attention to feeling – to the emotion and wonder that characterise poetry – was not, Mill believed, by any means incompatible with a 'scientific' approach (128–9). Arguing against the archetypical Romanticism of Keats, who famously bemoaned the murder by Newtonian optics of the wonders of a rainbow, he insists that 'the intensest feeling of the beauty of a cloud lighted by the setting sun, is no hindrance to my knowing that the cloud is vapour of water, subject to all the laws of vapours in a state of suspension' (129). And that conclusion brings us directly and conveniently back to history, for it was reached in part by his reading of Carlyle, whose writings seemed to him to be not so much 'philosophy to instruct' as 'poetry to animate' (148); 'I felt that he was a poet' (149). And as we have seen, he came to consider Carlyle's *French Revolution* as itself not so much history as poetry – an attribution that was intended not as criticism but as high praise, inasmuch as Carlyle, as historian, revealed the *poetical* aspects of reality – the *feelings* of those involved, and so the *truth*.

Conclusion

John Stuart Mill's aspiration towards a synthesis between science and poetry, rationality and feeling, had application not only to his own individual psychology but also – as he shows in his description of Carlyle – more generally to the academic discipline of history. An obvious implication of his advocacy was a historiography that recognised the importance, in any claims for 'truth', of *imagination* on the part of historians and of the evocation of *emotions* in their reconstructions of the past. And that this, in the event, largely failed to transpire may serve to explain at least in part why fictional representations of historians and history have often been sadly negative. For while there has continued always to be debate between supporters of 'Enlightenment rationalism' and 'Romantic imagination' (with all the associated intellectual baggage of those two basic and no doubt oversimplified positions), it is the former that has held sway in nineteenth- and twentieth-century historiography.

Indeed, the case of Mill, as described in his *Autobiography*, indicates that Dickens in *Hard Times* was not so much satirising (as might at first appear) as illustrating the intellectual emphasis in Britain at that time, in relation particularly to how that impinged on educational – and thence more specifically historical – theory (and indeed practice). Gradgrind's emphasis on facts, in conjunction with a repudiation of feeling and wonder, has particular relevance to history, and it is an emphasis which has fitted well with the aspirations of a subject determined to project its scientific credentials. We have seen above how historians have continued, up to the present, to claim academic respectability, cultural credibility, and political importance, through assertions of the detached, impartial, rational, empirical nature of their discipline. We have further seen how that scientific approach has been periodically challenged by a more 'romantic' tradition in which greater importance is attributed to the more 'poetic' side of human life. But historians representing that latter tradition have been relegated to territory well outside the mainstream, and below the salt – a territory to be characterised, negatively, as 'historical romance'. It is in this context noteworthy that Carlyle – so approved by Mill as a 'poetic' historian – continues so far out of fashion in theoretical terms that he does not so much as appear in the index of a compendium of Philosophies of History published in 2000 (and that despite the inclusion of Mill himself).[53]

We need not, then, be surprised that representations of historians, from without the discipline of history itself, should so often appear in an unflattering light – as being one-sided people, like Gradgrind and Mill before their respective conversions to a fuller conception of humanity, and so representing, in the words of Proust, 'a past made arid by the intellect'.[54] Fiction again can be seen to reveal a practical reality, or fact, or truth, about historical theory.

---

[53] Burns and Rayment-Pickard (eds), *Philosophies of History*.
[54] Marcel Proust, *Remembrance of Things Past* [1920–27], 3 vols; London, Penguin, 1983, vol. III, p. 905.

Further reading

Dickens, Charles, *Hard Times* [1854], ed. David Craig, Harmondsworth, Penguin, 1969.

Eliot, George, *Middlemarch* [1871–2], London, Oxford University Press, 1947.

Ibsen, Henrik, *Hedda Gabler* [1890], in *Three Plays*, trans. Una Ellis-Fermor, Harmondsworth, Penguin, 1950.

Lewis, Wyndham, *Self Condemned* [1954], Santa Barbara, Black Sparrow Press, 1983.

Lively, Penelope, *Moon Tiger*, London, Penguin, 1988.

Mill, John Stuart, *Autobiography* [1873], London, Oxford University Press, 1924.

Chapter 4

Fiction, history, and memory

An important meeting point for history and fiction lies in their respective attention to, and use of, memory. This chapter, then, first considers the importance of memory for historical evidence and then examines some treatments of memory in fiction, with particular reference to Marcel Proust and Daphne du Maurier. It concludes with a study of the critique of memory, and thence more generally of historical evidence, to be found in Penelope Lively's fiction.

Memory is central to the activities of both novelists and historians. In fact, it is central to the activities of anyone concerned to construct a narrative – a chronologically based story leading from an earlier beginning to a later end. For it constitutes the only tool we have for gaining any access to the past, and so for giving any account of what happened before the present moment. It is not surprising, then, that the importance of memory for the construction of our own (supposedly enduring) identities has also long been recognised, with David Hume most famously appealing explicitly to memory as the 'glue' that sticks together our pasts and presents, so enabling us to claim some personal continuity.

Some seventeen centuries before Hume, though, Plutarch, in his essay on 'Tranquillity and Contentment', had written of the need to keep a proper balance between past, present, and future, and to retain a connection between all three; for, in the words of his sixteenth-century translator, all are 'linked (as it were) and chained by the copulation of things past and present'. It is memory that enables that connection to be maintained, and it is that that the foolish man will reject – foolish, since as a corollary he will ignore the inevitably fleeting and elusive moment that is *now*, and thus allow 'everything to pass away and run as it were through a sieve'. Such foolish repudiators of memory are like the man in hell, who plaited a rope and failed to notice the donkey behind him, who ate his rope as soon as he had made it; whereas the wise, on the other hand, will take due note of what is behind them, and will be concerned with the weaving of memories into a thread, in such a way that they will provide some lasting sense of selfhood. They will incorporate memories, both good and bad, into a single harmonious whole; and that retention of the past in memory will enable it to live on in the present.[1]

Admittedly, even if we succeed in following Plutarch's advice, the memories thus utilised in the construction of our coherent narratives may not be entirely our own: we rely additionally on recollections of parents, siblings, friends, and others; on family photographs, perhaps, recording scenes that we might otherwise have forgotten; and the personal is often overlaid by the social – by cultural influences that steer our memories in ways that conform to a more widely accepted (and acceptable) past. But whatever the problems concerning what actually constitutes memory, there remains a heavy dependence upon it – in our daily lives, and in history as well as in fiction. For any records used – anything that historians refer to as 'evidence' – necessarily themselves derive from other people's memories of what happened. And of course it is commonly claimed that the most reliable evidence on which historians can draw is that derived from eyewitness accounts, or the memories of those who were themselves personally involved in the events in question.

Explicit recognition of historians' dependence on memory dates back at least to Thucydides, who claimed that his own work gained its reliability, and its superiority over mere fiction, by virtue of its basis in personal experience and evidence from contemporary eye-witnesses. 'Romances' about the past – poetic treatments of events such as those of Homer – were just that: figments of imagination, lacking any grounding in what 'really' happened. Homer dealt in myths, whereas historians, who firmly based their work on actual memories of people and events, could thereby claim to represent what really took place; given sufficient care in their use of memories, their histories corresponded with the actuality of the past – they were authentic, '*true*'.

The proper use of reliable memories as their foundations thus constituted the essential difference between history and romance: it was at the root of the contrast between 'fact' and 'fiction'. And that presupposition of history's superiority to fiction as a constructer of 'true' narratives (almost always

---

[1] Plutarch, Essay on 'Tranquillity and Contentment', in *Plutarch's Moral Essays*, trans. Philemon Holland, ed. E. H. Blakeney, London, J. M. Dent, c. 1911, pp. 175–6.

implying some linear passage through time) has persisted through to the present; it is what *defines* history – delimits it – in relation to fiction, and what justifies its widely acknowledged importance.

Yet when one comes to examine memory, its reliability comes immediately into question, and not least as an indicator of a regular linear trajectory through time. Historians themselves have of course long been aware of hazards associated with the evidential base of their work – aware, probably even from personal experience, that memory can play tricks, can delude us and mis-represent others, can appear to have a life of its own, detached from any 'real' experience, can adapt and get modified, can come to appear as unstable and as imaginatively based as fiction. Yet often they choose to ignore that.

Which is why novelists, as writers of what is readily admitted to be fiction, can sometimes provide more illumination on this subject – and on *historio-graphical* repercussions – than historians themselves. Tolstoy makes the point in *War and Peace* that, even in everyday life in peacetime, we are liable to mis-remember the past and fail to distinguish between our actual experiences and things we might have just imagined. The young girl Sonya, for example, claimed to have foreseen Prince Andrew's death, and genuinely believed that she had done so: 'what she had *invented* then, seemed to her now as *real* as any other recollection'. And such self-delusions are yet more likely under the stress of war: so Tolstoy describes the Russian officer Nicolai Rostov in glow-ing terms, as 'a truthful young man [who] would on no account have told a deliberate lie'. But although, as he later recounted his experiences, he 'began his story meaning to tell everything just as it happened . . . [yet] impercept-ibly, involuntarily, and *inevitably* he lapsed into falsehood'.[2] And Joanna Bourke has more recently cited a diary from the Great War, which indicates a similarly involuntary confusion between memory and actuality: 'One thing that I can remember seeing quite distinctly (although I never did, but dreamt it in the hospital – it was a true story nonetheless).' That extraordinarily hon-est (if confused) self-appraisal clarifies that at one level the veteran concedes the *fictive* nature of his memory, while insisting at the same time, but on another level, that his memory was nonetheless *true*.[3]

That apparent *inevitability* of distortion on the part of participants clearly has important implications for the validity of subsequent histories that are supposedly based on reliable eyewitness accounts; and it impacts in particular on descriptions of those who claim to have played a major role in the events

---

[2] Leo Tolstoy, *War and Peace* [1868, 1869], trans. Louise and Aylmer Maude, London, Oxford University Press, 1941, III.184; I.316 (my emphases).

[3] Joanna Bourke, *An Intimate History of Killing*, London, Granta, 2000, p. 9.

in question. It is significant that that critique of memory's reliability as a foundation stone of history appeared long since in Tolstoy's work of *fiction*; and in this chapter we shall go on to examine further examples of novelists *anticipating* other historical theorists and historians themselves.

Memory and historical evidence

First, though, we need to look at a positive promotion of history as the *antidote* to such defective and self-deluding memories. Michael Bentley, for example, has written of how 'history is precisely *non-memory*'. It is, rather, 'a systematic discipline which seeks to rely on mechanisms and controls quite different from those which memory triggers and often intended to *give memory the lie*'.[4] So far from being assimilated to history, it is history's specific function to act as a *corrective* to memory.

That oppositional stance has been adopted by some historians in the face of a veritable upsurge in the counter-claims of those advocating the priority of memory. Those advocates are sometimes critical of disciplinary history because it is seen as totally excluding, or at best minimising the importance of, such aspects of the past as play prominent parts in individual memories. This, then, constitutes another act in the enduring drama of the struggle between a 'scientific' and a more 'romantic' history: supporters of 'memory' here follow in the tradition of Sir Walter Scott and those who put emphasis on the subjective experience of past peoples; for them, individual memories provide a vital historical resource that enable a fuller, more rounded and possibly more colourful past to be recounted. As Avishai Margalit has noted, 'When history is contrasted with memory, history is habitually labelled as cold, even lifeless, whereas memory can be vital, vivid, and alive.'[5]

That contrast has been highlighted in a postcolonial context, where memory has been posited as an important corrective to orthodox historical narratives that have failed to take proper account of subordinate or 'subaltern' subjects. The disciplinary imperialism of history has been particularly evident in relation to the political and ideological imperialism of western powers; and proponents of memory see their advocacy as an aspect of not only personal but

[4] Michael Bentley, *Modern Historiography: An Introduction*, London, Routledge, 1999, p. 155 (my emphases).
[5] Avishai Margalit, *Ethics of Memory*, Cambridge, Mass. and London, Harvard University Press, 2002, p. 67.

also ethnic rehabilitation. The memories of the previously colonised and repressed may not always accord with the histories in which they see their pasts represented, and in such cases the actual memories (perhaps orally transmitted) of participants may (now in contradistinction to Michael Bentley) prove a useful corrective to 'official' or hitherto widely accepted histories. (We shall return to this in relation to African-American women's writing in Chapter 8.)

There may in these cases be some danger of indulging a sentimentality or nostalgia – or even, with associated appeals to the ineffable and sublime, a newly developing form of religiosity[6] – that conflicts with conventional academic practice; and few can fail to be aware of the recent resurgence of popular interest in (auto)biographies and memoirs, often designed to appeal to a voyeuristic public by recalling traumas from which it may feel smugly safe. But despite that hazard, and the associated risk of 'false memories' and fakes,[7] there is often an affecting immediacy in personal memories that is lacking in some (though by no means all) proper histories.

Admittedly, as Bentley claims, we can all be mistaken in our memories, confusing events, overlaying past circumstances with more recent experience, making anachronistic assumptions, and generally misremembering what happened. And at such times, historians can often provide help by resorting to archival evidence and consensual conclusions, and so establishing persuasive chronologies which we then feel bound to accept. That corrective function for history can certainly be seen to have a place in our construction of some narratives: there is, for example, an accepted historical record that, in the face of all my protestations, confirms the date of the outbreak of the Second World War, and confirms that the evacuation of British forces from Dunkirk preceded D-Day. Such factual records can indeed persuasively refute defective memories, and it is surely uncontentious that a wrongly remembered date or order of events should be corrected; in such cases 'memory' properly defers to 'history'.

But problems still arise when history purports to provide more than a chronicle of bare 'facts': as soon as historians attempt to make something of those facts, by putting them into some sort of narrative, they are bound themselves to rely on contemporary accounts – and those in turn inevitably rely on

---

[6] See e.g. the interesting essay by Kerwin Lee Klein, 'On the Emergence of Memory in Historical Discourse', *Representations* 69, 2000, 127–50.

[7] See e.g. Binjamin Wilkomirski, *Fragments: Memories of a Childhood, 1939–1948*, London, Picador, 1996. Published as an 'unselfconscious and powerful . . . masterpiece', it was later revealed as a fake. See further Chapter 8 below.

memory (the memories of those involved, or of contemporary reporters of what was then going on). So that, as soon as historians proceed from discrete 'facts' to their emplotment they are faced once again with all the problems associated with (potentially defective) memory.

And those problems look likely to be compounded in the near future, when, according to the claims and predictions of Wulf Kansteiner, we will enjoy the delights of new digital technologies and formats that will allow us (unashamedly) 'to *invent* the content of our memories'. In the immediate future, he suggests, 'the virtual world . . . will become the memory of choice'; which I take to mean that we may soon come to live with a 'virtual' or fantasy past, rather than any 'real' one, if that for whatever reason seems preferable. In certain respects, of course, we have always chosen our memories – selected some few, out of an infinity of potential competitors, to make a part of our past provide a base appropriate for our future aspirations – but it seems that we are now to be blessed (or is it cursed?) with the additional support of powerful 'virtual' back-up. Kansteiner's vision in this context of a 'postmodern nirvana of virtual remembrance' may provoke some suggestions for alternative and preferable nirvanas from old reactionaries like me; but we seem likely to agree that the developments envisaged by him would serve further to complicate the relationship of memory with 'history', and throw yet more doubt on the reliability of memory-derived historical evidence.[8]

That complications already exist, and that doubts about memory's reliability have long been held, may be seen in another meeting ground of history and fiction.

Memory in fiction

Marcel Proust

Proust is the novelist whose work is most obviously – indeed, most *obsessively* – concerned with memory. *Remembrance of Things Past* (1920–27) is how the title of his major work is translated into English in Scott Moncrieff's version; *In Search for Lost Time* would be a more literal rendering of the French *À la recherche du temps perdu*. Either way, that title alerts us to the most important

---

[8] Wulf Kansteiner, 'Alternate [sic] Worlds and Invented Communities: History and Historical Consciousness in the Age of Interactive Media', in Keith Jenkins, Sue Morgan and Alun Munslow (eds), *Manifestos for History*, London, Routledge, 2007, pp. 132, 140, 142.

treatment of memory in fiction;[9] and in his attempts to search for 'lost time' – time that now constitutes 'the past' – Proust confronts what are (at least in many respects) essentially the problems and issues by which any historian is faced.

That is not, of course, to suggest that there are not some differences between the autobiographical and intensely personal approach of Proust on the one hand, and, on the other hand, the more publicly orientated concerns and techniques of conventional historians. Most importantly, apart from the occasional citation of a note or letter, the former makes very little use of written records; he repairs to no archive in a search for documents, and he may thus seem to avoid the problems inherent in such data as are the historian's main resource. But in fact there is much overlap; for, as we have noted above, texts in archives are ultimately dependent on the *memories* of those who wrote them, or of those esteemed competent (as eyewitnesses, especially) to provide authoritative evidence. So when Proust tries to make some sense of his life, by composing it within a literary narrative (however unconventional), he faces many of the difficulties by which any storyteller, or writer about past times – and so any historian – is confronted.

For questions are immediately raised about the nature and function of memory. How are memories retrieved? How reliable are memories in respect of recovering what 'actually happened'? How complete are they? Or rather, what were the criteria for the choices and selections inevitably made in their formulation and retention? How partial are they, in relation both to some assumed 'whole' of the event in question, and to the inevitable 'bias' or prejudices of their author? In what respects is their validity to be questioned, as being (necessarily) 'subjective', deriving, as they do and must, from individual personalities each with their own emphases and interests? What has occasioned or determined the (sometimes sudden and unexpected) recovery of specific memories? Have they been (and can they be) deliberately recalled, or have they resurfaced to consciousness by some purely fortuitous contingency or subconsciously formed association? And what further potentially useful memories – memories that might affect the nature and direction of our stories – remain still buried and lost in a time past that is lost irretrievably?

---

[9] Proust's work is hard to characterise, but he does insist upon its *fictitious* nature: as narrator, Marcel explains that, 'In this book . . . there is not a single incident which is not fictitious, not a single character who is a real person in disguise.' *Remembrance of Things Past* [1920–27], trans. C. K. Scott Moncrieff and Terence Kilmartin, 3 vols; London, Penguin, 1983, III.876 (my emphasis). Future page references to this edition will be given in the text.

These, then, are some of the themes to be encountered in Proust's work – not always explicitly articulated as such, but always inherent and interwoven in his complex narrative. That is not to say that he necessarily encounters them, as it were, head on, or in a directly theoretical way. Indeed, as he makes clear through Marcel as his narrator, he has little time for literary theorists, who advocate a practical socio-political purpose for literature: their 'theories seemed to me to indicate very clearly the inferiority of those who upheld them'; for, themselves using 'hackneyed phrases', they paid no attention to language, but encouraged an over-intellectualised approach that was likely to result in a theoretical display tantamount to producing 'an object which still has its price-tag on it' (III.915–16).[10] Such over self-consciousness about what one is doing will, Proust believes, render one's productions somehow *inauthentic*: it is precisely the *unbidden* nature of the memories on which he focuses – memories such as are evoked by sensory perceptions. That is 'the mark of their authenticity . . . their essential character was that I was not free to choose them'; their *fortuitous* nature 'proved the trueness of the past which they brought back to life' (III.913).

The question of self-consciousness relates also to experiences themselves: again, Proust believes, *excessive* consciousness of what one is experiencing actually distances one from the experience; so that one is left unsatisfied, unfulfilled, as having in some way lost direct touch with the external world – lost its sense of immediacy, or *reality*; one has become *detached*. And that in turn has clear implications for how one describes an experience and reports it to others – which is where we revert obviously to the matter of historical evidence. For how does that intrusion of *distance* between subject and object (a requirement of any scientist from the time of Descartes) affect one's ability to perceive it 'truly', and then transcribe it into literary form – the form that constitutes an historical source?

Proust's own epiphanic moment (as described by Marcel) – the moment when he decides to try to make something meaningful of his life through the medium of literature – comes with his sudden awareness of the intrusion into his *present* consciousness of a *past* moment in all its complexity and completeness; when he realised that 'the past was made to encroach upon the present and I was made to doubt whether I was in the one or the other' (III.904). That memory, which so disorientates the recipient, confusing his chronology, comes unbidden, but somehow provoked by a seemingly inconsequential

---

[10] Cf. I.510, where M. de Norpois shatters Marcel's confidence by speaking against 'Art for Art's sake' and advocating something more than 'the manipulation of words in a harmonious manner'.

smell or sound or touch – the smell of a madeleine (I.50–51; III.899), the sound of a musical phrase (I.375), the touch of an uneven stone at one's feet (III.899–900), or the stiffness of a linen napkin (III.901). But its *recovery*, and its successful *assimilation* into the present, occasions a true happiness of both aesthetic and emotional dimensions (III.902f.) – a situation that sounds interestingly similar to that of the Dutch historian Johan Huizinga, who claimed, through the medium of a painting by Van Eyck (in 1902), to have experienced direct contact with the Middle Ages (about which he was then inspired to write), and who further (and similarly) claimed to have received, by looking at a seventeenth-century engraving, 'the conviction of an immediate contact with the past . . . an . . . almost ecstatic experience of no longer being myself, of a getting in touch with the essence of things, of the *experience of Truth by history*'.[11]

Proust's concern with the past derived initially from his personal need to make some sense of his life – to give his own existence some meaning; and his whole book (just like our own diaries or journals, if we keep them) can be interpreted as a record of that personal quest. His own resolution of an existential crisis ultimately involved the writing of a book, now widely acknowledged as one of the greatest literary works of the twentieth century. But while few will be competent to follow his lead in that respect, his psychological journey along the way may provide illumination for historians whose concerns, at least in some respects, coincide. For it is clear that, for all his avowed disapproval of 'theorists', Proust himself inevitably confronts numerous issues by which historians are concerned in practice. We shall now look briefly at some of these, including memory itself of course, and its use and validity as evidence, identity and narrative, relativism, and time.

In his search for personal meaning, Proust clearly feels a need to make some sense of a past that has culminated in his present: his present, in which he is feeling so discontented (even depressed), needs, he believes, to encompass a past. But looking back, that past seems far from unitary: it seems, rather, to be 'compounded of *so many different pasts* that it was difficult for me to recognise the cause of my melancholy' (III.890, my emphases). Those different pasts, or the truth about those pasts, need to fit together into something coherent (I.303–4); for (as Plutarch had seen) identities depend on an assimilation of past with present. And that is where the importance of memory comes in:

[11] On Proust as a mystic whose experiences transcend time and defeat death, see R. C. Zaehner, *Mysticism, Sacred and Profane*, Oxford, Clarendon Press, 1957, pp. 52–61. For 'Huizinga on historical experience', see Frank Ankersmit, *Sublime Historical Experience*, Stanford, Stanford University Press, 2005, pp. 119–39; quotation is from p. 126 (my emphasis).

Proust cites the example of waking up in a strange room – not knowing *where* he is, or *who* he is. Then, as he describes, memory comes to his rescue, reminding him of how he came to be where he was; it 'would come like a rope let down from heaven to draw me up out of the abyss of not-being, from which I could never have escaped by myself' (I.5–6); and he thus regains some sense of personal continuity and selfhood.

The retention of any such firm sense of identity is problematic, partly because (as we shall discuss further in Chapter 6) we are never simply *unitary* entities: 'none of us can be said to constitute a material whole, which is identical for everyone' (I.20), or indeed even for ourselves. 'In so many people there are different strata which are not alike', so we never know quite where we are in relation to others or to ourselves: Proust describes one character, Gilberte, as being 'like one of those countries with which one dare not form an alliance because of their too frequent changes of government' (III.710) – an example that illustrates the fact of 'a single individual being several different people for different observers . . . or even for the same observer at different periods over the years' (III.95). So that, as he explains in another case, 'There were . . . two M. de Charluses, not to mention any others' (III.893).[12]

This relativism of our perception is to be observed not only in our individualised characterisations of other people, but also far more widely – and in ways that directly impinge upon our apprehension of historical evidence. Proust writes in general terms of 'the uniqueness of the fashion in which the world appears to each one of us' (III.932), but also, and more particularly, about the impossibility of a universal perception which might enable us to see things simply 'as they are'. The example he gives of the views of Saint-Hilaire, indicating our inability to have our cake and eat it – to view from several (or even only two) points at the same time – has clear implications for history, or any other subject in which some 'objective' knowledge is the goal: what we see, what we experience, and what therefore we report (as the 'truth' of any view or situation) is inevitably dependent on the viewpoint we have chosen – which is but one viewpoint chosen from an infinity of other possibilities (I.114–15).

The relativism of our viewpoints can be seen sometimes in the way that our minds – or is it our actual perceptions? – are changed. That change can be brought about by the provision of alternatives through art; for it is the function of art to release us from the very narrow constraints of our own vision and to introduce us to other possibilities: 'Thanks to art, instead of seeing one world only, our own, we see that world multiply itself and we have at our disposal as

---

[12] Cf. III.761, where he writes of 'the law that a person is many different persons according to who is judging him'.

many worlds as there are original artists' (III.932). But change can also be effected through self-interest: evidence of events, or rationales for action, can be adapted, modified to suit some later need. Thus, we are told how Gilberte was revealed as having rewritten her own past, her own history of her departure from Paris early in the war, in 1914. She had gone to her country house in Tonsonville, and at the time she had given as the reason for her move a natural desire to escape from what seemed an imminent German invasion. But some years later she offered an alternative, and more heroic sounding explanation: she had forgotten the reason she had originally given, and in a new letter to Marcel, 'her departure . . . was presented *retrospectively* in a very different light . . . In a word, Gilberte was now persuaded that she had gone to Tonsonville not, as she had written to me in 1914, in order to escape from the Germans and be in a safe place, but on the contrary in order to face them and defend her house against them' (III.777–8, my emphasis).

As Proust writes a few pages later: 'So much for the value of evidence and memory!' (III.871). For that example makes patently clear one aspect of the problematic nature of historical evidence: if Gilberte leaves confusing and contradictory accounts of her own recent past, what are we to make of historians' ascriptions of motives to others in more complicated matters in the more distant past? And in a further example, where Proust does explicitly make the connection with historical evidence and practice, he draws attention once more to the inevitable relativism that results from the need to select:

> If, in the realm of painting, one portrait makes manifest certain truths concerning volume, light, movement, does that mean that it is necessarily inferior to another completely different portrait of the same person, in which a thousand details omitted in the first are minutely transcribed, from which second portrait one would conclude that the model was ravishingly beautiful while from the first one would have thought him or her ugly, a fact which may be of documentary, even of *historical importance*. (III.738–9, my emphasis)

Furthermore, fresh evidence can come to light which necessitates re-appraisal of our personal narratives and histories; and in this context Proust introduces a theme that is treated later and at greater length by Penelope Lively (as we shall see below). He describes, then, how his friend Monsieur Swann finds out about a single untruth apparently perpetrated by his lover Odette, and how that leads him to question their whole relationship. For 'he could feel the insinuation of a possible undercurrent of falsehood which rendered ignoble all that had remained most precious to him'. His trust was completely undermined, so that he felt forced to make a painful reappraisal of his life story, after 'shattering stone by stone the whole edifice of his past' (I.404). Such requisite personal reappraisals have obvious implications for histories too, which must likewise remain vulnerable to undermining and the shattering of their whole edifice.

Another subject that impinges most obviously on historical theory is that of time. Proust is particularly conscious of the way that past and present become muddled: 'our life', explains Marcel, is 'so careless of chronology, interpolating so many anachronisms into the sequence of our days', that, when thinking of his previous lover Gilberte, he found himself 'living in those – far older days than yesterday or last week', when he still loved her (I.691).[13] 'The nimble shuttles of the years', as he explains, 'weave links between those of our memories which seem at first most independent of each other' (III.879); and later in the work, with his memory jogged, he experiences various impressions 'at the present moment and at the same time in the context of a distant moment, so that *the past was made to encroach upon the present* and I was made to doubt whether I was in the one or the other'. His experience was effectively 'extra-temporal', existing *'outside time'* (III.904, my emphases); and it was through his realisation of this that Marcel came to conceive the ambition to recover 'the Time that was Lost' (III.904), those 'fragments of existence withdrawn from Time' (III.908). For most people, the past lies largely forgotten: 'their past is like a photographic dark-room encumbered with innumerable negatives which remain useless because the intellect has not developed them' (III.931). So, at another point where history and fiction meet, Proust's aim becomes to shine light into these dark corners – 'to make visible, to intellectualise in a work of art, realities that were *outside Time*' (III.971, my emphasis).

Daphne du Maurier

Daphne du Maurier is a particularly successful novelist and may seem an unlikely candidate for inclusion here as Proust's partner; but, for all her undoubted popularity and widespread appeal, she shows a general interest in history and historiography in a number of her writings, so is another example of an author who introduces related issues to a wider audience.

---

[13] The continuing presence of a past lover is of course a common conceit. See e.g. Thackeray, for a description of Henry Esmond's great passion for Beatrix – a passion that may long since have died and been relegated to the past, but which lives on in memory: 'such a past is always present'. Cited by Christina Crosby in her discussion of *The History of Henry Esmond*, 1852: see *The Ends of History: Victorians and 'The Woman Question'*, London, Routledge, 1991, ch. 2.

Interconnections of the past with the present are highlighted, for example, in *The House on the Strand* (1969), where the hero Richard Young takes a hallucinogenic drug which supposedly transports him on trips back six hundred years. He then seems, in an earlier incarnation as Roger Kylmerth, to directly experience life (or rather actually *live*) in that previous time; and the novel consists of two interwoven stories of past and present. That sort of 'time machine' conveyance backwards (or forwards) in time is not particularly original, but this book does confirm the author's interest in things historical – an interest that was central to her most famous work, *Rebecca* (1938), where concerns with *memory* are at the very core.[14]

For that hugely popular novel, although not explicitly concerned with 'history' per se, nonetheless presents a narrative that has much to do with the potential for tragedy arising from misunderstood or misinterpreted or uncommunicated pasts, from 'memories' that are perhaps projected on to others and inadvertently transmitted, and from narratives constructed from these and found later to be baseless.

The un-named 'heroine', or central figure, at the outset famously dreams that she returned to Manderley, the great country house in which and around which most of the novel is set. That reported dream sets a tone of nostalgic recollection of the past which pervades the whole book. A rather retiring and self-effacing character, the narrator initially believes that Maxim, the older man whom she meets and spontaneously marries in Monte Carlo, is still grieving for his first wife Rebecca – reputedly an exceptionally beautiful and talented woman who had been greatly admired by all who knew her. Arriving, after her honeymoon, at Manderley, our heroine is confronted by a considerable amount of evidence that appears unequivocally to support her deductions concerning Maxim's past: Rebecca's rooms in the now closed-off west wing remain as they had been during her lifetime, like a shrine to her, with clothes and other personal effects carefully preserved; the servants still refer to her with awe and respect, and maintain her ways of keeping house and garden and organising daily life; her private cottage on the beach remains similarly untouched, and looks just as it had on the night she sailed off in her small boat and was tragically drowned. Everything she sees and hears confirms the new young wife in her belief that Rebecca had been universally revered and uniquely loved by Maxim: she represents a formidable ideal, both in her own person and in her relationship with her husband, to which our heroine herself feels quite incompetent to aspire. And Maxim's apparent emotional withdrawal from her, and his own silence – even evasiveness – regarding the past,

---

[14] Daphne du Maurier, *Rebecca*, London, Victor Gollancz, 1938.

further confirms her in that interpretation of life at Manderley before her own arrival.

It was only later that the truth was revealed to her – a truth which proves to be the very opposite of what she had believed. Maxim finally confesses how Rebecca, far from being perfect, had been unfaithful and had become totally estranged from him: indeed, their relationship had broken down to such an extent that he had finally, in desperation, murdered her. All the seemingly obvious evidence that had lain before our heroine's eyes had been totally misconstrued; and her marriage and her life had to be built afresh on entirely new foundations – on revised perceptions of the past, rewritten histories.

It is not difficult to see, then, how this seemingly simple book – almost naïve in its romanticism (but still eminently readable) – actually succeeds in illustrating what must have seemed for its time a quite sophisticated approach to historiography. Our personal histories, no more or less than 'professional' public histories, are necessarily built on foundations that presuppose common-sense attitudes to empirically and psychologically deduced evidence, to a reasonable consistency in human nature, and to respective degrees of probability. So the narrative that the heroine constructs of the past is perfectly well-founded, and would have been confirmed by any historian working to the generally accepted rules of historical writing. Yet the assumed truth of that narrative could be demolished in an instant – could be shown to be not truthful at all, but based on misconceptions and misinterpretations that could not reasonably have been foreseen. And if that is the case in a comparatively straightforward situation involving few characters, how much more vulnerable are the more complicated histories of public events with casts of millions?

A critique of memory in Penelope Lively's fiction

For the student of historical theory, the novels of Penelope Lively are of particular interest, not least as providing a further critique of naïve attitudes towards memory and its confident use as historical evidence; and these novels again emphatically indicate that historiographical issues may actually be better presented to a wider public through the medium of fiction than, more conventionally, within the constraints of academic books and articles. Indeed, we might claim that the novels to be considered here together present, not simply an excellent example of fiction meeting history, but an impressive 'fictional' *popularisation* of seemingly recondite 'historiographical' matters (and 'popularisation' here is to be taken as a term of praise). Those matters include some major reassessments of history's nature(s) and purpose(s) in the light of postmodern and postcolonial challenges; but in this chapter I shall consider the question of *memory* in particular, as that relates to chronology, evidence, narrative construction, and truth. In this context, we shall look at *Moon Tiger* (1987), *City of the Mind* (1992), and *The Photograph* (2004), taking each of these in turn in their order of publication.

Moon Tiger[15]

The central character in *Moon Tiger* is an unconventional historian named Claudia. Amidst her numerous 'heresies' in relation to the nature(s) and purpose(s) of history, what concerns us here is that she is highly critical of conventional linear narratives, the validity of which she shows to be challenged through a consideration of problems associated with her own personal experience of *memory*. For memories, as she realises, do not come to us tidily, as a straightforward line of events, as they occur, one after another; rather, they may be suddenly provoked at random, with some of them unexpectedly highlighted in the jumble of our pasts. So when, for example, Claudia's sister-in-law Sylvia brings a poinsettia to her hospital bedside, it proves to be an 'unwitting brutality', since, like Proust's madeleine, it immediately transports her back in time – in her case, to poinsettias she had seen flowering in the desert during the war, when she was enjoying all too briefly the company of her lover Tom Southern, who was soon to die (100).

Tom himself, she was reminded, had explained how his wartime experiences, fighting in tanks in the desert, played havoc with normal perceptions of time: 'It's like the whole of life in a single appalling concentration. It does lunatic things with time. An hour can seem like a day or a day like an hour' (101). This is a frequently remarked upon phenomenon: as an historian of the wider picture, Fernand Braudel concludes 'that time moves at different speeds',[16] and similarly, with regard to literary representation, E. M. Forster explains that a narrative plot is 'something which is measured not by minutes or hours, but by intensity . . . when we look at our past it does not stretch back evenly but piles up into a few notable pinnacles'.[17] It is that sort of temporal disorientation that was suffered by Tom, who records in a diary that was much later retrieved by Claudia, years after his death, how 'I couldn't say now what

---

[15] Penelope Lively, *Moon Tiger*, London, Penguin, 1988. Page references will be given in the text.

[16] Fernand Braudel, quoted by Richard J. Evans, *In Defence of History*, London, Granta, 1997, p. 154.

[17] E. M. Forster, quoted by Frank Kermode, *London Review of Books*, 10 May 2007, p. 18.

came before what, where we were when, how this happened or that; in the mind it's not a sequence, just a single event without beginning or end in any proper sense' (196).

Those were the direct impressions of someone actually involved in events which would later be historicised – would be put tidily into a coherent linear narrative. And for that task, Tom should surely have been the ideal source, with his recorded memories likely to be claimed by later historians as the most reliable evidence: a first-hand eyewitness report – what could be better than that? And yet even at the time, the experiences seemed to him to be impossible to contain within any simple 'story-line'.

The problem for historians, then, is to know how best to re-present such a chaos of events. It is of course a general problem that relates to all experience, but it becomes particularly evident in periods of stress; and, as Tolstoy emphasises in *War and Peace*, war is the supreme example of irreducible chaos – or of chaos which can be reduced only by an arbitrary and subsequent imposition of an order for which we (and not the events themselves) are responsible. Perhaps, therefore, in such circumstances, a more appropriate model for historical writing might be that of a kaleidoscope, which can be shaken in order to produce many different colourful (but all still arbitrary) patterns.

That is what, as an historian, Claudia comes to believe (2); and it is actually exemplified by Penelope Lively in the construction of her novel, where past episodes of Claudia's life, in Egypt during the war, are interpolated into the narrative – resurfacing in her memory as that is jogged in various directions by people and everyday objects. The integration into the novel's narrative of her wartime episode in Egypt is one exemplification of Claudia's proposal for what she terms a 'realistic kaleidoscopic history'; and, as a literary technique, such interweaving is used also, and to notably good effect, in *City of the Mind*, as we shall see below.

Within Claudia's own narrative, though, there is an additional indication that Egypt itself, as a part of memory, is to be hugely important – both privately to her in her personal life and also publicly in its continuing cultural influence. On both these levels, it is clear that Egypt 'is *not then but now*, conditioning the way we look at things'. Memories are not confined to some isolated and self-contained entity we call 'the past': their *presence* remains with us, affecting, if not determining, what we are. That applies to Claudia herself, with her formative experiences during the war – including especially her one true experience of love. And it applies more generally in cultural history: Egypt is a country in which layers of history are closely interwoven, and relics of long distant times continue to exist and loudly resonate: 'Past and present do not so much co-exist in the Nile valley as *cease to have any meaning*' (80, my emphases). And that conclusively demonstrates, for historiography, the inadequacy of linear chronologies.

Claudia's awareness of that, as an historian, makes her critical more generally, not only of professional chroniclers, but also of those who, whether for personal or political purposes, attempt to cast their own tidy narratives over the inherent messiness of real life. Attending an international conference in a French chateau after the war, she is struck by how, with all its opulence, the venue itself appeared as 'a physical manifestation of *history as illusion* . . . I listened to well-fed complacent men and women designing the future and *rearranging the past*.' Acutely conscious herself that 'History is *disorder*, [she] wanted to scream at them – death and muddle and waste. And here you sit cashing in on it and *making patterns* in the sand' (152, my emphases).

That those patterns are not found within the sand of the past, but are our own constructions subsequently imposed upon it, is a lesson that some historians (for all Hayden White's theorising) might still be surprised to hear from their fiction-writing colleague.

City of the Mind[18]

One of the main themes in *Moon Tiger* – the ways in which the remembered past impinges on the present – is further illustrated in Penelope Lively's later novel *City of the Mind*. As an architect, the central character Matthew Halland is constantly reminded by London's physical environment of its previous histories: buildings evoke much earlier pasts, both through their embodiment of reworked styles of classical antiquity, for example, and by their own surviving traces of the times in which they themselves were built. Thus, at least for the architecturally informed, the Caryatids on St Pancras Parish Church in Euston Road provide obvious reminders of the Erectheion on the Athenian Acropolis; and for Halland himself, his practice's refurbishment project in Cobham Square is redolent of its original construction in 1823. Haunted by ghost-like reappearances from the past, he (no less than Tom in *Moon Tiger*) becomes temporally disorientated: it seems to him that, in a sense, 'everything is simultaneous', so that, as he drives around after lunch looking for a parking space, 'it is 2.25 (and still 1832)' (24). And more generally, 'driving through the city, he is both here and now, there and then . . . The whole place is a chronicle, in brick and stone, in silent eloquence, for those who have eyes and

---

[18] Penelope Lively, *City of the Mind*, London, Penguin, 1992. Page references will be given in the text.

ears' (2–3); and 'everything alludes to something else (9) . . . The whole place is one babble of allusions' (66).

Those allusions provoke, for many older Londoners, recollections of the wartime blitz; and that aspect of the war is vividly recalled here in a series of extracts interwoven with the main narrative – with descriptions of fires and crumbling buildings, deaths and rescues, and unexploded bombs. Thus, once again, through the novelist's literary technique, we are reminded of the inadequacies of linear narrative. For the past and present cannot be disconnected: 'There is no sequence in the city, no then and now, all is continuous' (210). And that experience of 'non-sequential' time requires re-presentation in historical as well as 'literary' writing.

In the public domain of the physical environment, then, memories are constantly jogged and the past brought back to present life; and a similar mechanism operates in relation to our private lives. So in the main narrative of the novel, we see how Matthew Halland is repeatedly reminded of his earlier experience: he catches sight of the moon and, with 'time dissolved', is transported back to his telescopic observations as a boy (2); he is reminded by an antique chair of his marriage to a now estranged wife, and he endlessly replays in his mind some of the events of that time – re-running and rewriting the narratives of his courtship and alienation and separation. And as he does so, certain events – conversations, small and almost imperceptible gestures – barely registered by him at the time, assume with hindsight a new significance; the past once more is rearranged.

Whether such rearrangements get one any nearer to a 'truth' is an altogether other matter; they would seem rather to be a part of an ever-ongoing process. But a warning is added concerning the reliability of any evidence by which such reassessments might be provoked; for evidence from the past – those 'primary sources' by which historians place such store – is not necessarily reliable at all. In particular, the hazards of taking paintings at face value are exposed: on a visit to a picture gallery, Matthew's new art historian friend Sarah explains that what is perhaps most significant about George Hayter's painting of 'The Reformed House of Commons, 1833', is that it is a fake – 'a splendid con'. It appears to provide invaluable historical evidence of a particular occasion, showing, or appearing to show, the faces of all 375 Members of Parliament; but in fact the individual portraits had been painted, not *in situ*, but in the artist's studio – and afterwards put together, to illustrate 'a moment that never was' (198).

Historiographical issues, then, of various kinds, are never far from the surface in this novel; but most important here is the author's illustration of the intrusiveness into memory of pasts both public and private, and of the ways that both, after requisite (and ongoing) rearrangements, are incorporated into the present – woven into the complex texture of everyday lives. *City of the Mind* also provides another example of how that complexity can be represented in literary form; so that in form no less than content it may prove suggestive for historical theorists and historians themselves.

The Photograph[19]

With her novel *The Photograph*, Penelope Lively returns with a vengeance to the rearrangement of the past, this time in relation specifically to personal memories, but again with obvious implications for historical writing more generally. Her story is basically concerned with the disruption of memories – and thence of whole lives – through the unexpected intrusion into consciousness of one seemingly trivial piece of additional information about the past. Interest in that theme (which we have seen previously treated by Proust) had been indicated years earlier in another of her novels, *The Road to Lichfield* (1977), where the central character, Anne Linton, learns to her amazement that her dying father had had a long affair. With that additional piece of evidence about her father's life, she had to rearrange not only his, but also her own, past; she herself had to begin 'the slow re-adjustment of the past, roaming to and fro across the years, without regard to chronology, sifting through a jumble of events and occasions'. That entailed recognising that her previous understanding of the past – her previous, supposedly truthful, personal history – needed fundamental reassessment; everything required reinterpretation in a new light, from a revised perspective. 'What I thought was thus, was otherwise. Things that appeared so, were not.'[20]

It is this theme which recurs centrally in *The Photograph*, where it is treated in far greater detail. The central figure here is Glyn, an archaeologist who is involved (with appropriate symbolism) in 'the interpretation of vanished landscapes' (2), and so is professionally aware that when 'some new and vital piece of information comes along . . . the whole historical edifice is undermined' (61). He knows in his professional capacity that 'There's always the possibility of startling new evidence that moves the goal posts' – with a drought, for example, revealing previously unsuspected geophysical features that then necessitate complete revision of earlier interpretations (61). But, despite that professional – and so *intellectual* – recognition, he is unprepared for the personal – and so emotionally freighted – parallel case, when he comes across

---

[19] Penelope Lively, *The Photograph*, London, Penguin, 2004. Page references will be given in the text.

[20] Penelope Lively, *The Road to Lichfield* [1977], Harmondsworth, Penguin, 1983, p. 54.

startling new evidence concerning his dead wife Kath, which seems to entail a similar moving of the goal posts, and indeed a fresh marking out of the whole terrain on which the game of his life had been played.

The new piece of evidence consists of an old photograph, discovered purely by chance. Taken from behind, it shows Kath holding hands intimately with her sister Elaine's husband Nick; and the postures seem quite obviously to imply an infidelity, previously unsuspected. As with Proust's Swann and Du Maurier's Rebecca, that newly acquired evidence clearly makes necessary a complete reappraisal of Glyn's past, including his personal relationships, and not least that with his own wife. Indeed, his whole 'understanding of the past . . . [was] savagely undermined' (6); his whole view of past events and people was thrown into doubt and question. For 'it appears that [things] were not as they seemed to be at the time, nor as I have believed them to have been ever since' (15). Particularly problematic for him is that Kath herself takes on a new ambiguity: she 'is both what she ever was, and she is also someone else' (12). And that of course has implications for his own self-identity and continuing sense of direction: 'I am confronted with . . . an unreliability about my own past' (100–101); and that has implications for the future. The dead are beyond reach, but 'The rest of us are still flailing around trying to make sense of things' (102) – trying to engage, at a personal level, with that historical 'tidying up' we saw described above in *Moon Tiger*.

With Glyn's own previous tidiness disrupted, others too become involved in his investigations and rearrangements of the newly opened past; others too have the validity of their previous perceptions and memories brought into question. Thus, for Kath's sister Elaine, 'A stone has been cast into the reliable, immutable pond of the past, and as the ripples subside everything appears different.' Her history is no longer as it has always appeared; certainty is succeeded by doubt. 'The reflections are quite other, everything has swung and shattered, it is all beyond recovery. What was, is now something else' (59). The memory of her sister fragments, and she is left with an image no longer 'clear and precise', but rather with someone who is now less clearly defined, 'a multiple Kath' – 'some composite being who is everything at once, no longer artificially confined to a specific moment in time' (153). A friend of her husband's, similarly, appears in a new light, his identity less definite: 'The Oliver who has been in her head these last ten or fifteen years disintegrates and is replaced by a new and different Oliver, one whom she does not know. Did not know' (59–60). Again, it is not only the past per se that is involved, but also the implications of that past for the present and future.

There are further important implications for Elaine's own immediate family. Nick, of course, cannot see why his newly discovered brief affair should not remain safely buried in the past where it belongs – 'cannot believe that something long since laid to rest can thus come bubbling up and wreck his life' (138); but Elaine nevertheless decides to end her marriage to him. And even their daughter Polly is affected by the newly destabilised past: for her, too, the existing order has been shaken, 'alien data have flashed up on the screen – uninvited and unwelcome . . . there are faultlines all over the place' (111). And in her unsettled state, she comes to realise the inadequacy of her own boyfriend, and resolves to leave him.

As the consequent disruptions multiply, his discovery of the photograph seems to Glyn to constitute 'a defining moment', establishing a new paradigm or framework, a new chronology within which the past could be inscribed: 'There was before the photograph, a time of innocence and tranquillity . . . Now it is after the photograph, when everything must be seen with the cold eye of disillusion' (115). And as he desperately tries to review his past, he comes to see his own memory as nothing better than an 'old pail with holes and rusty seams' (117); we may need our memories to 'confirm our passage through life . . . [and] tell us who we are' (114), but he realises that 'everything that he remembers . . . is shown to be faulty' (116).

That instability, deficiency, and unreliability of memory goes to the heart of histories both personal and public. At the personal level, memories provide the basis for our perceptions of ourselves and our immediate circle, and so of our identities and relationships; they provide the evidence on which to construct those narratives on which we depend to give our lives substance, meaning, direction. And at the public level memories no less constitute the basis of histories – providing those eyewitness accounts of events that count as the 'primary sources' on which historians rely. So in *The Photograph*, Penelope Lively can be seen to mount a serious challenge to historiography as a whole. Her main point is that one apparently insignificant item of newly discovered evidence can completely disrupt previous memories and perceptions of the past – can completely disrupt the whole evidential structure on which our histories are built. And who is to say when, out of the blue, such flies will turn up to contaminate our historical ointment?

These implications for the way we relate our (now destabilised) selves to the (now destabilised) past are of enormous theoretical and practical importance; for recognition of the need constantly to review the past and rewrite histories actually affects (or should affect) our actions in the future. But in the present context it suffices to note how a novelist – a writer of *fiction* – has most effectively shown the implications for *history* of the prospect of endlessly rearranging, and of periodically being forced to rearrange, our memories and so our perceptions and descriptions of the past.

Conclusion

In T. S. Eliot's play *The Cocktail Party* (1950), the psychological consultant Sir Henry Harcourt-Reilly proposes a prescription for some troubled guests: 'You will have to live with these memories and make them/ Into something new.'[21] Both of those instructions merit some discussion in the context of history and fiction. For it may not be immediately clear either that we *do* have to live with certain prescribed memories, or that we are in a position to manipulate memories in such a way as to make of them something *new*. The former seems to be contradicted by our propensity to forget those episodes in our pasts that we might prefer never to have taken place; and the latter appears to offend against the conventional belief that history – derived as it necessarily is from memories – is a retrieval of what actually happened, and not something that can be manipulated by us into something different, something new.

To take the first point first, it is of course clear that there are many memories that people – and even historians – have chosen *not* to live with. It would be quite impossible consciously to live with *every* available memory: as Carlyle observed, we need to forget some things in order to remember others; 'without oblivion, there is no remembrance possible'.[22] It is not – it could never be – the whole of our past that we retain: even in prospect, that would soon paralyse the brain and inhibit any further action; such commitment to the past would give us no time for the present, and we would all end up like Proust in his cork-lined room, having repudiated life for the sake of recovering times passed and lost. So the remembered elements of the past must be selected, chosen with some purpose in (or out of) mind; and those numerous aspects that have been, whether consciously or unconsciously, dismissed as unimportant and rejected as irrelevant or inappropriate for present needs, continue to lie, as Proust described, like negatives in a photographic darkroom, undeveloped. As such, they continue to exist, but may conveniently be forgotten.

But what is convenient may change, and memories deliberately discarded have a habit of recurring – of popping back into our consciousness unannounced. Through her representation of her family home with a guillotine in front, the sculptor Louise Bourgeois has indicated her wish to cut off, erase from the present, certain traumatic memories derived from her childhood. But however much we may strive in such symbolic ways to chop the past off, it is likely, as we say, to catch up with us: as Virginia Woolf describes, there

---

[21] T. S. Eliot, *The Cocktail Party* [1950], London, Faber and Faber, 1958, p. 182.
[22] Thomas Carlyle, *The Letters and Speeches of Oliver Cromwell*, ed. S. C. Lomas, 3 vols; London, Methuen, 1904, vol. 1, p. 6.

'comes the terrible pounce of memory, not to be foretold, not to be warded off'; or as Nietzsche puts it, a past event returns 'as a ghost . . . [to] disturb the peace of a later moment'.[23] Such unwelcome intrusions – memories of which we are made newly aware – may well introduce alternative conveniences and alternative demands, imposing long-forgotten episodes upon us and requiring us, for all the initial repulsion and discomfort and embarrassment, to embrace newly revealed skeletons in cupboards.

In personal terms, as we have seen above in the fictional case of Glyn in *The Photograph* – and as is also brilliantly shown by the American novelist Tim O'Brien, whose character John Wade embodies the dire effects of endeavouring to repress his memories of the Vietnam War[24] – such required reconstructions can pose a serious threat, by intruding upon and challenging the carefully constructed narratives that constitute our own and others' selves. But it becomes a therapeutic necessity in the interest of psychic health; for, as Eliot's Harcourt-Reilly goes on to clarify, 'Only by acceptance/ Of the past will you alter its meaning.' Only by admitting that something has happened can we hope to look at it in a different, and more positive, way; only by accepting it as a part of our past can we modify the part that it plays in our present personal narrative.

And no less in the public arena, self-images may need to be updated, in order to accommodate newly revealed, or newly accepted, aspects of a past that demand their place in history. The comparatively tardy acceptance and incorporation of their Nazi past by Germans is but one well known example. A disruption of public memory was effected by the capture and trial of Adolf Eichmann in 1961. Before that date, it has been shown, the memory of the attempted wartime extermination of the Jews and other 'undesirables' had largely been effaced – or certainly had not impinged upon the wider public, either in Europe or the USA, so that the term 'Holocaust', as descriptive of a specific historical phenomenon, had barely been applied.[25] What Eichmann's trial achieved was the stirring up of memory: the need for testimony – for witnesses – provoked remembrance, or rather made it permissible (even desirable and morally needful) for survivors to recall, articulate, face up to, what they had experienced. So that (initially in the cause of justice) horrific memories were necessarily incorporated, first, into the identities of

---

[23] Virginia Woolf, *The Waves* [1931], Harmondsworth, Penguin, 1951, p. 227; Nietzsche, *Untimely Meditations*, ed. Daniel Breazeale, Cambridge, Cambridge University Press, 1997, p. 61.

[24] Tim O'Brien, *In the Lake of the Woods*, London, Penguin, 1995, on which see pp. 142–46 below.

[25] See Peter Novick, *The Holocaust and Collective Memory*, London, Bloomsbury, 2000.

individuals, and thence into the wider consciousness that constitutes the identities of nations.

This issue is far from being confined to Germany, where such matters are now openly discussed. Other examples include the belated (and often still reluctant) admission by the French of their less than universal resistance to their occupying conquerors in the Second World War, and by the British of their own sometimes less than savoury imperial escapades. And that such matters of public memory and forgetting still persist is indicated by the reluctance of the Japanese and Turks to remember early twentieth-century events in, respectively, Nanking and Armenia.

As for Harcourt-Reilly's second point, any suggestion that memories can somehow be moulded nearer to the heart's desire at the whim, or instruction, of another would seem seriously to offend against the rules of traditional historiography; but the problem may lie in the interpretation of those rules. For the importance of history as a guardian of memories can hardly be disputed. Whether privately as individuals, or publicly as communities, we resort to memory for the fabrication and the maintenance of our identities; we look to narrative threads from past to present in order to establish continuities in, and meaning for, our selves. It is only by doing that, as Hume long since concluded, that we have any notion of who on earth we are – whether as individual psychological entities or socio-political groups or nation-states. It is the acceptance, then, the apprehension of, or laying claim to, a cluster of memories, that serves to underpin our individualities and identities – our very notion of our otherwise free-floating selves. It is in them (those evidential traces of our pasts), and in the carefully constructed narrative chain for which they each provide a link, that we find a root; and from that root, we may hope to find the potential for further growth and development.

It is not for nothing, then (as we have seen above with Proust), that we grope for some memory as we flounder into consciousness on awaking in an unknown room, in order to re-establish our feeling of self-identity; it is not for nothing that those in solitary confinement take care to make a mark each day, in order to maintain some sense of temporal continuity and coherence – a coherence that entails that their present does derive from a past. It is our memories of the past that serve to stabilise us in an otherwise amorphous (literally form-less), directionless and purposeless, confusing and chaotic present – serve as Saul Bellow's character describes, 'to keep the wolf of insignificance from the door'.[26]

---

[26] Saul Bellow, *Mr Sammler's Planet*, Harmondsworth, Penguin, 1977, p. 190.

And our evident need for memories has traditionally been fulfilled, at a public level, by narratives of the past produced by historians: from antiquity on, it has been history's avowed function to recall and re-present, and so retain, the past in present consciousness – effectively to make that past an essential part of, even a requisite foundation for, the here and now. The important question is, then, on what basis historians choose the memories – select the evidence – from which their narratives are constructed, and in accordance with what criteria they 'emplot' them, or include them in their stories. For there is, as we have seen, a *choice* involved: memories do not come with their own inbuilt meanings; meaning is bestowed upon the past by us – and that meaning, the direction of our tracks made through the past, will depend upon the direction that we wish to go in the future. We might, as Nietzsche advocated, redeem ourselves by taking charge of our past, and transforming every 'It was' into 'Thus I willed it!'; and we might, as St Augustine proposed some fifteen hundred years previously, from the extraordinary 'storehouse of memory', select possible 'actions and events *and hopes for the future*'.[27]

There have recently been some attempts by historians to reappraise memories, by interweaving narratives of groups previously considered as mutually exclusive and mutually hostile, in ways that might encourage recognition of a shared past. Examples of such attempted syntheses include those relating to (and re-relating) Arab and Israeli pasts, and to Jewish and non-Jewish German historical remembrance; and the purpose of such newly illuminated commonalities is to lay foundations for a future that might (indeed, must) likewise be shared, but henceforth with equality and mutual respect.[28]

To revert, then, to T. S. Eliot's Harcourt-Reilly: by accepting memories, we can do something with them that can be to our advantage, constructing narratives that lead to a more positive and hopeful future. His advice is not only in line with contemporary psycho-therapeutic practice, but also consistent with the use and critique of memory by the writers of fiction instanced above; and it may then be the case that, as a writer of poetry, Eliot too was ahead of the game in terms of historical theory and practice.

[27] Friedrich Nietzsche, *Thus Spake Zarathustra*, trans. Walter Kaufmann, Harmondsworth, Penguin, 1978, p. 198; Augustine, *Confessions*, trans. R. S. Pine-Coffin, Harmondsworth, Penguin, 1961, p. 216 (my emphasis).
[28] See further Chapter 5 below.

Further reading

Augustine, Saint, *Confessions*, trans. R. S. Pine-Coffin, Harmondsworth, Penguin, 1961.

Byatt, A. S. and Harvey Wood, Harriet (eds), *Memory: An Anthology*, London, Chatto & Windus, 2008.

Du Maurier, Daphne, *Rebecca*, London, Victor Gollancz, 1938.

Klein, Kerwin Lee, 'On the Emergence of Memory in Historical Discourse', *Representations* 69, 2000, 127–150.

LaCapra, Dominick, *History and Memory after Auschwitz*, Ithaca and London, Cornell University Press, 1998.

Le Goff, Jacques, *History and Memory*, trans. Steven Rendall and Elizabeth Claman, New York, Columbia University Press, 1992.

Lively, Penelope, *The Photograph*, London, Penguin, 2004.

Margalit, Avishai, *The Ethics of Memory*, Cambridge, Mass. and London, Harvard University Press, 2002.

Proust, Marcel, *Remembrance of Things Past* [1920–27], trans. C. K. Scott Moncrieff and Terence Kilmartin, 3 vols; London, Penguin, 1983.

Roth, Michael S., *The Ironist's Cage: Memory, Trauma, and the Construction of History*, New York, Columbia University Press, 1995.

Chapter 5

Fiction, history, and ethics

In their attempts to embrace a 'scientific' model for their subject, historians have traditionally repudiated any ethical involvement. It is argued in this chapter that, while some historians themselves are now belatedly rejecting that approach, it was writers of fiction who first offered a critique of 'detached' history, and who explicitly advocated the injection of a moral dimension into the subject, especially when provoked by personal experience of war. As case studies of fictional advocacy of ethically orientated history, we assess Tolstoy's War and Peace *and Wyndham Lewis's* Self Condemned.*

I am aware that this is to blaspheme against the sacrosanct school of what these gentlemen term 'Art for Art's sake', but at this period of history there are tasks more urgent than the manipulation of words in a harmonious manner.[1]

That quotation from Proust, despite not representing the author's own views, exemplifies an attitude, not only to history but to the arts and humanities more generally, that is displayed in critiques through the twentieth century, and not least through the medium of fiction. Writing in the early decades of that era, Proust, through the words of his character Monsieur De Norpois, foreshadows a widespread revulsion against an aesthetic tradition that seemed to isolate art and artists – including writers and philosophers and historians – within their own professional cliques. Intellectuals generally

---

[1] Marcel Proust, *Remembrance of Things Past*, trans. C. K. Scott Moncrieff and Terence Kilmartin, 3 vols; London, Penguin, 1983, 1.510. This quotation comes from a speech by M. De Norpois, whose opinion actually horrifies Marcel – whose own approach to literature is described at III.915–16.

Plate 1 Aristotle, who influentially distinguished sharply between history and fiction, is here seen teaching Alexander the Great (340 BC). 19th century wood engraving. akg-images Ltd.

Plate 2 Penelope Lively, a contemporary novelist who shows a particular interest in historiographical issues. Mark Gerson, bromide print, 1984. National Portrait Gallery.

Plate 3 Nineteenth-century school-room, as described by Dickens: painting by Albert Anker, 'The Village School' (1896). akg-images Ltd.

Plate 4 Daphne du Maurier's *Rebecca*: Joan Fontaine at Manderley (film, 1940). akg-images Ltd.

Plate 5 History, fiction, and film: film set for Tolstoy's *War and Peace* on Moscow's Red Square (1963). akg-images Ltd./RIA Novosti

Plate 6   An early advocate of ethical history: Wyndham Lewis, self-portrait, ink and wash (1932). National Portrait Gallery.

Plate 7 History and national identity: history lesson under National Socialism, Germany, undated. akg-images Ltd.

Plate 8   Virginia Woolf, whose novels reveal a particular concern with memory
and identity: Photograph by George Charles Beresford, platinum print, July 1902.
National Portrait Gallery.

Plate 9 The focus of concern in Don DeLillo's *Libra*: John F. Kennedy with his wife Jacqueline and Governor Conally shortly before his assassination, Dallas, 22 November 1963. akg-images Ltd./ullstein bild.

seemed to be cut off from the social and political realities of their time, and to disdain intervening at all in public life.

Such professional withdrawal could of course be construed by others as a virtue, and historians themselves were quick to justify their own aloofness from the immediate travails of their time. For, after all, the last thing they wished to be accused of was ideological involvement – especially after the blatantly nationalistic productions by British and German historians before and during the Great War. It was not for nothing that Julien Benda had reproached intellectuals for their betrayal of humanistic values – their failure, in the face of political pressure, to retain their independence and maintain those absolutes on which civilisation ultimately depended; they had become, as he accused, nothing better than 'men of politics who make use of history to support a cause whose triumph they desire',[2] and history, with its convenient justifications for nationalistic and imperialistic ambitions, had indeed been effectively enlisted to fight on both sides of the war. In the face, then, of subsequent accusations of ideological intrusions (such as are perennially levelled against those of whom we disapprove), a certain defensiveness was only to be expected; and that implied a retreat into disciplinary autonomy – an assertion of historians' own cool 'objectivity' and detachment from quotidian pressures.

In that context, Vera Brittain recorded how at Oxford in 1919, 'the second-year History School were in process of studying Tudors and Stuarts . . . detached from their past and their future and *completely unrelated to anything whatever* in time or space'.[3] And in such an intellectual climate, historians did not of course stand alone. Philosophers too tended to keep aloof from the practicalities of everyday life: R. G. Collingwood in the 1920s wrote of a recent philosophical revolution, which included the advocacy of 'a new kind of moral philosophy, purely theoretical, in which the workings of the moral consciousness should be *scientifically* studied as if they were the movements of the planets, and *no attempt made to interfere* with them'. The clear inference to be drawn was that 'for guidance in the problems of life', for *practical* advice, one had to look elsewhere; scientific detachment did not permit of interference. So that Collingwood went on to lament the appearance of a generation of students who regarded philosophy as nothing better than 'a futile parlour

---

[2] Julien Benda, *The Great Betrayal*, trans. R. Aldington, London, Routledge, 1928, p. 56.

[3] Vera Brittain, *Testament of Youth: An Autobiographical Study of the Years 1900–1925* [1933], London, Virago, 1978, p. 479 (my emphases). Vera Brittain herself, referring contemptuously to 'the smooth, patriotic selections of school history-books', endeavoured after the war 'to understand how the whole calamity had happened, to know why it had been possible for me and my contemporaries, through our own ignorance and others' ingenuity, to be used, hypnotised and slaughtered', in an attempt to prevent it happening again (pp. 354, 471).

game'. The subject had previously been taken seriously as actually affecting everyday life, as being practically useful in the resolution of human problems; but the new-style philosophers 'were proud to have excogitated a philosophy so pure from the sordid taint of utility that they could lay their hands on their hearts and say it was *no use at all*.[4]

With their similar emulation of scientific procedures, historians no less prided themselves on the practical uselessness of their subject: to be *useful* was not their concern; history was to do with *truth*, and was a subject to be studied purely 'for its own sake'. From the time of Galileo, the theoretical physicist was absolved from the responsibility of *applying* scientific knowledge – of determining, or even being concerned with, how theories might be put into practice; so that the twentieth-century nuclear physicist was not professionally concerned with any 'moral scruples' relating to the dropping of an atomic bomb – his concern being only with the fact that it was 'superb physics'. And in a similar way, historians felt themselves exonerated from any dirtying of hands. In the late nineteenth century Lord Acton accused his fellow historian Mandell Creighton of wanting 'to pass through scenes of raging controversy and passion with a serene curiosity, a suspended judgement, a divided jury, and a pair of white gloves'.[5] For Creighton, and for generations of historians who followed through the next century, 'objectivity' implied a detachment that enabled them to maintain their professional poise – their perceived non-judgmental 'even-handedness' and 'balance' – even as they waded in retrospect through the greatest monstrosities and inhumanities of their times.

Indeed, it is only recently, at the turn of the twenty-first century, that some historians have begun to question that cultivation of detachment, and that a serious debate has been joined about the purposes and possible *utility* of history in political and ethical contexts. Sven Lindqvist presents his material calmly enough in his *A History of Bombing* (2001), but his underlying purpose in doing so is profoundly moral; Dagmar Barnouw's *The War in the Empty Air: Victims, Perpetrators, and Postwar Germans* (2005) is described as reassessing 'victims' and 'perpetrators', for the practical purpose of encouraging a more inclusive 'historical remembrance for postwar generations'; and

---

[4] R. G. Collingwood, *An Autobiography* [1939], Harmondsworth, Penguin, 1944, pp. 36–8 (my emphases).

[5] Lord Acton, Review of Mandell Creighton, *A History of the Papacy*, in *The English Historical Review* 2, 1887, pp. 571–81. Cf. Lytton Strachey on Creighton 'picking his way with an air of calm detachment amid the recklessness, the brutality, the fanaticism, the cynicism, the lasciviousness' of such Renaissance spirits as Savonarola, Caesar Borgia, Julius II, and Luther. *Portraits in Miniature and Other Essays*, London, Chatto & Windus, 1933, p. 211.

Jamil Hilal and Ilan Pappe's *Talking to the Enemy* (2006) is similarly concerned with the construction of 'bridging narratives', in their case revealing the commonalities in Arab and Israeli pasts, in order for that revised history to serve as a foundation for a shared future. But while such new visions of an 'applied' history – history explicitly imbued with an ethical purpose – are to be welcomed, what is interesting here in relation to our theme is that such historiographical revisions were long since advocated by writers of fiction. Once again it seems that fictional critiques of history anticipated those made only much later by historians and historical theorists themselves.

Fiction and ethical history

That claim will be further substantiated in this section, which includes studies of two important critiques of detached and ethically uncommitted historiography within what are essentially 'fictional' vehicles.

First, though, it is worth noting that a particularly direct and full treatment of history and historiography in this context appears in a novel already considered briefly in relation to memory in Chapter 4. For Penelope Lively's *Moon Tiger* pays specific attention also to a critique of the detachment conventionally ascribed to historians as an appropriate (and indeed essential) characteristic – a detachment that denies them a subjective response to their objects of study, and that results in a lack of (or, rather, deliberate withdrawal from) moral involvement. The central character in this novel, the elderly historian Claudia Hampton, exemplifies a contrary approach, with her ambition to link her own personal autobiography to a universal history – and so to make some sense of her own life within its very much wider context.[6]

That plan, to integrate a personal and public narrative, is not of course without precedent or parallel, albeit on a rather less ambitious scale. Biographers generally try to contextualise their subjects' lives, and to give but two examples of historians who have more recently linked their own autobiographies with wider public events: Modris Eksteins has presented an effective interweaving of personal and public in *Walking Since Daybreak* (1999) – an account of the Baltic States in the twentieth century (including the Second World War), in which members of his own family are shown to have been deeply implicated; and Eric Hobsbawm has written an autobiography (2003)

---

[6] See Penelope Lively, *Moon Tiger*, London, Penguin, 1988. Page references will be given in the text.

which is similarly contextualised within the 'interesting times' through which he has lived.[7]

Those two examples have not (so far as I am aware) incurred the wrath of other historians, but, in her own rather more ambitious project, the fictional Claudia Hampton admits that she is actually setting out to shock – and expects to achieve that outcome, not least through her repudiation of detachment: 'Not for me', she defiantly insists, 'the cool level tone of dispassionate narration' (8). As a self-confessed 'populariser' and '*non-professional* historian', she has already been 'loftily disdained by some academics, angrily refuted by others' (59, my emphasis). For she has deliberately ignored the fact that history, as her brother reminds her, is conventionally 'grey stuff', and not the *colourful* 'spectacle' that she looks for and provides in what is denigratingly described as her 'Technicolor history' (186, 60).

That resort to a subjective and colourful representation of the past derives partly from Claudia's reluctance to accept conventional attitudes towards chronology. Time, as presupposed in the construction of orderly linear narratives, is a mainstay of professional historians; but Claudia confesses that as such it 'irritates' her, as being inadequate to represent her own experience. For she is aware that inside her own head, 'there is no sequence, everything happens at once'; so that 'a lifetime is not linear but instant' (68), with memories 'forever shuffled and reshuffled' like a pack of cards. Instead of aspiring, then, to be a sort of 'archetypal chronicler' (3) simply describing events, one after another, in their supposed order of appearance, she proposes (as we have already seen in Chapter 4) to adopt the model of a kaleidoscope, in which can be seen an infinity of colourful patterns arbitrarily imposed upon data, without any concern for temporal considerations.

Obviously implied in the promotion of that kaleidoscopic model is an acceptance of a relativism in terms of which we all see different patterns from different viewpoints at different times: in short, 'We all look at it [the past] differently' (2). So that we all, in the end, present very *personal* histories: 'my view of you is my own, your relevance to me is personal'; and so Claudia is criticised for 'once again subordinating history to her own puny existence'. But, as she responds: 'Well – don't we all?' (29) And the important point that follows from that is the requirement to *choose* the manner of relating our histories

[7] Modris Eksteins, *Walking Since Daybreak: A Story of Eastern Europe, World War II, and the Heart of the Twentieth Century* [1999], London, Macmillan, 2000; Eric Hobsbawm, *Interesting Times: A Twentieth-Century Life*, London, Abacus, 2003. I have subsequently been referred to Neil Sheehan, *A Bright Shining Lie* (1989) – 'a brilliant weaving together of one American soldier's personal history and his country's fateful efforts in Vietnam' (Robert Stone, *New York Review of Books*, 22 November 2007, p. 42).

to ourselves: the inevitability of our personal *involvement* implies the necessity of moral *choice* – and it is here that we are bound to confront the question of what history is actually *for*.

When Claudia as a young girl had posed that question to her teacher, she had received the conventional response (as it might still be given today, and often is, by teachers, politicians, and historians), that it 'is how you can understand why England became a great nation' (22). Dissatisfied with that answer, Claudia herself aspires in her own histories to make a moral point – a point about the transitory nature of the 'greatness' to which her teacher had referred. In her own historical work, then, she intends to 'devote a good deal of space to Memphis', a great Egyptian city in the time of the Pharaohs: once a political, religious, and cultural centre, of enormous wealth, power, and importance, it is now nothing more than 'a series of barely discernible irregularities in the cultivation and an immense prone statue of Rameses the Second. How indeed are the mighty fallen' (114).

Such reminders of human mortality and hubris have long been a by-product, if not explicit aim, of morally committed histories. In classical antiquity, Thucydides described how the imperialistic arrogance of the Athenians was followed by the humiliation of their own defeat; Geoffrey of Monmouth in the twelfth century was similarly concerned quite explicitly to show how earthly triumph quickly fades, describing how King William's 'corpulent stomach, fattened with so many delicacies, shamefully burst, to give a lesson, both to the prudent and the thoughtless, on what is the end of fleshly glory'; and his near contemporary Henry of Huntingdon drew the same moral from the death of Henry I and the stench that was said to have come from his corpse: 'Observe, I say, what horrible decay, to what a loathsome state, his body was reduced . . . and learn to despise what so perishes and comes to nothing.'[8]

As far as Claudia is concerned, that remains as the supreme moral lesson for history to teach; and it is related to the further more general point that, in histories that are inevitably subjective and relative, *some* moral point must *inevitably* be implied. Claudia's proposal explicitly to use her history to make a moral point – a point, in her case, about imperialistic hubris and mortality – indicates the possibility, and even inevitability, of intruding an ethical dimension into historical writing. Her critique of history's *nature* – her

---

[8] Geoffrey of Monmouth and Henry of Huntingdon, quoted by Robert W. Hanning, *The Vision of History in Early Britain*, New York and London, Columbia University Press, 1966, pp. 155, 228–9, n. 54. This same theme was of course pursued by Shelley in his poem 'Ozymandias'.

demonstration of history's relativity and of historians' subjective input – prepares the way for that newly proposed ethical *purpose*. These are matters much discussed now by contemporary historians and historical theorists, some of whom have similarly advocated, and in some cases demonstrated, an injection of ethics into historical writing; but I shall now go on to argue that that position had been further anticipated by other writers of fiction – and in particular by two very different novelists, Leo Tolstoy and Wyndham Lewis.

Leo Tolstoy

Like Penelope Lively's Claudia, Leo Tolstoy, writing in the later nineteenth century, is critical of both the nature and the purpose of history as practised in his time; and like her, he too proposes to inject into history a decidedly *ethical* dimension – in his case a pacifist message, opposing rather than glorifying war.

It is of course Napoleon's invasion of Russia in 1812 that is at the centre of Tolstoy's extraordinary study *War and Peace*.[9] Telling the stories of various characters within a closely observed and detailed historical context, the work is hard to define in terms of conventional disciplinary categories. The author himself rejected as a proper description both 'novel' and 'historical chronicle'; but despite being set within a specified historical context, and despite having far-reaching philosophical and ethical resonances, his story is clearly in its essence a work of *fiction* – and so qualifies for inclusion in our discussion here. Indeed, if we accept its characterisation by R. V. Sampson as a ' "novel" . . . meant to exemplify the correct method of presenting history', it can be seen as a highly appropriate subject for our case study.[10]

Tolstoy's interest in historical theory derived from, or at least was closely related to, his profound concern with man's inhumanity to man – a failing most obviously revealed in times of war. That perception of man's inhumanity has exercised writers through the ages: sparks of moral concern, if not blazing indignation, have been ignited through the personal experience of war from

[9] Leo Tolstoy, *War and Peace* [1868, 1869], trans. Louise and Aylmer Maude, London, Oxford University Press, 1941. All references are to this edition, in which three separately paginated Books are included in one volume.

[10] R. V. Sampson, *Tolstoy: The Discovery of Peace*, London, Heinemann, 1973, p. 161. The most widely known account of Tolstoy's philosophy of history is Isaiah Berlin, *The Hedgehog and the Fox: An Essay on Tolstoy's View of History* [1953], London, Weidenfeld and Nicolson, 1967; the most recent treatment is that of Hayden White, '*War and Peace*: Against Historical Realism', in Q. Edward Wang and Franz L. Fillafer (eds), *The Many Faces of Clio: Cross-cultural Approaches to Historiography, Essays in Honor of Georg G. Iggers*, New York and Oxford, Berghahn, 2007.

Thucydides to Tim O'Brien; and Tolstoy's own study of Napoleon's Russian campaign – which for him was recent history – was coloured by memories of his own military service in the Crimean War.[11] From that personal experience, he was led to question the conventional narratives presented by historians – narratives that (more so in his time than in ours) commonly attributed the outcome of events to the intervention of 'great men', and as a corollary minimised the role of individual responsibility in others.

Inadequacies in the approach of conventional historians included, Tolstoy believed, their seemingly widespread complacency in the acceptance of inhumanity and moral decline amidst the horrors of war. Such indifference could be shown only by those who remained physically and emotionally detached from the realities: whether in actual battles, or in later descriptions of those battles, detachment – although a professional requirement in the historical discipline as then understood – itself constituted a form of inhumanity. And so too did approval and praise for those who cultivated detachment in the context of warfare itself.

Thus, Tolstoy shows how the supposedly 'great' Napoleon himself, praised as he was 'by half the world . . . *had to repudiate truth, goodness, and all humanity*'.[12] It was only after he was forced to recognise his own impotence – his own inability to affect the course of events at Borodino (which he described as 'the most terrible of all my battles') – that he began to have doubts about the value of his whole enterprise. His celebrated strength of mind, which he liked to test by viewing the dead and wounded with equanimity, was finally overcome as he surveyed 'the terrible spectacle of the battlefield'. He became conscious of the powerlessness, not only of his once mighty army, but also of himself. He could do nothing to change the course of events, over which he was supposed to have control; 'and *from its lack of success* this affair, for the first time, seemed to him unnecessary *and horrible*' (II.539–40, 525, my emphases).

Recognition of the horrible nature of war comes earlier to other participants. When the Russian Emperor Alexander goes round a battlefield, he sees a wounded soldier being moved on a stretcher and hears him groan:

---

[11] Stendhal, who too had had personal military experience, serving as an officer under Napoleon, was an acknowledged literary predecessor: see his (much briefer) description of the Battle of Waterloo in *The Charterhouse of Parma* (1839).

[12] Cf. Alexis de Tocqueville's assessment of Napoleon as being 'as great as a man can be *without virtue*' (Hugh Brogan, *Alexis de Tocqueville: A Biography*, London, Profile Books, 2006, p. 404, my emphasis). Thackeray similarly, in *Vanity Fair* (which is set at the time of Waterloo), describes Napoleon as 'the great historic type of vanity' (Geoffrey Hemstedt, in Laurence Lerner (ed.), *The Victorians*, London, Methuen, 1978, p. 10).

'Gently, gently! Can't you do it more gently?' said the Emperor, apparently suffering more than the dying soldier, and he rode away.

Rostov saw tears filling the Emperor's eyes, and heard him, as he was riding away, say . . .: 'What a terrible thing war is: what a terrible thing!' (I.334)

It is terrible not least because men feel compelled to repudiate their natural human feelings towards one another, and to become totally *detached* from their enemy. Pierre Bezukhov notices how, amidst 'the stirring and deafening noise of the drums', one corporal's face changed, and even the sound of his voice – and 'he recognised that mysterious, callous force which compelled people against their will to kill their fellow men' (III.261–2). It was precisely that change in which Tolstoy says that he was most interested – '*in what way and under the influence of what feeling one soldier kills another*'. That, he believes, is one essential subject for historical enquiry – an enquiry recently undertaken by Joanna Bourke.[13]

And as Tolstoy clarifies, such enquiry indicates that moral transformations can occur in people with amazing speed, and work both ways. That is to say, people at war are not only suddenly moved negatively, to act inhumanely, but can just as easily be quickly converted by good example to a more humane disposition. During the Russians' evacuation from Moscow, as he describes, carts were being used to transport possessions and were being efficiently loaded by her family's servants, when Natasha became overwhelmed by compassion for the wounded soldiers who were being brought in, and insisted that the carts be reallocated for use by them. The servants were at first uncomprehending, and bemused by her counter-instructions; but as they too re-thought the whole situation, 'It no longer seemed strange to them but on the contrary it seemed the only thing that could be done', and they set about unloading the carts with great energy (III.59).

And such changing perceptions can even affect combatants themselves. As conditions for both sides deteriorate at the still indecisive battle of Borodino, the soldiers begin to wonder what it's all about: 'To the men of both sides alike, worn out by want of food and rest, it began equally to appear doubtful whether

---

[13] Leo Tolstoy, *The Raid and Other Stories* [1852], trans. Louise and Aylmer Maude, Introduction by P. N. Furbank, Oxford, Oxford University Press, 1982, p. 1 (my emphases). For Joanna Bourke's helpful attempt to answer Tolstoy's crucial question, see her *An Intimate History of Killing*, London, Granta, 2000. The American novelist Tim O'Brien (to be considered further in Chapter 6) also confronts this question in the context of the Vietnam War, attributing much to social pressures, and concluding that 'Men killed, and died, because they were embarrassed not to . . . just to avoid the blush of dishonour'. *The Things They Carried* [1990], New York, Broadway Books, 1998, p. 21.

they should continue to slaughter one another.' At that point, they stop acting automatically under orders, and begin, rather, to think for themselves; and 'At any moment these men might have been *seized with horror at what they were doing*, and might have thrown up everything and run away anywhere.' Even as an officer, Rostov begins to have 'terrible doubts', when he recalls his visit to the field hospital, crammed full of men 'with arms and legs torn off and in dirt and disease'; and as he contrasts that picture in his mind with an image of 'that self-satisfied Bonaparte', he asks, '*why* those severed arms and legs and those dead men?' (II.543; I.552, my emphases).

This questioning of the continuing acceptance of military values is central to Tolstoy's revisioning of history, and his own account exemplifies that emphasis. The conventionally 'great', from his standpoint, actually *lack* humanity. 'Not only does a good army commander not need any special qualities, [but] on the contrary he needs the *absence of the highest and best human attributes* – love, poetry, tenderness, and philosophic inquiring doubt' (II.308, my emphasis). So Tolstoy conversely promotes values that are diametrically opposed to those of the military, assigning a major role in that reversal to his character Prince Andrew. Portrayed originally as a brave young officer enthusiastically leading his men, Andrew is badly wounded at the battle of Austerlitz; and at that point, he is brought to question all his former values. He comes to realise the uncertainty and unimportance of everything he thought that he had understood perfectly before, and he feels compelled completely to reassess his attitude to war. That involves repudiating conventional values concerning 'honour', 'heroism', and any idea that war is simply a 'game': 'If', he concludes,

> there was none of this magnanimity in war, we should go to war only when it was worth while going to certain death . . . War is not courtesy but the most horrible thing in life; and we ought to understand that, and not play at war . . . let war be war and not a game.[14] As it is now, war is the favourite pastime of the idle and frivolous . . . [I]t is the highest class, respected by everyone . . . [H]e who kills most people receives the highest rewards . . . [T]hey kill and maim tens of thousands, and then have thanksgiving services for having killed so many people. (II.487–8)

[14] War did of course continue to be seen as a form of sport (which form depending on the social class of those involved) at least until the Second World War, during which one Brigadier Beckwith-Smith of the Coldstream Guards advised his men at Dunkirk to 'stand up . . . [and] shoot at [the German dive-bombers] with a Bren gun from the shoulder. *Take them like a high pheasant.*' (Quoted by Niall Ferguson, *New York Review of Books*, 30 November 2006, p. 28, my emphasis.) For other examples, see Joanna Bourke, *Intimate History*, pp. 233–4; and note p. 273 re the equivalence of the sporting and Christian spirits.

That indicates the essence of Tolstoy's own position – a position reached from personal experience in a war later characterised as 'completely pointless and manifestly avoidable . . . a completely futile waste of life'.[15] His own repudiation of military values, and of the inhumanity implied in them, is evident throughout the book and exemplified in sneering references to 'a stick called a "marshal's staff"', and to 'that sort of victory which is defined by the capture of *pieces of material fastened to sticks, called standards*'.[16] He is clear that traditional justifications for war (as still used in the twenty-first century) are nothing better than cynical political rhetoric: 'Since the world began and men have killed one another, no one has ever committed such a crime against his fellow-man without comforting himself with this same idea . . . the hypothetical welfare of other people' (III.359; II.545, my emphases; III.98).

'Hypothetical' is the key word there, and points up the self-delusions with which, in the perpetration of inhumane acts, we continue to indulge ourselves. Ideals of *glory* and *grandeur* continue to be manipulated: it is not for nothing that national kings dress up formally in army uniforms, and that military commanders (with their ubiquitous statues) are held up as exemplary figures. But such values, Tolstoy insists, essentially 'consist not merely in considering nothing wrong that one does, but in priding oneself on every crime one commits, ascribing to it an incomprehensible supernatural significance' (III.425).

How on earth, then, we are bound to ask, does this all come about? Who is responsible for what has happened and what happens? Those too are questions to which historians have addressed themselves, and, Tolstoy believes, their answers all too often resort again to the concept of the 'great man' – the great man who personally determines the course of history, and so absolves the ordinary person from any responsibility for what happens. It is in opposition to that distorted emphasis, that Tolstoy advocates a rethought historiography.

In denying the supreme importance of the great, heroic figure as the motor of history, Tolstoy was bucking the trend of his time – especially in the case of Napoleon, who, together with a few others such as Alexander the Great (and later Adolf Hitler), has almost invariably been treated by historians as an archetypal 'hero' (or anti-hero) who, whether for good or ill, by force of character single-handedly changed the course of history. The 'great man' theory of history had been influentially promoted by Hegel in his *Lectures on the Philosophy of History* (1837) and by Thomas Carlyle in his lectures *On*

---

[15] A. N. Wilson, *Tolstoy*, London, Penguin, 1989, pp. 101, 108.

[16] Cf. Carlyle: 'Have not I myself known five hundred living soldiers sabred into crows' meat, for a piece of glazed cotton, which they called their Flag' (*Sartor Resartus*, London, Ward, Lock, n.d., p. 148).

Heroes, Hero-Worship and the Heroic in History (1841); and it had then been deliberately reinforced in historical practice by Napoleon's own nephew in his *The History of Julius Caesar* (1865). Furthermore, with its implicit Hegelian justification for trampling down 'many an innocent flower' that may stand in the way, it was adopted with approval in a fictional context by Dostoevsky: in *Crime and Punishment*, the 'hero' Raskolnikov argues that 'great' individuals are above the law, and are justified in committing 'all sorts of enormities and crimes' in furtherance of their visionary objectives.[17] So it was against a currently fashionable view that Tolstoy rejected any such idea of an individual agent's privilege and potency.

It was by describing Napoleon's battles in detail, that Tolstoy justified his conclusion that the commander's personal input into events was far less than regularly imputed to him by historians. To them, with their need to make sense of the past, it was convenient for Napoleon to be seen as directing a succession of orderly events. But that was a retrospective vision; for in fact the complicated movements of men and horses and supplies, as they interacted on the battlefield, were so chaotic as to be out of anyone's control: 'Napoleon, who seems to us to have been the leader of all those movements – as the figurehead of a ship may seem to a savage to guide the vessel – acted like a child who, holding a couple of strings inside a carriage, thinks he is driving it' (III.253).

That is of course a characterisation that would hardly have appealed to Napoleon himself. In Tolstoy's account, and to change the metaphor, he liked to think of himself as a master chess-player, deliberately moving his pieces in both attack and defence, responding rationally to the counter-moves of his opponent, and finally homing in for the kill; so that, having inspected his forces before battle, it is in those terms that he states his decision: 'The chessmen are set up, the game will begin tomorrow!' (II.500).[18] But in fact, claims Tolstoy, war degenerates from that supposedly orderly model into something more akin to 'blindman's buff' (III.334), a game in which two players are blindfolded and one, seeking to escape, runs straight into his opponent's arms. As commander-in-chief, then, Napoleon was not so much a rational calculator, carefully disposing his forces in an orderly and rule-bound manner, but more akin to a blind man blundering around helplessly in a situation over

[17] Fyodor Dostoevsky, *Crime and Punishment* [1866], trans. David Magarshack, Harmondsworth, Penguin, 1951, pp. 275, 277. Here Dostoevsky follows G. W. F. Hegel, *Reason in History: A General Introduction to the Philosophy of History* [1837], trans. Robert S. Hartman, New York, Bobbs-Merrill, 1953, p. 43.

[18] Cf. Tolstoy's long-time friend and fellow officer S. S. Urusov (himself the author of a book on the 1812 campaign), who proposed that the bloody struggle for the Fifth Bastion at Sevastopol be settled by a game of chess (Sampson, *Tolstoy*, p. 116).

which he had no control; he was deluding himself (and historians) if he (or they) thought that he was in any meaningful sense in charge of the situation.

In fact, Tolstoy claims with the benefit of personal experience, battles are so chaotic that it is hard to descry any meaningful *order* within them, or any human *control* over them. It is bad enough in peacetime, when a government administrator might think he is in control, but only to find that when a crisis occurs, 'instead of appearing a ruler and source of power, [he] becomes an insignificant, useless, feeble man'. As with a man holding on to a ship with a boathook, all goes well so long as 'the sea of history remains calm'; but when a storm arises, and the sea starts heaving and the boathook no longer reaches, the delusion of control becomes impossible. And in wartime, the matter is yet more problematic: in the chaos of battle, 'The commander-in-chief is always in the midst of a series of shifting events and so he never can at any moment consider the whole import of an event that is occurring.' Retrospectively, an 'event' may seem to have a shape, with beginning, middle, and end; for 'the law of retrospection . . . regards all the past as a preparation for events that subsequently occur' – and that, as we have seen, provides the basis of histor-ians' narrative constructions. But at the time it is necessary to respond to a series of occurrences that lack any such tidy form; so that one general, for example, is described as being 'like a horse running downhill harnessed to a heavy cart. Whether he was pulling it or being pushed by it he did not know, but rushed along at headlong speed with no time to consider what this move-ment might lead to' (III.91, 8; II.399; I.341).

Despite everyone's intentions, then, the best laid plans inevitably come to nothing; and Tolstoy notes of one carefully calculated disposition of forces, that 'not a single column reached its place at the appointed time'. Men, he explains, 'had started in due order and, as always happens, had got some-where, but not to their appointed places . . . [A] few eventually even got to their right place, but too late to be of any use, and only in time to be fired at'. So it is hardly surprising that, in the heat of battle, any reports made by Napoleon's subordinates are '*necessarily* untrustworthy', sometimes derived from second-hand information, and always out of date (III.234, 240; II.519, my emphasis).

Yet it is of course on these deficient reports that Napoleon has to base his own instructions, with the inevitable result that any orders he gives bear no relation whatever to any reality on the ground: they 'had either been executed before he gave them, or could not be and were not executed'; and 'for the most part things happened contrary to . . . orders'. Thus, when, for example, 'the army retreated, [that] does not prove that Napoleon *caused* it to retreat, but that the forces which influenced the whole army . . . acted simultaneously on him also'; and he was in truth, as Tolstoy concludes, nothing more than a 'most insignificant *tool of history*' (II.519–20; III.279, 360, my emphases).

That is not of course how Napoleon or anyone else wants to see themselves, and they do their utmost to reverse the situation and make history *their* tool. Thus, those who have taken part in a battle generally describe it 'as they would like it to have been, as they have heard it described by others, and as sounds well, but not at all as it really was'. Self-delusion is rampant. One Russian general naturally wanted to take the credit for an operation that had proved successful, even though that success had been achieved only by pure chance: 'The general had so wished to do this, and was so sorry he had not managed to do it, that it seemed to him as if it had really happened. Perhaps it might really have been so? Could one possibly make out amid all that confusion, what did or did not happen?' And on another occasion we are told how Prince Andrew listened to a discussion held with officers – 'and to his surprise found that no orders were really given, but that Prince Bagration tried to make it appear that everything done by necessity, by accident, or by the will of subordinate commanders, was done, if not by his direct command at least in accord with his intentions' (I.257, 236).

In one way or another – and with enormous implications for historiography – we are virtually bound to deceive both ourselves and others. As we have seen in the previous chapter, we simply fail to remember or remember wrongly, finding it hard to remember at all without imposing on the past some structure – where a structure normally implies a series of discrete events that are strung together with causal interconnections and in narrative form. It is both the singularity and coherence (and so delimiting and definition) of 'events' and their respective positioning (especially in causal sequence), that Tolstoy questions. 'No battle', he insists, ever 'takes place as those who planned it anticipated'; nor does it ever take place in the orderly manner retrospectively ascribed to it by participants and historians.[19]

So what are we to make of those orderly narratives provided by historians, with their descriptions of 'wars and battles carried out in accordance with previously formed plans'? Tolstoy's uncompromising answer is that we have to conclude that any such idealised descriptions are simply false. Historians are bound to use 'the letters of the sovereigns and the generals . . . memoirs, reports, projects, and so forth'; and from these (no doubt respectable

---

[19] Proust likens a general's situation to that of a writer, 'who sets out to write a certain play, a certain book, and then the book itself, with the unexpected potentialities which it reveals here, the impassable obstacles which it presents there, makes him deviate to an enormous degree from his preconceived plan' (*Remembrance of Things Past*, III.783).

'primary') sources, they deduce aims and developments that never in fact existed; they 'have written the history of the beautiful words and sentiments of various generals, and not the history of the events' (III.242–3, 340, 342). It is easier to make sense of the past – to cast over it a tidy narrative – when the events of that past are perceived as having been rationally planned and executed by a few outstanding 'great men', whose own evidence helpfully supports that picture; but such accounts bear no relation whatever to any historical 'truth'.[20]

Tolstoy's repudiation of the 'great man' theory paves the way for his recommendation of a more ethically orientated historiography, in which the 'exemplary' figure is radically redefined. And here there is at the very heart of *War and Peace* an unresolved contradiction concerning human agency and freedom. For Tolstoy on the one hand wishes to insist on the individual's ability to act autonomously, but on the other hand reserves his highest praise for the man who bows to the inevitability of destiny, or the 'fate' that governs history. This ambivalence or ambiguity or contradiction, between our seem- ingly instinctive wish for, and consciousness of, *freedom*, and our recognition of scientific laws that preclude its possibility by indicating the *necessity* of actions and events – 'the insoluble mystery presented by the *incompatibility of freewill and inevitability*' (III.523, my emphasis) – is widely experienced; and its exploration itself becomes for Tolstoy one of history's main concerns. (I wonder if this may be related to one of Joanna Bourke's conclusions concern- ing the difficulty of reconciling combatants' assertions that they were 'only obeying orders' – thereby devolving responsibility elsewhere – and their need nonetheless to retain a sense of their own autonomy and agency and indi- vidual responsibility.[21])

Thus, he illustrates historical inevitability by analogy with clockwork. In his description of the Russian army at Austerlitz, for instance, he likens it to a mechanical clock, in which springs and cogs, pulleys and levers interact to produce certain required effects. When, at the instigation of the Emperor, the army started moving, it 'was like the first movement of the main wheel of a large tower-clock. One wheel slowly moved, another was set in motion, and a third, and wheels began to revolve faster and faster, levers and cogwheels to work, chimes to play, figures to pop out, and the hands to advance with regular

[20] Rousseau too scorns historians who purport to tell about the causes of victory and defeat 'with as much assurance as if [they] had been on the spot'. They are in reality *inventing*, for 'A tree more or less, a rock to the right or to the left, a cloud of dust raised by the wind, how often have these decided the result of a battle without anyone knowing it?' Jean Jacques Rousseau, *Émile* [1762], trans. Barbara Foxley, London, J. M. Dent, 1911, p. 200.

[21] See Bourke, *Intimate History*, p. 370.

motion' (I.336–7). Once the initial step had been taken on the periphery, individual parts within, long dormant, were triggered into life, and the whole ground into action with a slow but sure inevitability.

That mechanical inevitability in the movements of an army is paralleled in events as they developed after the retreat from Moscow: 'The tightly coiled spring was released, the clock began to whirr and the chimes to play.' And caught up in that situation, the Russian commander-in-chief Kutuzov, unable any longer to 'check the inevitable movement . . . gave the order to do what he regarded as useless and harmful – gave his approval, that is, to the accomplished fact' (III.233). Within a course of events that were unfolding in a quasi-mechanical way, Kutuzov appeared to have no more choice than the serried ranks of soldiers caught up within the confines of their various deployments; so he simply went along with what had been otherwise determined.

Indeed, from that predetermined course of events there was no escape for anyone. On his entry into Moscow, Napoleon made various pronouncements and issued specific instructions. 'But strange to say all these measures, efforts, and plans . . . did not affect the essence of the matter but, like the hands of a clock detached from the mechanism, swung about in an arbitrary and aimless way without engaging the cogwheels' (III.249). They lay somehow outside what was actually taking place, outside the mechanism of what was actually happening, and therefore had no ability to impinge on them or alter them.

In the more general context of historical development, individual battles themselves become seen as small parts of a larger mechanism – a remorseless ongoing process in which and by which all humans are entrapped. So the battle of Austerlitz, for example, which seems at the time such a great and exceptional event, takes its place as one small part of an infinitely wider picture: for all the 'passions, desires, remorse, humiliations, sufferings, outbursts of pride, fear, and enthusiasm' then experienced, it constituted nothing more significant than 'a slow movement of the hand on the dial of human history' (I.337).

In this mechanistically orientated universe, one's understanding of mechanics – of how the universe is actually constituted – takes on additional importance. Tolstoy periodically reiterates his belief that humans do well simply to *accept* a degree of inevitability in their lives. Individuals play their own (however small) part in a grand design that transcends their own individuality; and there can be moral virtue in recognising the part that small cogs play in the smooth working of a machine. Those who do not understand mechanics may think that a small shaving, that falls into a machine by chance and gets tossed around in it, is actually an important component; but in fact it is hindering the machine's working, whereas 'the small connecting cog-wheel which revolves

quietly is one of the most essential parts' of it. Historians who fail to understand this will leave out of account such quietly modest commanders as
Dokhturov, of whom Tolstoy clearly approves. In such cases historical silence
can be the clearest testimony to a man's merit; he is one, like his compatriot
Konovnitsyn, who exemplifies those 'unnoticed cog-wheels that, without
clatter or noise, constitute the most essential part of the machine' (III.270,
274).

The concept of some predetermined (or even providentially ordered) destiny is revealed most clearly in the case of the Russian commander-in-chief,
Kutuzov – a man much maligned (and not least by historians), but of whom
Tolstoy holds the highest opinion. For Kutuzov, as Tolstoy explains, 'under-
stands that there is something stronger and more important than his own will
– the *inevitable* course of events': 'By long years of military experience he
knew, and with the wisdom of age understood, that it is impossible for one
man to direct hundreds of thousands of others struggling with death, and he
knew that the result of a battle is decided not by the orders of a commander-
in-chief, nor the place where the troops are stationed, not by the number of
cannon or of slaughtered men.' Rather, there was some 'intangible force'
which he watched and guided 'in as far as that was in his power' (II.447, my
emphasis, 526).[22]

It was after Napoleon's retreat from Moscow that (as we noted above)
Kutuzov finally lacked the power to guide events, when (as with the Iraqi
retreat along 'The Highway of Death' from Kuwait in 1991) the pressures
upon him to attack and harry the retreating army proved irresistible, and he
was finally unable any longer to check what was already an *inevitable* outcome.
Despite that belated capitulation, Kutuzov was later criticised and openly
accused of blundering: he had held out too long against the pressures from all
sides. But Tolstoy strongly defends him: 'Such is the fate, not of great men
. . . but of those rare and always solitary individuals who discerning the will of
Providence submit their personal will to it.'[23] He had had his eye on something

---

[22] Eric Hobsbawm has recently written in similar vein about the Hungarian Revolution of
1956, noting that 'in retrospect, given their historical context, there is an *air of inevitability
about the flow of events*, as there is about the direction of a great river'. 'Could it have been
Different?', *London Review of Books*, 16 November 2006, p. 3 (my emphasis). See also
Christopher Hitchens' (highly questionable) assertion relating to the Iraq war, in a debate,
28 January 2003: 'The United States has placed itself *on the right side of history*' (quoted in
New York Review of Books, 27 September 2007, p. 16, my emphasis). And for Nietzsche on
'amor fati', see *Ecce Homo*, trans. R. J. Hollingdale, London, Penguin, 1979, p. 65: 'I do not
want in the slightest that anything should become other than it is'; cf. p. 68.

[23] Submission to the pattern of a design beyond our present vision is a recurring theme in
Tolstoy: on a more personal level, see the reiterated assurances in *Anna Karenina* that 'things

beyond apparent short-term expediency: he 'alone amid a senseless crowd understood the whole tremendous significance of what was happening'. But that was bound to prove less than endearing to the mass of people who lacked such vision, so 'he repeatedly expressed his real thoughts with the bitter conviction that he would not be understood'. And sure enough, Tolstoy laments, 'The hatred and contempt of the crowd punishes such men for discerning the higher laws' (III.360–62).

Discerning and living in accordance with such 'higher laws' remains the responsibility of individuals – and their ability to do that seems not to be compromised by any 'inevitability'. So having denied the effectiveness of great men, Tolstoy puts the 'ordinary' person back in control. Thus, at the battle of Borodino, it was not the commanders who did the killing, but the common soldiers: 'Napoleon shot at no one and killed no one. That was all done by the soldiers.' Individual soldiers, then, are responsible for their own actions: 'The French soldiers went to kill and be killed at the battle of Borodino not because of Napoleon's orders, but by their own volition.' Their actions were not in reality controlled by their commanders: as we have seen, 'it was not Napoleon who directed the course of the battle, for none of his orders were executed and during the battle he did not know what was going on before him' (II.498–9). So moral responsibility for whatever is done reverts to the individual.

Each individual, then, does well to seek his or her own salvation: rather than following the crowd or some charismatic leader, humans need to find their own happiness – and they will do that not by theorising but through practical experience. It is thus through his own suffering and deprivations in captivity that Pierre comes to conclude that 'man's highest happiness' lies in freedom and the ability to choose one's own way of life. He comes to the realisation that 'there is no condition in which he need be unhappy and not free'; his 'inner freedom . . . was independent of external conditions' (III.259, 324, 385). So he can remain an autonomous individual at all times, enabled to resist the pressure of others' assumed power.

That very practically orientated conclusion would affect the way Pierre lived in the future; and education more generally – and that includes the discipline of history – would also benefit from such a practical emphasis. The 'plain farmer' Nicholas, we are told, 'laughed at theoretical treatises', and was all the

will shape themselves' (Tolstoy, *Anna Karenina* [1877], trans. Louise and Aylmer Maude, Oxford, Oxford University Press, 1995, pp. xv, 5, 447). Here Tolstoy again follows Hegel, who had written of 'world-historical individuals' who grasp the concept of 'a higher universal, make it their own purpose, and realise this purpose in accordance with the higher law of the spirit' (*Reason in History*, p. 39).

more successful for doing so; and the army general Pfuel, conversely, is criticised for being 'one of those theoreticians who so love their theory that they lose sight of the theory's object – its practical application'. As with agricultural and military matters, so too with historical, we need to avoid becoming remote from everyday practical – and so ethical – concerns: Tolstoy refers scathingly to 'a present-day professor who from his youth upwards has been occupied with learning – that is with books and lectures and with taking notes from them' (III.439–40; II.303; III.420–21); and that is a picture which, consistent as it is with other representations of historians considered in Chapter 3, remains familiar today.

In conclusion, then, it is clear that *War and Peace* provides another important exemplification of the way that history meets fiction: it is a work of fiction that incorporates a critique of historiography and more particularly a recommendation that history be used for ethical – and more specifically humane anti-war – purposes. Tolstoy's careful analysis of battles, which exposed their ultimately impenetrable chaos, is emblematic of the past more generally; and the spurious nature of historians' more ambitious (scientistically derived) claims is thereby revealed. For as he explains, by various strategies historians contrive to cast a seemingly simple and straightforward narrative over events that by their very nature defy such simplistic treatment. Those strategies importantly include the assumption of a controlling intelligence – whether in the form of Providence or 'genius' or 'greatness', or even just faith in narrative coherence – that ensures an orderly development towards some rationally devised end. The apparently chaotic behaviour of individuals then comes to be viewed from the historian's perspective as actually a purposeful contribution to a preordained plan, all making perfectly good sense in the longer term. That is how history is written. But the resultant histories, Tolstoy insists, are only interpretations imposed retrospectively, with the benefit of hindsight and a filter that excludes as irrelevant anything that doesn't fit; and as often as not they project values that are far from humane.

Narratives claim to be authoritative by virtue of their derivation from 'primary' sources, and especially the evidence conveyed by eyewitnesses who have actually been involved in the events under review. But when such sources are investigated, they turn out on the whole to come from those leaders and commanders whose evidence we have seen to be far from reliable. So a different emphasis may be not only highly desirable but actually possible; and histories duly reformed could focus on, and project, an entirely different, and preferable, set of values – detachment replaced by human and ethical involvement.

Wyndham Lewis

Tolstoy, in this or any other context, may seem oddly paired with Wyndham Lewis (1882–1957): the former a widely renowned guru in his own time, and the author of a work frequently acclaimed as the greatest ever novel; the latter a man who quickly lost critical favour (through his then unfashionable interest in homosexuality and allegedly fascistic[24] leanings), and remembered now, if at all, as a somewhat eccentric satirist, novelist, painter, and (with Ezra Pound) founder-editor of *Blast*, mouthpiece of the early twentieth-century literary and artistic movement known as 'Vorticism'.[25] But what the two men shared was a personal experience of war, which led in each case to an interest in historical theory and, more particularly, to a shared concern with injecting an ethical dimension into historical writing.

In Wyndham Lewis's case, there are early references to historiography in *Time and Western Man* (1927) where, in a discussion of time and Spengler's 'chronological philosophy', he effectively repudiates the then conventional view of the historian as detached recorder of the truth about the past. Despite a popular conception of the historian as an 'incorruptible recorder of *the truth*, and nothing but the truth', producing 'a true account of something as it *really* happened', history, claims Lewis, can in fact never be more than one *version* of the past, presented with some *purpose* in mind; it is inevitably 'seen through a temperament of a certain complexion, and intended to influence its generation in this sense or in that'.[26]

Lewis reveals a continuing interest in historiography – with references to such practitioners as Ranke, Bury, and Butterfield – in *The Writer and the Absolute* (1952), a wide-ranging survey of the earlier twentieth-century cultural scene. But of most direct relevance to our theme here is his treatment in a novel published in 1954: *Self Condemned* is a fictional work but one in which the central character, René Harding, is clearly based on his own life. Significantly, he is a Professor of History who believes that his own academic discipline is effectively a 'racket' ripe for reform (118); and in certain respects

---

[24] As Lewis's mouthpiece in his semi-autobiographical novel, René Harding is advised that *The Times* had described him as 'fascist-minded': 'quite likely it did', he responds, 'since many people have been called that recently, simply because they had made a remark of an unenthusiastic kind about communism'. Wyndham Lewis, *Self Condemned* [1954], Santa Barbara, Black Sparrow Press, 1983, p. 128. Future page references will be given in the text.

[25] Since writing this, there has been some renewed interest shown in Wyndham Lewis, with an exhibition of his Portraits at the National Portrait Gallery, London, summer 2008.

[26] Wyndham Lewis, *Time and Western Man*, London, Chatto & Windus, 1927, p. 263.

that projected reform consists with what we have just seen being advocated by Tolstoy.

Professor Harding is represented as being in his late forties, and as having, like Tolstoy and Wyndham Lewis himself, lived through the experience of war – in his case, the Great War of 1914–18; and he can see (now shortly before the outbreak of the Second World War) that a resumption of armed conflict is imminent. It is in that context that he comes to conclusions about history not dissimilar from those that we have seen R. G. Collingwood expressing about Philosophy.[27] The perceived problem in both cases is that the subjects appear to have no practical importance: in the face of a forthcoming catastrophe, they seem altogether impotent, unable in any way to avert it; they are effectively *useless*.

So history, as Harding comes to believe, is 'as harmless a thing as could well be imagined' – an anodyne theoretical construction of no practical consequence. It is concerned with the recital of such banalities as 'William the Conqueror 1066 and a list of the wives of Henry VIII' – what Collingwood referred to as 'that putrefying corpse of historical thought, the "information" to be found in text-books'.[28] It has no bearing at all on what really matters in the present: its concern is only with 'the past, the long ago'; it has become 'synonymous in the popular mind with something *distant*'. And if perchance it approaches the present, and 'gets so near to us that it hurts, [then] naturally we no longer regard it as *history*' (118–19). And a corollary, no doubt advantageous to the subject, is the belief that, so long as it retains its distance and stays with things remote in time, it can be safely left to its own devices. Disciplinary autonomy is thus bought at the price of irrelevance.

For as soon as history does approach nearer to the present – something that Harding himself had allowed in his own notorious *Secret History of the Second World War* which, predating the actual outbreak of that war, makes a 'dramatic jump into the middle of the *unfinished* history of our time' (81, my emphasis) – problems inevitably arise. That is the case not least because a part of history's function is to expose what lies beneath the surface of events; so that, in the course of their researches, historians inevitably unearth and lay bare the intricacies of political machinations – 'become privy . . . to the dark secrets' of the ruling classes. And that way leads the route to political intrusions into history. For when dealing with the near-contemporary, or what is close at hand,

---

[27] Collingwood's thought was certainly known to Lewis, who actually quotes from what he refers to as 'an unpublished MS' – a manuscript that later took form as *The Idea of History* [1946], Oxford, Oxford University Press, 1961, pp. 77–8: see *Self Condemned*, pp. 92–3.

[28] Collingwood, *Autobiography*, p. 54.

history itself becomes perceived as something of potential *use*; and in those circumstances historians in turn are liable to be exposed to political pressures. And long before the exposures of Michel Foucault and his successors, Harding comes to realise that historians are expected to conform, their function being to underpin the status quo: 'All kinds of things are expected of him [and] he is supposed to *conform to accepted views* of every sort' (56, 119, my emphasis).

This has particularly important implications for Professor Harding's (and Wyndham Lewis's) major concern – with war. Orthodoxy requires, for example, that in any discussion of the Great War the blame for 'so senseless a crime' is put, not on the government, but on the people: it was the clamorous 'anger of a great people demanding action' that forced the government to give way and go to war – that is how it is to be presented. So the historian is forced to go along with official propaganda – to 'adhere to the reality of the world of slogans' – and is unable openly to examine what lies beneath the rhetoric. History, as Julien Benda too had indicated, thus loses its own identity and prospective value, and comes to resemble nothing more than 'an Armistice Day speech' (119).

It is thus complicit (just as Tolstoy had previously charged) in the continuing glorification of war itself. The exclusion of real *historical* analysis from recent events enables men to continue 'proudly unrolling the blood-stained and idiotic record of their past', without proper scrutiny; and it is then small wonder that preparations for yet another war should be reported 'as if it were an international football match which was being staged in an unusually elaborate manner'. Furthermore, and making matters worse, support in these proceedings is provided by the *religious* arm of government, so that 'From a million pulpits sing-song voices assure us that war is a holy thing' – something, incidentally, confirmed both by Vera Brittain, who wrote of how 'dons and clerics were still doing their best to justify the War and turn it into England's Holy Crusade', and by a senior training officer of the time who boasted that the 'Christian Churches are the finest blood-lust creators which we have' (119, 93, 43, 182).[29]

As a further result of its own ideological involvements, any attempts to reform history as an academic discipline are bound to meet with resistance: vested interests are ubiquitous, and 'the conspiracy to perpetuate the ten-millennia-long system popularly known to us as "history" is well organised'.

---

[29] Brittain, *Testament*, p. 126; Bourke, *Intimate History*, p. 289, who also (p. 268) quotes Ian Serraillier, a poet from the Second World War: 'The new commandment's "Thou shalt kill/in order to effect God's will".'

Whether from theological or political motivations, the content – the subject matter – of histories is included for reasons considered to be valid, so that any proposal to modify that content, by excising some events and adding others, is sure to provoke hostility from somewhere. To take but one illustration, 'the Catholics would not give up the reign of Henry VIII in any axing of the past, for that reign is rich in evidence of the kind they want'; and with history similarly providing useful underpinning for other theological and political positions, 'there is nothing to justify the hope of the immediate end of the glorification of the unselective past as "history"' (85, 355). (With that concept of 'the unselective past' we would of course now take issue, but the allegation of ideological interests and intrusions continues loudly to resonate.)

Furthermore, as Professor Harding realises, the problem is exacerbated by the fact that any reform of history must involve more widely ranging reassessments elsewhere – indeed, nothing less than a 'revaluation, moral and intellectual, throughout society'. His own aim, therefore, involves not just the bringing about of disciplinary change (an ambitious enough enterprise in itself), but nothing less than the amelioration of society as a whole. For he has come to believe that 'the slush and nonsense, the pillage and carnage which we have glorified as "history" . . . throws us back upon the futility of our daily lives, which also have to be condemned'. A reformed history, so he hopes, in which the 'slush and nonsense' has been replaced by something more edifying, might provide a better model for our own everyday lives: instead of presenting 'the bloody catalogue of their backslidings', a more worthwhile history would record 'the passions of men to stop sane'. Rather, that is, than regularising (and thereby implicitly legitimising) the negative, history would aspire to exemplify the positive: reverting to the long outdated model of history as moral teacher, anything 'unworthy of man's attention', any 'action which is so revolting that it *should not* have happened' (even if it did) should be expunged from the historical record; the emphasis on *quantity*, or ascription of importance only to such matters as affect large numbers of people (of whatever 'unvarying mediocrity and criminality'), should be replaced by a focus on *quality*; and 'the principal figures in the history-book should be those heroic creators who attempt to build something' (95, 351, 212, 93, 354, 86).[30]

Implying as that does some supposedly new degree of *choice* for historians with regard to the past – with how they are to select from it and with how they

---

[30] Rousseau similarly writes of history characteristically painting 'men's evil deeds rather than their good ones': *Émile*, p. 199. And cf. Hegel, who notes that periods of happiness and harmony constitute mere 'blank pages' in history; it takes a crisis – something bad – to provide a story. See Martin Davies, *Historics*, London, Routledge, 2006, p. 69.

are to go on to treat their selections – Professor Harding's approach to his subject remains fraught with its own difficulties, some of which have become more clearly exposed during the last half century (when Wyndham Lewis's self-professed emphasis on *theory* of history has become more widely shared). First, of course, traditional history is itself hardly 'unselective' (as described above): it may, as having become unquestioningly accepted and established as an orthodoxy, have acquired the appearance of being so; but numerous revolutions in the subject, inspired lately by a proliferation of minority interest groups, have revealed the extent to which all historical treatments are, of necessity, *selective* in their various attempts at 'glorification of the . . . past' (or of an infinity of pasts).

Second, Wyndham Lewis makes it clear through his professorial mouthpiece that he is himself well aware that '*All* history is written with a bias'; and the historian, as René Harding early concedes, is 'the servant of the ruling class'. 'Bias', then, is seen as a problem only when that bias is one of which we disapprove, and for Lewis himself that applies when the ruling class is communist: it is in relation specifically to Soviet Russia that Harding warns that when history 'is written with a state-organised bias . . . great harm ensues'. But despite that particular citation, the danger is of course universal. 'For if you falsify past events methodically, you very soon authorize or indeed command that present events be systematically falsified also' (118, my emphasis, 56).

In these anxieties about the very practical political effects of totalitarian control of history, Lewis shares concerns with another of his now more frequently cited contemporaries (about whom he himself wrote at some length[31]). In George Orwell's dystopian vision, *Nineteen Eighty-Four* (1949), the power of the past is equally well recognised: there, 'No written record [and that of course includes history] . . . ever made mention of any other alignment than the existing one', and leaders are well aware, in the words of their Party slogan, that 'Who controls the past controls the future'.[32] For Orwell, as for Lewis, 'History' (now in Professor Harding's words) 'includes the *present* as well as the past' (118, my emphasis).

The crux of the matter here, though, becomes for Lewis's protagonist (as it has become for us) the openly conceded *universality* of historical 'bias'. For that implies in turn the absence of *any* 'standard of objective reality'; and as with Julien Benda, the lack of any absolute or ultimate criterion of truth in history is seen to be, for any society, 'a very bad thing'. Without such a

---

[31] See *The Writer and the Absolute*, London, Methuen, 1952, esp. pp. 153f.
[32] George Orwell, *Nineteen Eighty-Four* [1949], Harmondsworth, Penguin, 1954, pp. 30–31.

concept, intellectuals generally are liable to get seduced by fleetingly fashion-able theories, whether in sciences or the arts; and then they lose the ability 'to preserve the *individual* judgement intact, immune from contagions of popular hysteria'. So as in our own postmodern times, 'the problem of prob-lems is to find anything of value intact and undiluted . . . to discover any foothold (however small) in the phenomenal chaos' (118, 351), or, as Lewis writes elsewhere, some 'unchanging criterion of continuous validity . . . some steadying principle'.[33]

It is the quest for some such 'steadying principle' or 'foothold' that still engages historians and others, so that here too Wyndham Lewis seems to speak directly to us as his intellectual heirs (or, perhaps better, he is an ancestor whom I have deliberately chosen as exemplary). And his message is instructive, for René Harding's recognition of the absence of any requisite 'foothold' – "I hate these twentieth-century *Absolutes*!" (135, original empha-sis) – leads to his *resignation* in two senses of the word. First, it provokes his professional resignation – a resignation required by his own integrity when he realises the incompatibility of his own intellectual conclusions with the then current orthodoxies of the discipline he is paid to profess. To the consterna-tion of family and friends, he resigns from his respected academic position – a decision that sets in train a number of events, including his emigration to Canada, which culminates in the novel's tragic outcome. And second (and in the story later), it leads to a personal and emotional resignation – a resignation to (or resigned acceptance of) the academic status quo that is finally, and despite previous resistance, required by his own emotional need for some 'static finality in which the restless intellect might find repose' – the sort of peace that he had witnessed (and at that time rejected) during his convales-cence, after his wife Hester's suicide, with the theologically orientated inmates of the College of the Sacred Heart (380).

One resignation, then, is ultimately succeeded by another, so that René Harding's life may be seen as a tragic failure, with his ideals finally forced out of him by various pressures – including not least his own emotional pressures for survival – to conform to a current 'reality'. His proposed reformation – rethinking, reconfiguration – of history as a subject of social and human importance represents a utopianism that was (and maybe still is) hopelessly *un*-'realistic'; so that his friend Professor McKenzie is surely justified in including him amongst those dissatisfied with life as lived hitherto – amongst those who demand 'that man should remake himself and cease to live upon the paltry, mainly animal plane we know'. That puts him out on a limb: such

[33] *Writer and Absolute*, pp. 19 (my emphasis), 149.

ideals are not widely held, and thinking 'in a manner in which one is not allowed to think', he early becomes, as he describes himself, 'an outsider, almost a pariah' (315, 18).[34]

Life as 'an outsider' can, as shown in the case of Harding himself, prove difficult and even literally unbearable. But that is the role assigned, here in his fictional representations, by Wyndham Lewis to historians, and more generally to intellectuals. As again with Julien Benda, their responsibility must be to retain their own ideals, and by reference to those, in the face of all external and internal pressures, 'to preserve the[ir] individual judgement intact'. Well aware of our 'susceptibility to contagion' from contemporary fashions, and of the great 'pressure to achieve conformity', Lewis aspires to remain aloof from any intellectual or political party, or 'group-pull': excessive allegiance to one's own community, he insists, must prove 'fatal', for it implies the admission of temporal constraints – a form of parochialism – and results in one's 'critical faculties becom[ing] atrophied'. It is, then, precisely the function of the intellectual 'to provide some master prophylactic against obsessional contagions', and somehow 'to keep himself *different*'.[35]

As the writer's mouthpiece, René Harding himself, for all his evident idealism, is realistic enough to remain aware of the limitations of his own prospective influence: he may make his personal gesture or statement (which he does by resigning his position), but other people, as he recognises, are unlikely to be much impressed. 'Men do not', as he well knows, 'turn their lives upside down in response to the summons of a professor of history' (95). Yet for all its 'impracticality' and the ultimately dire personal consequences of his action, Professor Harding's initial stand in relation to his subject remains exemplary; and his insistence on the moral responsibilities of historians – responsibilities that encroach upon fields far wider than their own narrow historical specialisms, and impinge on 'real life' – remains an issue worthy of debate in the early twenty-first century.

From that debate Harding in the end removes himself, effectively (and no doubt understandably) capitulating to personal and professional pressures. But it is at the cost of becoming 'a glacial shell of a man' – 'only a half-crazed replica of his former self'. And the denial by others of the importance of such matters – their attempted ethical detachment – may lead to similar 'emotional

---

[34] Cf. p. 163: 'ostracism accompanies the act of repudiation'.

[35] Lewis, *Writer and Absolute*, pp. 19, 148, 193, 143, 53, 141. This is a theme treated also in an essay 'The "Detached Observer"', in *Rude Assignment*, London, Hutchinson, 1928, pp. 69–72. And cf. *Self Condemned*, p. 134: 'to have everyone thinking in exactly the same way about everything is, humanly speaking, a nightmare'.

amputations', and to the revelation of being, like some of Harding's later colleagues, 'unfilled with anything more than a little academic stuffing' (407,
402, 421) – as being 'the hollow men' described by T. S. Eliot (another contemporary of Lewis), 'the stuffed men/ Leaning together/ Headpiece filled
with straw . . .'. In such a situation, deprived of moral significance, historians
as well as history can do little more than 'whisper together' with 'dried voices
. . . [that]/ Are quiet and meaningless'.[36]

Once again, then, we have in the case of Wyndham Lewis a writer of fiction
who deals with some serious – indeed central – historiographical issues concerning both the nature and the prospective purposes of history; and in his
promotion of a refigured history as a practically orientated *ethical* enterprise,
he appears as well ahead of contemporary theorists.

Conclusion

Briefly to conclude, then, I have argued in this chapter that, just as we previously saw in relation to history's nature, so too regarding its purpose, writers
of fiction have on occasion anticipated historians and historical theorists, by
adopting a position advocating ethical involvement, that is only now (in some
cases over a century later) becoming more widely (though still by no means
universally) accepted. My two main examples here have been the widely dis-
parate figures of Leo Tolstoy and Wyndham Lewis, both of whom we have
seen, as a result of their own direct experience of war, to propose an ethically
directed history with a specifically humanitarian and pacifist agenda.

But those are only two of a number of possible examples: to bring the discussion of such issues forward in time, one could cite, with his experience of
the Second World War, Kurt Vonnegut; and, as a veteran of the Vietnam War,
Tim O'Brien. We shall discuss the latter at greater length in the following
chapter, but in relation to the former, we can note here briefly that Vonnegut
deliberately uses history as a basis for writing a work that is, again, specifically
intended to have an ethical dimension. His novel *Slaughterhouse-Five* (1969),
although obviously fiction, is based on his personal experience of the bombing of Dresden in 1945 – an experience he survived through being incarcer-
ated, as a Prisoner of War, in a meat cellar some three storeys under ground.
For a wider view of events at the time, Vonnegut made use of David Irving's

---

[36] T. S. Eliot, 'The Hollow Men', in *Collected Poems, 1909–1962*, London, Faber and Faber,
1963, p. 89.

historical work, *The Destruction of Dresden* (1963); and – most relevant for us here – he records his *moral* purpose in presenting his own historically based, but satirical and fictional account of what went on. In what is an essentially anti-war message, he explains his aim as being to 'catch people before they become generals and presidents and so forth, and you poison their minds'. To 'catch people' for that purpose, it may be easier to attract them in the first place with fictional, rather than strictly historical, works; but the aim is still avowedly practical and directed at the 'real' world. In Vonnegut's words – and as Tolstoy and Wyndham Lewis might have said about their own works – 'it is to encourage them to make a better world'.[37]

The subject of this chapter, then, has been to do with another meeting point between fiction and history, and more particularly with fiction-based recommendations for the injection of ethics into a reinvigorated history. That (as we saw explicitly recognised in the case of Wyndham Lewis but as is implicit too in Tolstoy) requires not only a disciplinary revolution but also some form of *personal* renewal – a veritable revisioning of one's own *identity*. And that leads us on directly to the following chapter.

Further reading

Berlin, Isaiah, *The Hedgehog and the Fox: An Essay on Tolstoy's View of History* [1953], London, Weidenfeld and Nicolson, 1967.

Bourke, Joanna, *An Intimate History of Killing*, London, Granta, 2000.

Harlan, David, *The Degradation of American History*, Chicago and London, University of Chicago Press, 1997.

Jenkins, Keith, *Why History? Ethics and Postmodernity*, London, Routledge, 1999.

Lewis, Wyndham, *Self Condemned* [1954], Santa Barbara, Black Sparrow Press, 1983.

Tolstoy, Leo, *War and Peace* [1868, 1869], trans. Louise and Aylmer Maude, London, Oxford University Press, 1941.

Wilson, A. N., *Tolstoy*, London, Penguin, 1989.

---

[37] Kurt Vonnegut, in Robert Scholes, 'A Talk with Kurt Vonnegut, Jr.', in Jerome Klinkowitz and John Somer (eds), *The Vonnegut Statement*, St Albans, Panther, 1975, p. 109.

Chapter 6

Fiction, history, and identity

Here we shall consider the interrelation of history and fiction in the matter of identity, noting the frequently asserted importance of history for personal and public identities, and the inevitable intermingling of history and fiction in the formulation and maintenance of those constructs (or the very meaninglessness of their attempted distinction in that context). As case studies, we examine the construction of an historian's 'new self' described by André Gide in The Immoralist, *and the attempted manipulation of memory in the interests of acquiring a new identity, illustrated by Tim O'Brien in his novel* In the Lake of the Woods.

It has become a truism, a platitude of contemporary life, that history underpins identity. In other words, there is wide agreement that we cannot possibly know who or what we are without some awareness of our pasts. And that is the case both for individuals and for communities, nation-states (and their constituents), and larger socio-politico-economic agglomerations. With regard to the former, genealogical investigation is rapidly becoming a whole new 'industry', with family archives supplemented by websites and televised investigations; while for the latter, self-interested appeals to justificatory histories grow by the day.

The current interest in identity-conferring or identity-confirming pasts coincides with a perceived fragmentation occurring at both personal and public levels. There is no need here to add to the numerous studies of 'modern selfhood' and its comparatively recent development (over the last three centuries or so),[1] but it is necessary to note the frequently cited condition of

---

[1] See in particular Charles Taylor, *Sources of the Self: The Making of Modern Identity*, Cambridge, Cambridge University Press, 1989.

insecurity that has resulted in modern times from the emancipation of individuals from the previous constraints of long-established social hierarchies. We are no longer born into an identity, whether as lord or peasant, butcher or baker – the rich man in his castle or the poor man at his gate: on the contrary, much time and energy is now expended on 'finding oneself', whether through extensive world tours or transcendental meditation. And unsurprisingly, demands grow upon the professions that are believed to provide help in this (paradoxically self-conscious and often self-regarding) quest – those genealogists, biographers, psycho-therapists, and historians of course, who are expected to facilitate the retrieval of pasts that will provide the foundations for enduring (and preferably interesting and attractive) personalities.

Similarly on public levels of social community and nation-state, there seems to be an increasingly felt need to identify with particular pasts in order to embrace a shared springboard for propulsion into the future. Small groups, whether socially or ethnically derived, seek shared backgrounds as a basis for cohesion; and national leaders, as they witness accelerating political fragmentation, look to the past in their search for shared values that they hope will serve as inspiring models for future integration. (Since I drafted this chapter, John Tosh has duly written of how history can 'be used to intensify the sense of *belonging* to a group . . . by *anchoring it securely* in shared narratives of the past'; and a senior member of the British Opposition, alarmed by new proposals for the national history curriculum, has insisted that 'Our national story [sic] can't be told without Churchill at the centre [sic]'.[2])

With various requirements and demands, then, for fulfilling personal and public narratives, the interests of history and fiction once more meet. For narrative construction, as we have already seen, but will further review in the next section, is an activity in which it is difficult, if not impossible, to draw hard and fast distinctions between the supposedly 'factual' claims of history and the admittedly imaginative input of fiction. And, in relation specifically to identity, an additional complication has to be faced: that, contrary to some earlier beliefs (as well as to some that endure), both 'human nature' itself and 'individual identity' are not necessarily static entities that persist through history and through individual lifespans – they are not fixed 'essences' that we can simply identify and thereafter utilise as unquestionable resources – but are, rather, to a greater or lesser extent our own social and personal, *and provisional*, constructions.

---

[2] John Tosh, *Why History Matters*, Basingstoke, Palgrave Macmillan, 2008, p. ix (my emphases); Michael Gove, Shadow Secretary of State for Children, Schools and Families, reported in *The Independent*, 26 August, 2008, p. 7. Note Gove's evidently enduring belief in a single, unitary 'national story' that can be told within a narrative boasting a single, unitary 'centre'.

'Human nature' in that context becomes, not something to which one has to become resigned ('well, it's just human nature, isn't it?', as, with a question that is only rhetorical, we accept the latest atrocity), but is something to be defined in our own terms, here and now – a model or target to which humans can aspire. Admittedly, without some notion of a shared 'humanity', the practice of history becomes virtually impossible, since it is what allows us to assume the possibility of understanding those past others, into whose lives and beings we endeavour sympathetically to penetrate. As the historian Henri Pirenne noted, 'one cannot comprehend men's actions at all unless one assumes in the beginning that their physical and moral beings have been at all periods what they are today.'[3] History must presuppose some commonality. But that is only to reveal or to re-emphasise some of the problems inherent in current historical practice, for that fundamental changes in human activities and responses do take place over time seems undeniable. In most of the West, for example, public torture and executions are now, unlike a few centuries ago, considered inhumane, or literally incompatible with (even diametrically opposed to) being 'human'. And similarly with individual identities: these are revealed as being less – or, rather, more – than monolithic; they (or we) are multiple, possessed of numerous alternatives which, largely as a matter of choice, we alternately conceal and reveal, disown and adopt. That too admittedly makes the task of historians, as they seek to comprehend and then explain the diverse and often contradictory actions of past individuals, more difficult, if not impossible. But there would be few today who would claim, even for themselves, a unitary and unchanging selfhood; and the voluntary adoption of, and the determined search for, an *alternative* identity will be the subject of our case studies later in this chapter – both of which illustrate once more the close connection between fiction, history, and historical theory.

History, fiction, and the construction of identities

If one accepts the contingency and instability and multiplicity of an individual's selfhood, then it is interesting to note that it is writers of fiction, rather than historians, who have first come to terms with that, and who have more

---

[3] Henri Pirenne, quoted by Rhodri Hayward, *Resisting History: Religious Transcendence and the Invention of the Unconscious*, Manchester, Manchester University Press, 2007, p. 4. Cf. Hegel: 'The concept of human nature must fit all men *of* all ages, past and present.' *Reason in History: A General Introduction to the Philosophy of History* [1837], trans. Robert S. Hartsman, New York, Bobbs-Merrill, 1953, p. 21.

recently made something positive out of what might initially have seemed to be a problem. That it might pose a problem for historians is fairly obvious, since their practice is based on the presupposition of an enduring personality: it is that that enables them to attempt to provide a coherent and integrated account of a past person's actions. So, for example, we might ask how many times attempts have been made to 'explain' a notorious agent such as Adolf Hitler by reference to his past – to his childhood, family background, early experiences in the First World War – on the assumption that it was one and the same person under investigation. That too is the assumption of the psycho-therapist, who seeks understanding of the present as the culmination of a rational (and so comprehensible) development from the past. And it is of course an assumption made in everyday 'common sense': why else should we talk of a person known to us as acting 'out of character'?

Yet the lack of a consistent and unitary personality has also long been recog-nised, at least in theory. In classical antiquity, while Thucydides was insisting on the longevity (or even immortality) of a consistent 'human nature' that would forever guarantee the usefulness of his history (as containing lessons that were universalisable, transcending time), the dramatist (and so for our purposes representative of poetic fiction) Euripides revealed some conse-quences of a 'split' (far from consistent) personal identity. To take but one, albeit extreme, example from his play *The Bacchae*: the mother of Pentheus is shown as transformed from her presumably rational, law-abiding (if not repressed) everyday self, into a wild and beast-like creature who delights in tearing her own son limb from limb. She thus manifests that 'divided selfhood' about which Plato had already theorised when he wrote of the different 'pulls' or internal pressures to which humans are subject – the wish to look, for instance, at a road accident, the results of which we do not really (at another level) wish to see.

That duplicity (if not multiplicity) of selfhood becomes a commonplace of Christian morality, where it has been accepted from the time of St Paul that one part of us cannot resist doing what another part of us would have us refrain from; but it is another dramatic poet who provides the model of a yet more complicated series of personalities, in terms of which 'each man in his turn plays many parts'.[4] Shakespeare's 'parts' may theoretically run in a temporal series, but in practice they may well get muddled; and with such a proliferation of personalities or identities, who anyway is to select the 'real' or common thread that bestows any continuity or consistency?

---

[4] For Shakespeare's 'Ages of Man', see *As You Like It*, Act II, scene vii.

Shakespeare's model of actors on the stage of life is re-adopted in the twentieth century by the American novelist Philip Roth. Through his character Zuckerman, he confesses:

> All I can tell you with certainty is that I . . . have no self, and that I am unwilling or unable to perpetrate upon myself the joke of a self . . . What I have instead is a variety of impersonations that I can do, and not only of myself – a troupe of players that I have internalised, a permanent company of actors that I can call upon when a self is required, an ever-evolving stock of pieces and parts that forms my repertoire. But I certainly have no self independent of my imposturing, artistic efforts to have one. Nor would I want one. I am a theatre and no more than a theatre.[5]

Zuckerman's 'stock of pieces and parts' must be derived from his experienced past, but that past – that history of his – does not result in (let alone guarantee) any independent, autonomous identity that can be seen to derive (naturally or rationally or explicably) from that past.

Philip Roth is there fulfilling a prophecy made earlier in the century by another writer of fiction, Virginia Woolf, who remarks on the way that individuals gain their own sense of self, not through intense self-scrutiny, but from other people – from the reactions and reflections back that they receive from those around them; and she rightly predicts that 'novelists in future will realise more and more the importance of these reflections, for of course there is not one reflection but *an almost infinite number*'. That indeed is a recurring theme in her own fiction. 'Nobody sees anyone as he is', we read in *Jacob's Room* (1922); for humans (like any objects of perception, only more so) are not simple unitary entities that can be thus readily defined and identified – so 'It is no use trying to sum people up' (any more, we might add, than it is any use trying to sum up 'the past', having supposedly seen it 'as it was').[6]

That recognition of impenetrable complexity is ascribed by Virginia Woolf to her fictional characters, many of whom reveal uncertainties about their own selves. Bernard in *The Waves* (1931) is exemplary as he ponders: 'What am I? I ask. This? No, I am that . . . it becomes clear that I am not one and simple, but complex and many.' With that realisation, other people's various expectations (and consequent requirements) can prove sometimes positive – as when

---

[5] Philip Roth, *The Counterlife* (1986), quoted by John Banville, who describes that novel as 'unquestionably his [Roth's] masterpiece, and certainly his most intricate and subtle creation'. *London Review of Books*, 4 October 2007, p. 23.

[6] Virginia Woolf, 'The Mark on the Wall' in *A Haunted House* [1944], London, Grafton, 1982, p. 44 (my emphasis); *Jacob's Room* [1922], London, Panther, 1976, p. 28.

Miss La Trobe in *Between the Acts* (1941) exclaims that, 'You've stirred in me my unacted part' – but at other times (and perhaps more frequently) tiresome. For their overly simplistic conclusions fail to do us justice; they derive, not from interest in us, but rather from their own priorities: 'we are not simple as our friends would have us, to meet their needs'; 'they do not understand that I have to effect different transitions; have to cover the entrances and exits of several different men who alternately act their parts as Bernard.'[7]

So, as he goes on to explain, 'I am more selves than Neville thinks'; 'I am not one person; I am many people.' Like Shakespeare's actor, he has, he recognises, in his time played many parts, ranging widely in character: 'For I changed and changed; was Hamlet, was Shelley, was the hero, whose name I now forget, of a novel by Dostoevsky, was for a whole term, incredibly, Napoleon; but was Byron chiefly.' It is small wonder, then, that when he looks for himself, seeking a definitive identity, he finds that self elusive: ' "He is gone! He has escaped me!" For there is nothing to lay hold of. I am made and remade continually.'[8]

A part of the reason for that continual remaking is that he responds differently to different people: 'Different people', as he acknowledges, 'draw different words from me.' And also different identities; for 'To be myself (I note) I need the illumination of other people's eyes'; 'My being only glitters when all its facets are exposed to many people.' Without those other people to confirm him in his various aspects, Bernard finds himself an insubstantial shell, 'full of holes, dwindling like burnt paper', and not able to be 'entirely sure what is my self'. That uncertainty induces a panic: he feels a need to 'dig furiously like a child rummaging in a bran-pie to discover myself'. But in the end he is still not sure of what he finds or of who he is: 'I do not altogether know who I am'; he is ultimately 'a man without a self'.[9] How, then, can any historian hope to pin him down – identify him as an integrated subject for biography, or rationally explain his actions?

---

[7] Virginia Woolf, *The Waves* [1931], Harmondsworth, Penguin, 1951, pp. 64, 76; *Between the Acts* [1941], London, Granada, 1978, p. 112. In the visual arts similarly, Marcel Duchamp for instance questioned the stability of identity, including his own, and went to the lengths of creating an alternative (female) selfhood named Rrose Sélavy (a play on 'Eros, c'est la vie'), who 'signed' most of his works in the interwar years. He later (1960) referred to 'a little game between "I" and "me" ' (Tate Modern Exhibition 'Duchamp, Man Ray, Picabia', May 2008).
[8] *The Waves*, pp. 76, 237, 214, 114. One of Penelope Lively's characters enjoys similar (but fictional rather than historical) literary fantasies: 'She had been Tess and Natasha and Catherine Earnshaw and the girl in *Rebecca* and more ambitiously Madame Bovary and Anna Karenina.' *Perfect Happiness*, London, Penguin, 1985, p. 187.
[9] *The Waves*, pp. 114, 99, 159, 185, 237, 245.

Our reliance on other people for the construction of our identities (an insight incidentally utilised by promoters of mobile telephones – evidently essential equipment when 'I am who I am because of everyone'[10]) is a concern also of Virginia Woolf's contemporary, the poet T. S. Eliot, who picks up the same point in his play *The Cocktail Party* (which we consulted in Chapter 4 on the subject of memory). Here the character Edward confesses that, if he is to have any hope of finding out who he himself is, he needs first to know the nature of his wife Lavinia: 'I must find out who she is, to find out who I am'; for his own identity is, as in Bernard's case, reflected back at him by her. But therein, as Eliot, through his character of the Unidentified Guest/Sir Henry Harcourt-Reilly, observes later in the play, lies an additional complication. For identities reflected back to us in that way are only ever temporary: we can never really grasp them, for we are, as it were, always one step behind in our observations of others and ourselves: 'What we know of other people/ Is only our *memory* of the moments/ During which we knew them. And they have changed since then.' They too, like us, are in a state of constant (or inconstant) flux, so it is only them as they were in the past that we remember; by the time that we think of them, they have already moved on. 'To pretend that they and we are the same/ Is a useful social convention . . . [but] We must also remember/ That at every meeting we are meeting a stranger.'[11] Grasping at a solid identity in that ever-changing complexity of interconnections and reflections, it is hardly surprising that Franz Kafka should have confided to his diary, that 'I hardly have anything in common with myself.'[12]

But those fiction-based insights into the construction of identity impinge, again, directly on historical theory; for we are left here with something closely akin to the construction of any other narrative. And that is shown, once more, to be a matter of response and selection – a matter of choosing from a potential infinity of possibilities; and those possibilities are bound to derive from a past, the story of which will include in part a supposedly 'historical' component (appropriately supported by empirical evidence), and in part an admittedly 'fictional' one (resulting from more imaginative reconstructions). So that again the supposed unity of remembered identities fragments. As a 'fictional' character in one of John Banville's novels recalls, of a woman by whom he had been much affected in his childhood: 'No doubt for others elsewhere she persists, a moving figure in the waxworks of memory, but their version will be

---

[10] Orange advertisements, London, summer 2008.

[11] T. S. Eliot, *The Cocktail Party* [1950], London, Faber and Faber, 1958, pp. 33, 72–3.

[12] Kafka, Diary entry, 8 January 1914; quoted by Martin L. Davies, *The Prison-House of History*, New York, Routledge, 2009.

different from mine, and from each other's. Thus in the minds of many does the one ramify and disperse.'[13]

This may perhaps all seem obvious enough, but it is only much later that historical theorists have caught up with these conclusions, arrived at by writers of fiction from the earlier twentieth century. Thus Keith Jenkins, influenced here by Jacques Derrida, has recently written, in terms not dissimilar to those of Virginia Woolf, T. S. Eliot, Philip Roth, and others, of the self 'constantly being made and re-made, read and re-read, written and re-written, incessantly and interminably'. And Amy Elias has written similarly of the self as 'a dialogic process rather than a singularity, and . . . always defined by interaction with the other', quoting M. Eskin on the unceasing 'oscillation between the other's "aesthetic completion" of me and my own assertion of incompleteness and infinite potential'.[14]

Even now, however, it remains unclear whether historians themselves have fully come to terms with the inherent instability of their subject matter, and the difficulty, if not impossibility, of re-presenting subjects that are ever in a state of flux – subjects whose identities at any time are inevitably an inextricable mixture of 'fact' and 'fiction', of what can be empirically demonstrated and what is attributable, rather, to fantasy and imagination.

'A new self!': André Gide and a revision of history

I remember shouting aloud, as if my calling could bring him to me: 'A new self! A new self!'[15]

As that quotation indicates, André Gide's novel *The Immoralist* (1902) is concerned with the question of identity; and it will serve here as a particularly appropriate subject for a case study, since, in this work of *fiction*, the issue is tied up closely with *history* – both its nature and its purpose. The main theme is presented through the portrayal of the central character Michel, who is himself an historian, and who experiences a moment of epiphany, when (as described in the quotation above) he realises the possibility of adopting a 'new self'.

---

[13] John Banville, *The Sea*, London, Picador, 2005, pp. 118–19.
[14] Keith Jenkins, *Refiguring History*, London, Routledge, 2003, p. 60; Amy Elias, 'Meta-historical Romance, the Historical Sublime, and Dialogic History', *Rethinking History* 9, 2005, pp. 167–8.
[15] André Gide, *The Immoralist* [1902], trans. Dorothy Bussy, Harmondsworth, Penguin, 1960, p. 52; subsequent page references will be given in the text.

Being an historian, Michel is well placed to demonstrate the close inter-relationship between history and identity: indeed, his change of identity – his adoption of a new selfhood – indicates a proposed change in the very nature and purpose of history (as a discipline) itself. His own development represents the replacement of one sort of history by another, the old by the new; so that once again we see an early challenge to disciplinary and educational orthodoxies, coming not internally from an actual practitioner, but externally from a writer of *fiction*.

Gide, then, shows two very different kinds of historian, but with both kinds embodied (successively) in the same central character – the one before Michel's moment of illumination, the other after it; so the former is looked back to, retrospectively, as past and discarded, while the latter is portrayed as a present possibility, with implications for the future. So fundamental are the differences between these two that Michel seems to himself to be confronting not just a disciplinary revision, but also by implication the adoption of a whole new personal identity, a whole 'new self'.

Neither model of an historian (the earlier or later Michel), as presented here by Gide, is particularly alluring. The older, the traditional and orthodox model, is (as we are coming to expect now) a detached and desiccated type, reminiscent of George Eliot's Casaubon and others in the Dryasdust tradition, far removed from any practical experience of, or even concern with, 'real life'; while the new proposed replacement appears as an amoral relativist, gloating solipsistically in his own romantic individualism. Still, the personal transition involved in Michel's development from the one to the other, which lies at the very heart of the story, is clearly meant to be seen as progressive: it is exemplary – offered by Gide as something to be universalised by anyone to whom the light of truth has been revealed.

So Michel looks back at himself in the past, and is distressed by what he sees. Even the seemingly great virtue of 'stability of thought' (157), to which he had, as a conventional historian, formerly laid claim with some pride, now appears as something negative, for it has come to denote a lack of movement and of life. 'In the old days', he explains, 'I had taken pleasure in this very fixity, which enabled my mind to work with precision; the facts of history all appeared to me like specimens in a museum, or rather like plants in a herbarium, permanently dried.' That 'immobility', that 'terrifying fixity' of the past, is what makes the historian's work easier, or even possible; it is just *there*, as the proper object of his study. But for the later Michel it has, with all its fixity, come to constitute 'the immobility of death', a way of looking at the past which makes it all too 'easy to forget they [those specimen 'facts'] had once upon a time been juicy with sap and alive in the sun' (49–50).

So Michel comes to see his own past historical studies as being themselves detached from life – as being a sort of 'abstract and neutral acquaintance with the past', which in itself illustrates 'mere vanity' (64). And as such it denotes an activity in which he could no longer take any satisfaction or pleasure. Indeed, on the contrary, when visiting ancient sites in Sicily he finds that his historical learning actually militates against enjoyment: it 'became an encumbrance and hampered my joy'; so that 'I ended by despising the learning that had at first been my pride' (50). His own specialist work began to appear to him as 'senseless', inasmuch as it was far removed from the important questions of life; and he came to see that his professional colleagues were for the most part similarly remote from what really mattered, more interested in their researches than in living well. Indeed, they were 'on the verge of considering life merely as a vexatious hindrance to writing'; so it was small wonder that he 'found very little more pleasure and no more emotion in talking to them than in consulting a good dictionary' (88).

What Michel, like so many other students of history from Thucydides on, had originally believed was that he could learn some lessons from the past: on the assumption that that past resembled the present, 'I had actually dared to think that by questioning the dead I should be able to extort from them some secret information about life' (137). That remains of course for many an optimistic hope and a justification for studying the subject. But Michel came to realise that no such learning from the past was possible, and that the *important* questions of life could never be answered by looking back in that way.

It was his discovery or identification of the nature of those important questions that changed him so fundamentally as to make him feel that his previous studies were now irrelevant: 'the studies that up to then had been my whole life now seemed to me to have a mere accidental and conventional connexion with myself' (50). For they failed to address what he came to realise was the central issue: his own self-knowledge and his own identity. So he asks: 'inasmuch as I was a man, did I know myself at all? I had only just been born and could not as yet know *what* I had been born. It was that I had to find out' (51); and in the matter of finding that out, of finding out what constitutes humanity, history provided no help at all. 'How could the ancient past have answered my present question?' For his present question related not to what had been done, but to what might be done *better*: 'What can man do more? that is what seemed to me important to know. Is what man has hitherto said all that he *could* say? Is there nothing in himself he has overlooked? Can he do nothing but repeat himself?' (137).

So we are back with the old Aristotelian distinction between what has been and what might be. For Michel, history's concern with what has been, at the expense of a more poetic consideration of what might be, rendered it useless in answering life's fundamental questions: it was focused on a supposed past actuality which served only to reinforce a present that resembled it; it implied (as Martin Davies has more recently insisted[16]) only 'more of the same'. And he became increasingly aware that something more than that was needed – something whose existence, far from being revealed, was actually being *concealed*, overlaid and hidden, by contemporary culture: 'every day there grew stronger in me a confused consciousness of untouched treasures somewhere lying covered up, hidden, smothered by culture and decency and morality' (137). And the recovery of that undefined 'treasure' was the only possible objective for historians to set themselves: there could be no 'interest in historical studies except as a means of *psychological* investigation' (137, my emphasis) – investigation, that is, into human selfhood and aspiration, concerning *how to live*.

This is one point where we are immediately reminded of the eighteenth-century French philosophe Jean-Jacques Rousseau, who may be seen to anticipate Gide here and in a number of important respects; for he too was concerned with the central problem of how to live. As he puts it in his educational tract *Émile* (1762), '*Life* is the trade I would teach him.'[17] No less than Michel, he advocates a return to the 'natural' life that has been overlaid by supposedly 'civilised' developments. So in his *Discourse on the Arts and Sciences*, he specifically argues against what is conventionally termed 'progress': humans in his view have become the more corrupted, the more alienated from 'nature' they become; so that it is desirable to revert to the structures and values of earlier times in order to live well. 'From our earliest years', he asserts, 'a foolish education clutters up our minds and corrupts our judgement.'[18]

He goes on similarly to insist in *Émile*, that the 'civilised man' has become nothing better than 'a slave'. Liberation from slavery must be the aim, and that could be achieved only by 'fix[ing] your eyes on nature, [and] follow[ing] the path traced by her'; for it is 'an incontrovertible rule that the first impulses of nature are always right'. Ignoring, or rather positively rejecting, orthodox generally accepted values, the 'truly free' man 'desires what he is able to perform, and *does what he desires*': that is the 'fundamental maxim' underlying

---

[16] See Martin L. Davies, *Historics: Why History Dominates Contemporary Society*, London, Routledge, 2006.

[17] Jean-Jacques Rousseau, *Émile* [1762], trans. Barbara Foxley, London, Dent, 1911, p. 9 (my emphasis).

[18] Jean-Jacques Rousseau, *Discourse on the Sciences and Arts*, in *The Collected Writings of Rousseau*, ed. Roger D. Masters and Christopher Kelly, vol. 2, Hanover and London, University Press of New England, 1992, p. 17 (translation adapted).

Rousseau's education for his pupil Émile, and it later forms the starting point for Michel's philosophy.[19]

As with Michel, too, Rousseau selects History for particular consideration and critique. It is, he suggests, a 'ridiculous error' to impose a study of history upon children too young to have developed their own moral bearings. The subject is thought to be within their grasp, as being 'merely a collection of facts'; but the narration of mere 'physical and external movements' is valueless, teaching 'absolutely nothing'. Indeed, that 'factual' approach robs the study 'of all that makes it interesting, giv[ing] neither pleasure nor information': what is required, rather, is the admission of a moral dimension, enabling some real understanding of causes and effects. In this respect, Rousseau can be seen as a forerunner, not only of Gide but also of Dickens and those other fiction-based critics, all of whom we have seen asking or at least implying the same old question: 'But what is meant by this word "fact"?'[20]

The epiphany, or moment of revelation, that led to Michel's own professional and personal re-evaluations was brought about through a serious and prolonged illness, from which he nearly dies. The secret of life, as he explains, is the secret 'of one who had known death' (90). It is the possibility and proximity of death that provokes his awareness of the potentialities of life and of his own selfhood, and that new awareness involves a changing of perspective in which he is helped on his way by his friend Ménalque. Ménalque conveniently articulates in a coherent form some conclusions towards which Michel has for some time been independently moving: it is he who first explicitly formulates the model of amoral individualism that is to lie at the heart of the new historian, and it is he who practically exemplifies in his own life and actions the theoretical position towards which Michel had been finding his way.

Thus Ménalque is clear from the outset that he cares nothing for conventional morality. He is not concerned to live as others think he should live: acceptance of other people's judgements in such matters is nothing more or less than an abnegation of personal responsibility. So, he insists, 'my only claim is to be natural, and the pleasure I feel in an action, I take as a sign that I ought to do it'. From that highly individualistic (and, one might say, convenient) perspective, those people who simply follow convention 'live in a state of psychological distortion': afraid of being themselves, or of making individual choices, they passively accept models or patterns imposed upon them by others. They are fearful of their own potentialities – of what they themselves as autonomous individuals might prove to be: 'It is his own self that each of them

---

[19] *Émile*, pp. 10, 14, 56, 48 (my emphasis).

[20] *Émile*, p. 74.

is most afraid of resembling.' So they set up patterns or models by which to live and develop, but without even choosing these for themselves: each simply 'accepts a pattern that has been chosen for him'. Yet it is, of course, as Ménalque insists, just that part of each individual which *differentiates* him from all other people that, from its very rarity, 'makes our special value'. So it is surely ironic that 'that is the very thing people try to suppress'. They 'think they love *life*', but all they do is 'go on *imitating*' (100, my emphases).

Recounting these theories to Michel, Ménalque was preaching to the already converted, for what he was saying was exactly what his friend had said a month earlier to his wife Marceline. But there was nonetheless a fundamental difference between their respective positions: Michel realises that Ménalque is not just formulating *theories*, but is actually living out his beliefs in *practice* – applying them to real life. And in that practice lies his superiority. For 'alas, how pale words become, when compared with deeds!' Ménalque's life, he realises, indeed his 'slightest action [is] a thousand times more eloquent than my lectures' (97).

In his emphasis on practice, his friend does, as Michel notes, lie in a long tradition of moral philosophy: 'How well I understood now that the great philosophers of antiquity, whose teaching was almost wholly moral, worked by example as much – even more than by precept' (97). It has, then, long been considered necessary to *live* one's philosophy; and that necessity continues. As we have seen R. G. Collingwood, Wyndham Lewis, and others insisting some decades later, academic subjects should not be removed from real, practical life: if they become overly theoretical and remote from life, they die. 'Do you know the reason why poetry and philosophy are nothing but dead letter nowadays? It is because they have severed themselves from life' (106). They keep themselves 'as far away as possible from the disturbing reality', and while they may seem to be alive, they are not even aware that they are so (88–9).

And historians themselves can be seen to suffer from that same malaise. They too profess a subject that lacks contact with the practicalities of life. In fact, with its focus on the past, history positively militates against proper attention being paid to the present and future. So the past is something from which, in proto-postmodernist manner, Ménalque has succeeded in actually liberating himself: 'I do not want to recollect', he explains; for 'I should be afraid of preventing the future and of allowing the past to encroach on me. It is out of the utter forgetfulness of yesterday that I create every new hour's freshness' (196).

Consciousness of the freshness of every new hour is what needs to be cultivated: that was the lesson taught by Michel's near brush with death. The present moment is what is all-important: 'I was conscious of nothing in life but what the moment brought, but what the moment carried away' (60). For Michel, both as individual person and as historian, that newly awakened awareness marked a decisive break from his former life. After his long illness, 'I had thought I should rise again the same as before and be able without difficulty to reknit my present to my past'; but he could not do so (49). 'When . . . I wanted to start my work again and immerse myself once more in a minute study of the past, I discovered that something had, if not destroyed, at any rate modified my pleasure in it . . . and this something was the feeling of the present.' Henceforth, for him, history could not simply be studied, as we continue to say, 'in its own right': it had to include involvement with the present. 'Nowadays', explains Michel, 'if I still took any pleasure in history, it was by imagining it *in the present.*' And that has implications for how historical work is done, for, as Michel continues, 'the great political events of the past moved me less than the *feeling* that began to revive in me for the poets or for a few men of action' (49–50, my emphases).

That intrusion of feeling is, of course, highly significant, marking a turn from the conventional ideal of rational detachment to one of romantic involvement. What Michel is effectively doing is repudiating the intellect in favour of the emotions. 'Oh', he exclaims, 'if only I could rid my mind of all this intolerable logic!' (147). More important than thought is feeling: 'I thought of nothing; what mattered thoughts? I *felt* extraordinarily' (42). Michel's autobiography at this point begins uncannily to resemble that of John Stuart Mill, which we considered in Chapter 3, and marks a renewed emphasis on 'romanticism' in historiography, such as we have noted in the work of twenty-first-century theorists like Frank Ankersmit.

That vividly experienced *feeling* affected, in true romantic fashion, Michel's relationship with the external world of nature: 'it seemed to me that it was no longer with my sight alone that I became aware of the landscape, but that I *felt* it as well by some sense of touch, which my curious power of sympathy illimitably enlarged' (114). And that feeling of direct contact with nature had implications for memory – and thence for history too. For, as with Proust's savour of his madeleine, and as with Huizinga's claim to have enjoyed direct experience of the Middle Ages through the trigger of a painting by Van Eyck, 'the whole past suddenly rose up, as though it had been lying in wait for my approach to close over and submerge me'; and all Michel had to do was listen 'to the voice of my past as it recalled the slightest details to my memory' (70). As he describes elsewhere, 'my reawakened senses now remembered a whole ancient history of their own – recomposed for themselves a vanished past' (39).

In some way, then, the individual past is being directly retrieved, and with it an 'authentic' selfhood that has somehow become buried in that past and supplanted. 'The miscellaneous mass of acquired knowledge of every kind that has overlain the mind gets peeled off in places like a mask of paint, exposing the bare skin – the very flesh of the authentic creature that had lain hidden beneath it'; and it becomes Michel's self-imposed task to rediscover 'that authentic creature'.[21] The 'tabula rasa' of his mind at birth had to be retrieved, cleansed of all its subsequent inscriptions: the usurper – 'the creature who was due to teaching, whom education had painted on the surface' – is to be despised and 'shaken off'. Comparing himself to a palimpsest, he 'tasted the scholar's joy when he discovers under more recent writing, and on the same paper, a very ancient and infinitely more precious text'; buried beneath the new was some relic of the old, something that, despite its value, had been superseded and, in John Donne's words, 'forgotten and lost'. But in order to reach and read that older and more valuable text, it is 'first of all necessary to efface the more recent one' (51). So, in his Rousseauesque quest for original innocence, Michel applied himself to 'systematically condemning and suppressing everything which I believed I owed to my past education and early moral beliefs' (52). His aim now was to reveal the 'perfectible being' underneath; his only interest lay in 'striving after this unknown and vaguely imagined perfection' (53).

That process of cleansing implied, first, repudiating his own previous historical pursuits inasmuch as they involved too much interest in the past; so that, even while still in Sicily, he declined to visit ancient sites: 'Deliberately disdainful of my learning, and in scorn of my scholarly tastes, I refused to visit Agrigentum' (52); for that had become for him an irrelevance and a distraction. And on his return home, he completely revised his series of lectures, pouring into them, he says, 'all my newly born passion', and applying his theory of individual psychology to the wider field of history. For just as the original authentic individual had become contaminated by later accretions, and so lost to consciousness, so too, his thesis ran, more generally, had culture. It too, having originally been pristine and creative, had become atrophied and dead. It too, originally life-enhancing, had become nothing better than a constraint on creative thinking, a veritable '*destroyer* of life'.

Thus, referring to the later classical period, Michel explains:

I depicted artistic culture as welling up in a whole people, like a secretion, which is first a sign of plethora, of a superabundance of health, but which

---

[21] Again cf. Rousseau: 'God makes all things good; man meddles with them, and they become evil.' *Émile*, p. 5. And Keith Jenkins similarly writes of 'the possibility of new thoughts free from the shackles of history and ethics'. *Why History?: Ethics and Postmodernity*, London, Routledge, 1999, p. 29.

afterwards stiffens, hardens, forbids the perfect contact of the mind with nature, hides under the persistent appearance of life a diminution of life, turns into an outside sheath, in which the cramped mind languishes and pines, in which at last it dies. Finally, pushing my thought to its logical conclusion, I showed Culture, born of life, as the destroyer of life. (90)[22]

Such grandiose pronouncements always leave their authors vulnerable, and other historians, Michel ironically notes, 'criticised a tendency, as they phrased it, to too rapid generalisation'.

Their criticism, like that of contemporary historians in the context of postmodernism, may have been induced, not only by the appearance of disciplinary extravagance, but also by fear; for Michel's newly proposed model of history did of course additionally imply a rejection of the moral structures inherent in modern culture. It was, so he suggested, only by repudiating those moral constraints, that so inhibit individuality, that people can recover their own 'authentic' selves; and it therefore becomes an important function of history to act (now in Foucauldian mode) as a liberator, by revealing the roots of those constraints and the ways that humans have become imprisoned by them. It is their unthinking acceptance of principles derived from others that leads him to the seemingly extreme assertion: 'I hate people of principle' – an assertion with which Ménalque agrees, inasmuch as such people 'never do anything but what their principles have decreed they should do' (101), failing, that is, to consider the specificities (and so propriety) of their application.

One may be reminded here of Derrida, who insists on the need for moral decisions to be made, not from the supposed authority of generalised templates, but rather by reference to the particularities and specificities of any unique situation; there is never ever any 'given' answer to moral dilemmas, in which we are always and unavoidably confronted by the ultimate 'undecidability of the decision'. 'I invent the who, and I decide who decides what', as Derrida writes, sounding not unlike Michel. Or, as Keith Jenkins has asserted: 'for my decision to be mine, it has to be, in the end, ungrounded . . . my responsibility' – which is another reason why 'It is no good having a history here to "tell you what to do".'[23]

So what we are facing here – what, through the characters of Ménalque and Michel, is being recommended by Gide – is not only a psychological rebirth,

---

[22] Cf. John Burrow in relation to Tennyson: 'All cultures, institutions and creeds are ultimately liable to petrify into formulae and must then be cast off.' Laurence Lerner (ed.), *The Victorians*, London, Methuen, 1978, p. 136.

[23] Derrida, quoted by Jenkins, *Why History?*, p. 39; and see p. 21.

but also (as contributing to that) a revised historical study and a repudiation of conventional morality. That is all, of course, an exciting (or frightening) prospect, as re-visions and new beginnings are. As Michel describes his own renaissance: 'There was more here than a convalescence; there was an increase, a recrudescence of life, the influx of a richer, warmer blood' (52). But that comes at a price – the price of personal, historical, cultural, and socio-political stability. And that, it seems, even a century on, may still be a price too high to pay for the acquisition of a new history and thereby 'a new self'.

Another new self: Tim O'Brien and the manipulation of memory

Another more recent (indeed, contemporary) writer of fiction who has shown great interest in the formation of identity and its relationship with the past – with history and memory – is Tim O'Brien. His book *In the Lake of the Woods* (1995) centres on the experience of John Wade, who is so appalled by what he sees and does in the Vietnam War – and in particular the notorious My Lai massacre – that, having 'lost touch with some defining part of himself',[24] he tries to reconstitute and redefine that self. Like Gide's Michel, then, he attempts to fashion a new identity – a new self – which in his case necessitates the removal from consciousness of a part of his past and so the rewriting of his history.

O'Brien's book more generally invites further consideration of the whole relationship between fiction and history, and it once more serves to blur any sharp distinction between the two. For, on the one hand, it is decisively claimed by the author as a work of fiction; yet, on the other hand, problematic treatments of the past lie at its very core, and these inevitably (albeit implicitly) provoke related questions concerning the actual nature and purpose of history. Thus, in an introductory disclaimer O'Brien is insistent that his novel is to 'be read as a work of *fiction*', and that all the characters are his own imaginative inventions. But the story that he tells is heavily reliant on a 'real' historical

---

[24] Tim O'Brien, *In the Lake of the Woods*, London, Penguin, 1995, p. 147; further references will be given in the text. This book is the subject of an extremely interesting essay by Bruce Franklin – 'Kicking the Denial Syndrome: Tim O'Brien's *In the Lake of the Woods*', in Mark C. Carnes (ed.), *Novel History: Historians and Novelists Confront America's Past (and Each Other)*, London, Simon & Schuster, 2001, pp. 332–43. See also Joanna Bourke, *An Intimate History of Killing*, London, Granta, 2000, esp. ch. 6.

past; and the very form of the novel invites comparisons with historical procedures, with some chapters providing 'Evidence' (from diverse but variously relevant contextualising sources), and others offering a 'Hypothesis' (rather than definitive account) of what occurred – that latter approach underpinning the lack of certainty and narrative closure within the novel as a whole. There are footnotes, too, in orthodox historical mode to 'real' authorities (such as books and court testimonies), with references duly provided for quotations; and there are also a number of authorial comments inserted from time to time – notably concerning Vietnam, where O'Brien actually served in the infantry in 1969.[25] It is, then, perhaps unsurprising that the book should have received a prize from the Society of American Historians in 1995, for the best novel that year on an *historical* theme.

Within that theme, and most crucially, is the matter of memories and their attempted suppression: it is their insistent intrusion into present consciousness that ultimately leads towards an apparently tragic outcome in the case of the main character, John Wade. For Wade's experience in Vietnam continues to haunt him, despite his best attempts to forget and suppress memories of actions and events from which he wishes to dissociate himself. His perceived need for a new identity – a new self – derives in particular from his having been caught up in the notorious massacre at the village of My Lai (or Thuan Yen) on 16 March 1968. O'Brien's brilliantly conveyed descriptions of that event provoke recollection of Tolstoy's earlier insistence on the unreliability of eyewitness accounts of the chaos inherent in any battle: a straightforward narrative may be applied afterwards, with the benefit of hindsight, or the disbenefit of vested interests, but participants and agents at the actual time may well have been wandering in a haze of uncomprehending and disorientated disbelief.

Indeed, as we read here (and as has been reported from elsewhere in other conflicts), for those fighting it, the whole war in Vietnam was something of a mystery: 'Nobody knew what it was about, or why they were there, or who started it, or who was winning, or how it might end' (72–3). It was being fought a world away from home; the terrain was alien; the enemy was usually invisible, and not easily (if at all) identifiable from civilians; danger and death could come from any direction at any moment; nothing was clear-cut, nothing definite – except perhaps the experience of losing friends and colleagues. And

---

[25] Tim O'Brien's actual experience in Vietnam is more fully described in *If I Die in a Combat Zone* [1973], London, Flamingo, 1995: see esp. chapter 13 and fol. concerning My Lai, one year after the massacre. And see also *The Things They Carried* [1990], New York, Broadway Books, 1998 – another book described on the title page as 'a work of fiction', but written in autobiographical mode about the experience of war in Vietnam.

in that context of confusion, mystery, uncertainty and fear, frustration follows, and a desire to take it out on anyone or anything. So Lieutenant Calley (an historical figure of the time) is described as raging against nature, pointing his gun at the earth and firing twenty rounds into it, and then shooting at the grass and palm trees. And so in My Lai, he and his men simply shoot at any living thing that moves – animals and men and women and children and babies.

In O'Brien's account, then, we read of how John Wade, known (from his lifelong interest in magic) to himself and his mates as 'the Sorcerer', enters the place:

> Just inside the village, Sorcerer found a pile of dead goats.
> He found a pretty girl with her pants down. She was dead too. She looked at him cross-eyed. Her hair was gone.
> He found dead dogs, dead chickens.
> Farther along, he encountered someone's forehead. He found three dead water buffalo. He found a dead monkey. He found ducks pecking at a dead toddler . . .
> Simpson was killing children. P[rivate] F[irst] C[lass] Weatherby was killing whatever he could kill. A row of corpses lay in the pink-to-purple sunshine along the trail – teenagers and old women and two babies and a young boy. Most were dead, some were almost dead. The dead lay very still. The almost-dead did twitching things until PFC Weatherby had occasion to reload and make them fully dead. (107)

That extract, with its deadpan style, gives some idea of the haze through which Wade goes through this experience; and after encountering many further atrocities, we are told that 'all he could do was close his eyes and kneel there and wait for whatever was wrong with the world to right itself'. It seemed to him that such things could not be happening, could not have happened, could not be real; and in the end, his only way of coping with them was to try to forget. ' "Go away", he murmured . . . (108) . . . and in the months and years ahead . . . the impossibility [of what had taken place] itself would become the richest and deepest and most profound memory. This could not have happened. Therefore it did not' (109).

John Wade's presentation of a new self thus requires the obliteration of a part of his past – and that necessitates in turn both falsification of public records (that primary evidence on which historians rely) and also personal forgetfulness. So we read how he contrived to make significant amendments to the army records, making it appear that he was not even a member of the Company responsible for the events of that day: his own part was officially 'written out' of history – an excision that remained unidentified until an investigation following his attempted entry into national politics. But the more personal problem anyway remained – of how to write the whole thing out of his own mind.

With that aim, he 'did his best to apply the trick of forgetfulness' (147). For 'all you want is to forget'; and actually 'none of it ever seemed real in the first place' (186). So for Wade, it was like making his mind into a blackboard – a strategy he had learnt as a child – in order to 'erase the bad stuff' and replace it with 'pretty new pictures' (133). He 'punched an erase button at the centre of his thoughts' (213); and for much of the time, his sorcerer's trick worked: 'over time the whole incident took on a dreamlike quality, only half remembered, half believed' (268). It became a secret 'so secret that he sometimes kept it secret from himself' (73). But Virginia Woolf's 'terrible pounce of memory' could not in the end be evaded: visions came back to haunt him, of an old man whom he had shot, having mistaken his wooden hoe for a weapon, and of the murderous PFC Weatherby, whom he had also shot when he smiled down at him as he lay at the bottom of an irrigation ditch.

The elimination of the past from memory, and thence from the self, proves to be, then (as we have already noted in Chapter 4), not so easily accomplished. The wish to do so is understandable enough, and as one who had personally experienced not dissimilar episodes, Tim O'Brien himself sympathises with his 'fictional' character's attempt to forget: *'from my own experience* I can understand how he kept things buried, how he could never face or even recall the butchery at Thuan Yen' (p. 298, n. 127, my emphasis). He concedes the necessity of that coping strategy, which somehow 'makes reality unreal' and includes the making of 'erasures'; and he confesses that his writing may well be his own way of remembering and coming to terms with his past.

Somehow, in short – as Dominick LaCapra has argued in relation to 'extreme events' – the past has to be accommodated rather than jettisoned, memories 'worked through' rather than excised.[26] In John Wade's 'fictional' case, the ultimate outcome of his attempt to manipulate memory remains uncertain, with the end of his story left deliberately unclear; but from the evidence of earlier parts of the novel, the immediate results of his attempted suppression of the past prove wholly negative, with his public reputation and political career in ruins, and his private relationships and marriage utterly destroyed. His attempt to present a new identity decoupled from his past proved disastrous, and served further to re-emphasise the need for a coherent

---

[26] See e.g. Dominick LaCapra, *History in Transit: Experience, Identity, Critical Theory*, Ithaca and London, Cornell University Press, 2004.

biographical narrative – however much that may always have to be a blend of the historically 'factual' and imaginative fiction.

Conclusion

The mixing of fact and fiction in the construction, and in the attempted reconstruction, of identity is indicative of a less than consistent and coherent selfhood. Both André Gide's Michel and Tim O'Brien's John Wade exemplify personalities that are, in some sense, 'split', internally divided; and in their very inconsistency they exemplify also, if not a universal condition, then at least a human type that recurs in literature and life. For the development of an 'alter ego', an alternative self, seems not uncommon; and it can serve to enable an individual to get the best of both (or many) worlds – sometimes to fit into a variety of social groups and contexts, against which at other times he or she might choose to rebel.

That sort of inconsistent behaviour may seem to smack of schizophrenia, and it certainly points to problems for historical explanation and representation, for which a degree of consistency is generally presupposed. But literary representations of flexible, complex, or divided, identities date back at least to the nineteenth century – the iconic example of *Dr Jekyll and Mr Hyde* (1886) being a fictional account by Robert Louis Stevenson of a man with a personality split between extremes of good and evil. Such treatments of unstable identities, or 'divided selves', proliferate through the twentieth century, when they become a regular theme within such books and films as *The Three Faces of Eve* (1957) – which is loosely based on the true story of a woman who veered between self-effacement and more extrovert behaviour – and these works, it is noteworthy, are evidently intended somehow to *disconcert* their readers and viewers – that is, to unsettle them from their unthinking acquiescence in the integrity and seamlessness of personal identities.

Yet that propensity to unsettle derives, perhaps, from their representation (albeit in an extreme manner) of a condition that is recognisably universal. And it is disconcerting to realise the limits of our ability to understand, explain, and predict – disconcerting in real life and also in the theoretical reaches of academia. For the former, it does seem desirable to have the ability to sum people up, to categorise them within certain types or groups, so that we can then feel reasonably competent to foretell in various circumstances how they are likely to respond. And generally, of course, we succeed in doing that, on the admitted basis of evaluating probabilities. Which renders us the more uneasy when we fail – when that friendly guy next door turns out to be a rapist, or the trusted financial adviser is revealed as a fraudster. In such cases, the narrative in which we have inscribed people is disrupted – or, to put it more critically, invalidated; it no longer enables us to understand their pasts as we have done previously, much less predict their futures. So those earlier narratives are exposed as having been nothing more reliable than fiction all along.

And that has obvious and profound implications for the more theoretical matter of historiography. Anomalous behaviour – or behaviour that fails to cohere with people's identities as we have hitherto perceived and defined them – serves as a serious challenge to professional procedures. For in such a situation, we are bound to accept either that our previous model was inadequate, in that it failed to predict or account for what happened, or that people simply act in unpredictable and inexplicable ways – in which case (unable to perceive any possibility of explanation) we might as well give up the whole practice of history forthwith. Either way, the supposedly 'scientific' and *factual* character of history is challenged: our 'take' on the past – in the case of identities both personal and public – has been found to need revision; it is exposed as having been defective, as having been (at least in part) no more reliable than *fiction*.

Further reading

Gide, André, *The Immoralist* [1902], trans. Dorothy Bussy, Harmondsworth, Penguin, 1960.

LaCapra, Dominick, *History in Transit: Experience, Identity, Critical Theory*, Ithaca and London, Cornell University Press, 2004.

O'Brien, Tim, *In the Lake of the Woods*, London, Penguin, 1995.

Taylor, Charles, *Sources of the Self: The Making of Modern Identity*, Cambridge, Cambridge University Press, 1989.

Woolf, Virginia, *The Waves* [1931], Harmondsworth, Penguin, 1951.

Fiction and the functions of history

We have so far been considering the meeting of fiction and history with regard, mainly, to the latter's nature – to the perennial question, 'What is history?' In this chapter we turn more specifically to the closely related question of its purpose: 'What is history for?' That question we have already seen raised by Penelope Lively's fictional historian Claudia Hampton, and also by such writers as Tolstoy and Wyndham Lewis with their proposals for the injection of an ethical dimension into the subject. Here, after some preliminary discussion, we look at it more closely by reference first to Thomas Pynchon's V *and Don DeLillo's* Libra, *which reveal political dimensions, and second to Graham Swift's* Waterland *with its conclusion that history's function may be to teach a recognition of our own limited ability to provide explanations.*

All history classes should ask, What is the point of history? Why history?[1]

The history teacher in Graham Swift's novel *Waterland* has one particularly awkward pupil who insists on asking about the *point* of the subject, about what history is actually *for*, and *why* it should be studied. History teachers no doubt learn to expect such questions from sceptical students, but they nonetheless sometimes find it hard to answer them satisfactorily. For it is a question not often asked by historians themselves, who tend simply to assume the intrinsic value of their subject: for them, it does not need external justification; it is not *for* anything else; it is just good for 'its own sake' – or for constituting an important part of the more general human pursuit of truth.

---

[1] Graham Swift, *Waterland* [1983], London, Picador, 1992, p. 106.

And the trouble is that, once it is seen that history is always and inevitably history *for* some purpose, it becomes harder, if not impossible, to deny its less than wholly 'factual' nature.

Partly to avoid that problem, the question of history's function is often answered by reference to its methodology. It is claimed that the subject necessitates (or at least encourages) the acquisition of a number of practical skills that can subsequently be deployed elsewhere – skills such as analysis, the use of evidence, the formulation of hypotheses, the presentation of logically structured arguments, and so on. These skills can be learnt through 'doing' history, and can then be usefully 'transferred' to other contexts. History in a sense becomes a means to a more general educational (and thence work-orientated) end.

Where the focus is thus on *methodology*, questions may arise concerning the propriety of various approaches – whether, for instance, the emphasis should be on analysis or empathy – but the subject matter of histories in that context need hardly be an issue. But when attention does turn to history's *content*, further questions inevitably arise about what that content actually *is*, or should be, and how and why one subject, rather than some alternative, is included in what has come to be the generally accepted story of how we got to be where we now are; for that story is often claimed, by politicians as well as by historians, as having an important function in revealing a shared heritage, and so forming the basis for social, national, and even supra-national cohesion. As we considered above in Chapter 6, the narrative of history is widely assumed to be of vital importance for the construction of identity; so it is hardly surprising if the content and the nature of that narrative periodically becomes subject to review.

But when it is reviewed, history's whole problematic relationship with fiction once more comes to the surface. For 'history' is seen to be not some natural monolithic structure, which is just there, to be taught and learnt (like elementary mathematics or physics of the natural world), but rather a hybrid entity incorporating choices made with particular purposes in mind. Where the totality of the past remains elusive, appropriate selections are made for purposes thought to be appropriate; and questions then immediately arise about who made the selections, and who decided on what was to be considered 'appropriate' – what their motivations were, and why they had them. It becomes clear that history may serve to provide morally desirable examples for emulation, or to supply purposeful narratives to confirm identities, or to justify institutional structures, wars, national boundaries, imperial destinies, or indeed anything at all. But it is thereby additionally revealed as an arbitrary construction, shot through with choice and contingency, and, for all the claims to the contrary, a blend of evidentially based 'facts' and imaginative 'fictions'.

History, the pursuit of fact, and 'fabulation'

It is worth recalling that it has always been claimed that the fundamental purpose of history is to record 'the truth' about the past – in (no doubt overly) simplistic terms, to leave a true or *factual* record of what actually happened. Historians, wrote Sir Philip Sidney in the late sixteenth century, have truth, or 'veritie . . . written in theirs fore-heads'. Their job is to bring 'images of true matters, such as indeede were done, and not such as fantastically or falsely may be suggested to have been doone'; they are 'bound to tell things as things were'.[2]

Sidney there distinguishes clearly between history, which records the truth about actual past events, and, by contrast, fiction, the concern of which is with imaginative reports of things that may not even have actually happened. Yet the blurring of the two is immediately apparent, and Sidney himself has little confidence in the ability of historians to fulfil the seemingly simple function assigned to them. For he realises that they rely on earlier authorities who may themselves be less than reliable: the historian, he says, bases his own authority 'upon other histories, whose greatest authorities are built upon the notable foundation of Heare-say' – and mere hearsay, or reports from other people of dubious reliability, is hardly a satisfactory foundation for a supposedly true and authoritative record. And unreliability is compounded when we realise that the historian often finds himself recording events, the causes of which remain unknown to him; so that inasmuch as he suggests a cause, he is operating not so much as an historian but rather as a poet. 'Manie times, he must tell events, whereof he can yeelde no cause: or, if hee doe, it must be poeticall' – an indication that, when he is at his best, the historian is in fact, however paradoxically, exercising those speculative and imaginative characteristics that are conventionally assigned to the poet (someone with whom he is traditionally contrasted); or, as Sidney concludes, 'the best of the Historian is subiect to the Poet'.[3]

---

[2] Sir Philip Sidney, *An Apologie for Poetrie* [1595], ed. Evelyn S. Shuckburgh, Cambridge, Cambridge University Press, 1891, pp. 4, 20–21.

[3] Sidney, *Apologie*, pp. 15, 21–2.

As a further paradox, it can be seen that it is the poet, rather than the historian, who succeeds in telling the truth, or who at least avoids the imputation of lying. For the poet disdains to be subjected to the rules imposed upon the historian, and since he never claims to tell the truth, he can hardly be accused of failing to do so. The historian, on the other hand, through his ambitious claims in the face of all the associated problems, does expose himself to such criticism. Aspiring to tell the truth, he ends up failing to do so, and although that may be for good reason, he can then be justifiably accused of lying: 'the Historian, affirming many things, can in the cloudy knowledge of mankinde hardly escape from many lyes'.[4]

Finally, as another indication of the historian's failure, Sidney notes how he does not even fulfil his other main (and this time moral) function – that traditional function of providing examples for wider emulation. For he is, of course, as an historian in Aristotelian mode, not concerned with what should be, but he must, rather, focus on what *is* (or was). That is, he is bound to record what actually happens – and that, alas, is often far from being what we think *ought* to happen. In other words, in this 'real' world, evil people sometimes prosper at the expense of the good; so that the historical record might well have an effect diametrically opposite to what is hoped for – actually encouraging the wicked in their ways, and frightening others away from doing good. In Sidney's words, 'the Historian, being captived to the trueth of a foolish world, is many times a terror from well doing, and an incouragement to unbrideled wickednes'.[5]

That message, of the essentially negative effect of history as a record of human evil rather than good, is (as we have seen in Chapter 5) reiterated in the twentieth century by Wyndham Lewis. But on the whole, it seems that history's effect has been perceived as beneficial, showing, as histories generally do, a steady progress from a less favoured past to a preferable present. For historians have tended to structure their narratives in such a way as to indicate a trajectory in line with their own interests – whether those be the development of social structures and political institutions, or scientific and technological achievements, or the ability of artists accurately to portray nature and the human form. It is that teleological development, or development in the context of, and towards, some predefined 'end', that was identified and criticised by Herbert Butterfield as 'the Whig interpretation' of the past – an interpretation that was inherently reassuring about the present and optimistic about the future, but was of course open to the charge of bias (or something less than strict 'factuality'). From an alternative standpoint, doom-laden histories could (and sometimes did, and do) chart a steady decline, whether in terms of 'culture' (however defined) or human sociability or some other yardstick by which their authors are impressed. But dentistry usually gains the day, with few wishing to venture, even imaginatively, for their treatments back in time. So that it becomes the function of historians, on the whole, to provide reassurance about things overall getting steadily better.

Even the chronological procedures used by historians appear to imply such progress: as Julian Barnes – significantly a writer of fiction – has noted, their very dating system, in which, obviously, year succeeds to year, seems to indicate a natural forward progression. As we look *backwards* in time, 'civilisation' seems to recede – so that we are amazed when we encounter the wonders of ancient Egypt, which seem in some respects to equal, if not surpass, our own; and as we go *forwards* in time, we expect improvement – improvement defined in terms of the way we live today (so in material rather than spiritual ways). Dates, then, as Barnes (writing here as the author of a fictional 'history of the world') concludes, 'want to make us think we're always progressing, always going forward'. So 'we allow ourselves to be bullied' by them: we readily accept them as the structural framework for our historical narratives, since they back up our self-justificatory stories; they may recede backwards into prehistorical darkness, but they open up ahead into posthistorical illumination.[6]

And that in itself serves an important purpose, for despite appearances history is not, of course, a straightforward account of 'what happened'. (How could the infinite ever be bounded within a finite work of any kind?) It is, rather, 'just what historians tell us' – and having a vested interest in keeping us, as well as themselves, sane and happy, what they tell us is a story that derives from 'fabulation', as Barnes calls it – a story that reveals 'a flow of events, a complex narrative', but one that, for all its complexity, is ultimately to be seen as 'connected, explicable', with one thing leading logically on to another, displaying 'connections, progress, meaning'. Without the stability provided by such a narrative, 'we fret and writhe in bandaged uncertainty'; so naturally 'we make up a story' that will account for any lacunae in our knowledge or for any aspects of our past that we would rather be without – 'to cover the facts we don't know or can't accept'. With that function, history in the end is inevitably in part made up, *fictive*: 'Our panic and our pain are only eased by soothing *fabulation*' – by making up stories that enable us to feel all right; and then 'we call it history'.

[6] Julian Barnes, *A History of the World in Ten 1/2 Chapters*, London, Picador, 1990. Quotations are from pp. 241–2.

It is, then, once again a novelist, a writer of fiction, who clarifies in a highly entertaining way that an important function of history is to reduce an essentially unstable and complex past to a story or narrative that provides reassurance. Reassurance is achieved by the inclusion of causally connected explanations, by the avoidance of any negativity and the appearance of steadily progressive development, and above all by the bestowal of meaning on a past, the contemplation of which otherwise leaves us insecure and riven with anxiety. And – bringing us back decisively to our theme of history's meeting and relationship with fiction – it is recognised that any such story, any such narrative, is bound to be not, in the traditional sense, factual, but (at least in part) inevitably *fictional*, a 'soothing fabulation'.

The fictive nature of history's components is evident not least from the patently contrived nature of much of the evidence on which it is (often so confidently) based. We have already noted how literary texts, even where these purport to represent eyewitness reports, are inevitably partial – in both senses of that word, as implying both a limited and also prejudiced selection from the whole. But the scepticism properly due towards these needs to be extended to other forms of evidence, which may initially seem more reliable. Photographs and film, in particular, exude an aura of authenticity – appearing, as they often do, to convey a (if not the) truth about a past event in a supposedly 'objective' manner, free of any personal input or deception. The camera, as we are told, 'never lies': it produces fact, not fiction.

But even photographs – documentary evidence par excellence, as it might seem – can be fictive, as can be seen from the example of Joe Rosenthal's famous image of American marines raising the Stars and Stripes on the summit of Mount Suribachi on Iwo Jima in 1945. This not only won the Pulitzer Prize at the time, but it has also become 'perhaps the most reproduced photograph in American history', and even 'an icon of US patriotic virtue' – being mimicked, for instance, in a photograph of firemen raising a flag at Ground Zero (after 9/11) on 12 September 2001. But that image, so emblematic of American hard won victory, and even constitutive now of a part of national identity, was actually a picture of a second flag-raising, staged, with a larger flag, after the fighting had died down. What initially looks like reliable historical evidence of what actually happened, spontaneously and disingenuously recorded by one there at the time, is revealed as in some sense inauthentic, as something posed later 'for the camera' – as not 'factual' after all, but essentially a 'fake'.[7]

History's ability to make us feel good – to make sense of events, and leave an impression of meaning and purpose – indicates one of its most important

---

[7] David Simpson, *London Review of Books*, 29 November 2007, pp. 25–7.

functions; but it fulfils that function by itself proving to be a hybrid mixture of fact and 'fabulation'.

Functions and fictionality

We shall return to that theme in our discussion of *Waterland* later in this chapter, but first let us consider how other functions assigned to history further reveal the inherently fictional nature of the subject – or at least the intrusion into histories of elements that are far from being strictly 'factual'. Most obvious – but not for that reason necessarily always acknowledged – is the ideological function long enjoyed by history of supporting some particular political position.

So, for example, historians have periodically been recruited in a revolutionary role – have been required to provide appropriate genealogies to underpin the claims of aspirants to power, and to compose historical trajectories that consist with (if not appear to necessitate) plans for future change. Millennia before the Christian era, Egyptian Pharaohs took care to have their names inscribed in lists that revealed their own legitimacy as successors to previous rulers; in Roman times, the prospective emperor Augustus contrived to consolidate his position through establishing links with eminent ancestors, tracing back his lineage to the very founders (however mythical) of his city; and using essentially similar techniques more recently, Adolf Hitler sought to have his credentials confirmed with the help of an historical narrative that, despite his humble birth, connected him with the glamorous achievements of earlier German nationalistic heroes. Where history has been used in that way to support the claims of would-be rulers, whether in the form of emperors, dictators, or kings, there is rarely much reason to disguise the imaginative input of creative propagandists; and few would wish to question the 'fictional' quality of such annals and narratives, constructed as they are for overtly political ends, and designed for a public assumed to be either naïvely credulous or too fearful to deny their 'historical' validity.

But history has also been utilised to underpin revolutionary political actors on the other, or more democratic, side: most notably, the French revolutionaries self-consciously modelled themselves on such earlier republican heroes as the Roman Brutus, acclaimed as a justified tyrannicide for the part he played in assassinating Julius Caesar, the alleged aspirant 'dictator'. Either way, for political supporters of 'left' or 'right', history has been summoned as an ally – as including a content that can be amended, remoulded, refigured, re-narrativised, in order to fit in, as required, with any programme or eventuality. And what that helps to show, once more, is that such histories can never be straightforwardly 'factual', but contain within their narratives (constructed with whatever diverse motivations) elements of what are best described as 'myths' or imaginatively contrived 'fictions'.

What is also shown from these examples is that history's function, whether again used by the political left or right, is the essentially conservative one of providing justifications, for the assumption or for the maintenance of power, from *continuities* from past to present – and thence to future. It is designed to *reassure*, by providing persuasive explanations that indicate a steady and progressive march (in any direction we choose) in which we can (and should) all keep safely in step; for that is what is ordained and *natural*.

For those continuities, initially manufactured but subsequently presupposed, include not least (as we considered in the preceding chapter) notions of what it is to be a human being. One cannot explain another person's or another people's actions without assuming that they possess, or have possessed, characteristics not too dissimilar from our own. Without the assumption of some such uniformity of character and motivation, they must remain outside our understanding – characterised, for our convenience, as 'others', such as primitive savages or the simply insane (with whom we do not need to be concerned). So the result is a levelling off of human potential, with appeals to a 'human nature' supposedly fixed and exemplary, and justifications in terms of 'it was ever thus', or 'well, what can you expect?' Terrible atrocities, as we learn from Thucydides, were committed in the Peloponnesian War, including in particular a massacre at the little town of Mycalessus in 413 BC, in which no living being survived a surprise attack from the enemy; so that, when we read of My Lai, another site of military atrocities, in 1968, we can seek refuge for our outrage in past parallels, and shrug them off as predictable outcomes of an ever-present and enduring aspect of 'human nature'. History seems, once more, to *justify* the present – to make it 'only natural'.

Yet the account that Thucydides left was inevitably only partial – referring to only a part of what happened. And it is possible that some other part – a potential part that has long since been lost to memory – may have told a different story and left a different impression, with at least some redeeming model of human behaviour. For in our own time, there have been many reports of the notorious massacre by US Marines at My Lai in Vietnam that have omitted (or just marginalised) the episode of Hugh Thompson – the helicopter pilot who, in defiance of what at the time was seeming 'normal', refused to join in the killing but acted independently to rescue those he could. That anomalous behaviour of one man constituted what might seem to be a minor episode in relation to the whole event, and one that could easily have been left unnoticed and unrecorded. But it could (and perhaps should) be reintroduced as the central, the most important part of the history of that day – as providing an alternative and preferable model of what human beings might become.

Would that then, we might ask, constitute a *distortion* of the historical narrative, making it less than an accurate and authentic, and so 'factual', record of what went on? Or would it be just as 'true' – only history told from an alternative perspective, with a different evaluation of what was ultimately important, and recording, as Wyndham Lewis proposed, a more positive view of 'human nature'? (For people, perhaps, as Coleridge insisted, 'should be weighed, not counted'.) These questions at the very least confirm again the contingency of historical narratives – the element of choice, including moral and political choice, involved in their construction. And that serves to highlight further the point that such narratives are far from being straightforward 'factual' representations of 'what actually happened', but are, inevitably, *constructions* for particular purposes, owing much to what would conventionally (and disparagingly) be called imaginative 'fiction'.

Fiction, history, and politics

In a book published too late for my extended critical attention here, Timothy Parrish has argued that 'fiction in the postmodern era has become both the primary medium for arguing about what history *is*', and also 'the critical genre for understanding *how history is made*'.[8] That has clear implications for our discussion here concerning the *functions* – and especially the ideological functions, as just discussed – of history. For if we investigate history's nature and its mode of construction, we can surely deduce the motivations that may lie behind it – the *purposes* of those who produce it. So in our examination of the functions of history, we are brought back once more to fiction, and must take account of Parrish's argument that, in a number of American novels (including Don DeLillo's *Libra*, which I consider below) historians' motivations and purposes are revealed as blatantly (although not always knowingly) political.[9]

[8] Timothy Parrish, *From the Civil War to the Apocalypse: Postmodern History and American Fiction*, Amherst, University of Massachusetts Press, 2008, pp. 34, 37 (my emphases).
[9] Other novelists discussed by Parrish include William Faulkner, Cormac McCarthy, Toni Morrison, Thomas Pynchon, Joan Didion, and Denis Johnson.

That is by no means a new claim or revelation: the ideological under-pinnings of history have been recognised through the centuries. But we need nonetheless to take notice here once again that it is writers of fiction who, in a widely accessible form, have more recently provided historiographical illumination – who have, that is to say, deliberately and explicitly shed light on one of history's darker corners, by revealing afresh the *inevitability* of its ideological involvement and its function as a vehicle for politics.

That involvement was the subject also of an earlier work concerned with fiction and the representation of history, which has come to my attention all too recently. In *Jarring Witnesses* (1994), Robert Holton's focus is on narrative construction. He examines, first, novels by Joseph Conrad, Ford Madox Ford, and William Faulkner, and argues that these, through their presentation of coherent stories wherein (despite, or in the face of, challenges) a strict control is maintained on '*which voices are permitted to narrate*', may be seen as continuing to represent the political orthodoxies of modernity.[10] But he goes on, in the second place, to analyse examples of writing by others who in post-modernity challenge those long held orthodoxies. Importantly, hitherto excluded African-American women repudiate conventional forms of narrative and introduce new – previously repressed but now insistent – voices; and I shall refer briefly to these again in the following chapter. But I'll concentrate here on his discussion of another 'heterodox' work, Thomas Pynchon's *V*. And, not least because I personally find this example of postmodern fictional writing less than immediately transparent, I am pleased to acknowledge my considerable indebtedness to Robert Holton in this section.

Thomas Pynchon, V[11]

Thomas Pynchon's *V*, first published in 1963, is described by Holton as 'a postmodern historiographical novel – a novel about historical representation as well as about historical events'.[12] In terms of historical events, it ranges from 1894 to a 'present' in 1956. Through a series of episodes, from nineteenth-century Egypt, through early twentieth-century colonial South-West Africa, to the Suez Crisis, we follow – albeit (speaking for myself) at times with some difficulty – the fortunes of a discharged US sailor, Benny Profane, and of the

---

[10] Robert Holton, *Jarring Witnesses: Modern Fiction and the Representation of History*, Hemel Hempstead, Harvester Wheatsheaf, 1994, pp. 152–3 (my emphasis).

[11] Thomas Pynchon, *V* [1963], London, Picador, 1975. Page references will be given in the text.

[12] Holton, *Jarring Witnesses*, p. 245. The 'postmodernist' credentials of *V* are disputed by Brian McHale, *Postmodernist Fiction*, New York and London, Methuen, 1987.

central character, Herbert Stencil, as he seeks to track down the elusive 'V' of the book's title. But the various episodes described are not treated in chronological order; nor are they constrained within a straightforward linear structure; and the focus upon each shifts in a seemingly random way, being sometimes described from as many as eight different viewpoints.

Even in its structure, then, this partly 'historical novel' displays an alternative form of writing about the past; and it is indeed centrally concerned with *historiography* – with how and *why* history is written as it is. For Pynchon early describes our general situation as living within a 'History' that might be conceived as 'rippled with gathers in its fabric', such that we may be 'at the bottom of a fold' from which, despite the confidence with which so many histories have been written, our vision is severely restricted. In a passage reminiscent of F. H. Bradley's description of 'how, with every fresh standing-ground . . . comes another view of the far-lying past from a higher and new level',[13] Pynchon writes of how 'Perhaps if we lived on a crest, things would be different. We could at least see' (155–6). But we don't; so we have to make do with what is only a partial view, each of us grasping at fragments of evidential data to build up 'his own rat-house of history'. Every individual, the author suggests, seeks to build 'his own rat-house of history's rags and straws', taking from the totality of possibilities only what he personally (for whatever reason) wants; and in that state of extreme relativism, with everyone having 'their private versions of history', there must be about 'five million different rat-houses' in the city of New York alone (225).

With these concerns, and with its implicit critique of current practice, Pynchon's novel seems, as Holton notes, interestingly to anticipate postmodernist theorising – notably pre-dating even the works of Hayden White. For as with White later, we are brought back to the central issue of narrative – those smoothly running stories, whether fictional or historical, that seem to include everything within their embrace, and to tidy all those potentially awkward bits and pieces into the sort of neat package with which most of us feel aesthetically and emotionally comfortable. It is the presuppositions that underlie the construction and acceptance of such monolithic narrative structures which are challenged in Pynchon's fiction, just as they are to be later by postmodern historical theorists. And the way this is done in the novelist's case is, at least in part, by practical demonstration – by the fragmentation of his own story, which is broken up into constituents that do not come together in any obvious, or seemingly natural, way. By the use of that technique, Pynchon

[13] F. H. Bradley, *The Presuppositions of Critical History* [1874], ed. Lionel Rubinoff, Chicago, Quadrangle Books, 1968, p. 86.

deliberately questions the propriety of orthodox literary procedures, in a way that has implications for anyone who tells a story – and that of course includes historians.

For the point here again is that the sort of straightforward narrative that is generally presupposed in historical writing – just taken as 'natural' – actually conceals a host of events, attitudes, experiences, people, that fail to fit into or cohere with that dominant narrative. And the acceptance of a single 'hegemonic' narrative, which determines boundaries and defines the very acceptability or admissibility (or even perceptibility) of historical evidence, is of course a *political* move – a move *designed to exclude* the concerns of other peoples, whether those other peoples are different by virtue of race, or gender, or anything else.

Recognition of the political/ideological underpinning of historical narratives, and of their consequent power to reinforce and maintain – as well as to challenge and subvert – existing socio-political structures long pre-dated Thomas Pynchon, and can be seen most interestingly in the work of some African-American women writers of fiction from the later nineteenth century to the present. These are of interest, as Robert Holton shows, not least in their demand that the pasts of the previously excluded and near-forgotten be remembered, that the memories of their struggles, humiliations, and injustices, be kept alive – and I shall return to that theme in my final chapter.

Pynchon's own method in this context does not make his novel any easier to read or comprehend: in the absence of any single narrative in which all threads are neatly woven together into a comforting coverlet, the reader may well feel left out in the cold – floundering, somewhat perplexed and disorientated, not knowing how to understand anything or what conclusions, if any, are to be drawn. For what is central? What is peripheral? Who or what is more or less important? Where are we actually going? Without some authorial guidance on these matters, how are we to know what is 'right' or 'true' or even 'real'?

And that of course is all a part of the point: the reader's confusion is emblematic of a more general situation. For those questions arise also in the case of histories, where tales are told from a supposedly static and external viewpoint, assumed (in reputable works) to be 'objective', at a point of equilibrium and 'balance', from which all sides can be dispassionately assessed and we can be reliably informed of what the central issues are, who the major figures and who the merely 'minor', and above all the intended direction of travel. So what Pynchon does is to question the validity of crucial professional beliefs and procedures – revealing a host of gaps and fissures that narratives are intended to conceal, and thereby raising questions rather than supplying ready answers, and eroding any confidence we might have had about ever getting to know what has 'really' been going on. And in that way, as Holton notes, space is opened up to allow for other voices and experiences, alternative interpretations and evaluations. And the analogy with historical representation is obvious.[14]

Fiction's function here, then, is to reveal the political function of histories in which narratives have (necessarily) excluded as well as included, in which heroes and villains, perpetrators and victims, winners and losers have all been readily identified. Their identification depends upon the acceptance of fixed boundaries – boundaries that facilitate categorisation and seem to be naturally occurring as they divide one group or class of people from all others. Those divisions result from the way that 'reality' is currently perceived and presented – conveniently (for some) defining everything and everyone in terms of prevailing or dominant beliefs. And their re-presentation in historical narratives serves to confirm and reinforce them.

It is those orthodoxies of narrative construction that Pynchon sets out to subvert. So we read, for example, of one character, Mondaugen, who crosses a ravine that leads symbolically from the limits of one world to another, and thus arrives, as Holton describes, 'at the conditions of possibility of *another state of mind*'.[15] That transgression of conventional expectations is paralleled by the experience of a confused college boy, who is caught between his middle-class upbringing and the attractions of a more bohemian lifestyle: confronted by the need to choose between them, he is unable definitively to make up his mind. Rather, 'he will straddle the line . . . never stopping to wonder why there should ever have been a line, or even if there is a line at all'. Like those divided selves we considered in Chapter 6, 'he will learn how to be a twinned man . . . straddling until he splits up the crotch' (58).

In that same, sometimes uncomfortable, indeterminacy of identity, Stencil – reminiscent here of Virginia Woolf's Bernard – 'always referred to himself in the third person [which helped him] appear as only one among a repertoire of identities'; and, to confirm that schizophrenic impulse, he deliberately sought out places and experiences that were unfamiliar and uncharacteristic of him

[14] In Holton's words, Pynchon is indicating 'a heterodox discursive space . . . in which narratives of alterity, of non-synchronous and discrepant experience may be articulated', and in which 'jarring [non-conforming, non-consistent] historical witnesses might testify and be heard'. *Jarring Witnesses*, p. 241. Holton takes his use of 'jarring' from F. H. Bradley, who wrote of 'a host of jarring witnesses, a chaos of disjoined and discrepant narrations': *Presuppositions*, p. 85.

[15] Holton, *Jarring Witnesses*, p. 234 (my emphases).

as he had previously been (62). Later we read of how 'Stencil had all the identities he could cope with conveniently right at the moment'; so he was perhaps himself emblematic of 'contemporary man in search of an identity', identifiable only as 'He Who Looks for V' – the identity of whom (or which) is itself elusive, inasmuch as 'he didn't know what sex V might be, nor even what genus or species' (226).

The question recurs, then, of what in more general terms 'reality' actually is – that reality, including past reality, which it is the function of history to re-present 'as it was'. As a British agent, Stencil's father had pondered diplomatic situations and concluded that 'no Situation had any objective reality: it only existed in the minds of those who happened to be in on it at any specific moment' (189); like Tolstoy's military men, who all had their own versions of a battle, everyone had their own 'take' on any matter, so that 'short of examining the entire history of each individual participating . . . short of anatomising each soul, what hope has anyone of understanding a Situation?' (470). And that question can be taken to refer more generally to any historical event: Stencil Senior's lack of hope has problematic consequences not only for diplomacy, but also for historians hoping to record what happened. In their attempts to homogenise evidence and produce an inclusive and coherent narrative, they go beyond mere 'facts', and blurring once more any assumed boundaries between history and fiction, their work becomes enveloped in 'a nacreous mass of inference, poetic licence, forcible dislocation' (62).

Following fiction's lead, then, it becomes history's function to reveal by whom and for what purposes (potentially multiple) realities have been determined. Their sustenance by traditional historical procedures was what Pynchon was bringing into question; and his critique of histories that were supposedly ideologically neutral, but in fact conservatively committed, anti-cipated later theoretical approaches. It is, further, now widely recognised that 'history' embraces (or can embrace) far more than previously assumed, being potentially *limit-less*. It resembles 'V', as a 'sublime' which serves as the ill-identified object of an endless quest: itself changeable, it offers different possibilities at different times; it is to be desired, cherished, and pursued,[16] but never finally attained.

That continuing historical quest, though, signifies something further: namely, *discontent*, which translates in socio-political terms to *dis*ruption – the breaking down of boundaries hitherto accepted as 'definitive', natural, and necessary. The questioning of what *is* – of what is just accepted as the norm –

---

[16] This is of course disputed by some theorists.

itself becomes an important function for history as it encroaches on the previously poetic domain of *what might be*; and that function has been increasingly realised over the decades since Thomas Pynchon wrote. Once again, then, we can see that a fiction-based challenge to historiographical orthodoxies has proved to be a precursor of later theoretical critiques, as well as a model for the revision of practical procedures.

Don DeLillo, Libra[17]

Another postmodern work of fiction that provides insight into the functions of history is Don DeLillo's *Libra* (1988), which has been described by David T. Courtwright as 'a meditation on the nature of history itself', and of which Timothy Parrish writes that, 'perhaps no other postmodernist novel has so transparently and brilliantly dramatised the effect of the modernist narrative revolution on the practice of history'.[18] The focus of the book is on the assassination by Lee Harvey Oswald of US President John F. Kennedy on 22 November 1963 – an event of which Nicholas Branch has been hired by the Central Intelligence Agency to write a 'secret history' – and, in an effort to understand what 'really' happened, the author traces (episodically rather than chronologically) the (assumed) perpetrator's life from his childhood in New York to his own death in prison at the hands of Jack Ruby.

The admitted *secrecy* of Branch's prospective history already highlights an important point with which DeLillo is concerned here: that history is politically controlled; so that, just as Thomas Pynchon had indicated in *V*, one function of history is *political*. For history has to be controlled somehow; someone has to take the responsibility for constructing, from the chaotic jumble of data from the past, a narrative which, by its persuasive coherence, will then indicate a 'reality' about that past. And – as George Orwell long since made clear – those who construct and control that narrative of the past will control and help to construct also the story of the future. Which is a function far too important to be left to mere historians.

What in this context DeLillo makes clear by his own literary techniques is that any required narrative is conspicuously absent from the mass of data surviving from the event in question. The Warren Commission, which

---

[17] Don DeLillo, *Libra* [1988], London, Penguin, 1989. Page references will be given in the text.

[18] David T. Courtwright, 'Why Oswald Missed: Don DeLillo's *Libra*', in Mark C. Carnes, (ed.), *Novel History: Historians and Novelists Confront America's Past (and Each Other)*, London, Simon & Schuster, 2001, p. 78; Parrish, *Civil War*, p. 22.

investigated Kennedy's assassination in the immediate aftermath, published in 1964 a report that even then consisted of 888 pages, supported by no fewer that twenty-six volumes of evidence; and of course additional data continued to surface thereafter, provoking further questions and theories of alleged conspiracies, and ever greater lack of certainty. So DeLillo's historian Branch, even focusing on just one specific episode, is overwhelmed by the vast, and ever growing, amount of material pertaining, both directly and indirectly, to the case; and he becomes aware, in company with Hayden White (as we have seen in Chapter 1), that any coherent narrative will have to be imposed rather than being simply found.

That places a huge responsibility on the historian, who feels that he 'must study everything. He is in too deep to be selective.' So confronted by an impossible task, he begins to sound like George Eliot's Casaubon, with his years of accumulated notes but 'precious little' finished prose (59). Just like Casaubon and like too Ibsen's laborious Jörgen Tesman, and no doubt many real-life historians, 'He takes refuge in his notes. The notes are becoming an end in themselves.' Like so many others, he 'has decided it is premature to make a serious effort to turn these notes into coherent history. Maybe it will always be premature. Because the data keeps coming in . . . The past is changing as he writes' (301).

To compound the historian's problems, that actual data – the 'facts' themselves – are often ambiguous, inconsistent, and self-contradictory: 'There is enough mystery in the facts as we know them, enough of conspiracy, coincidence, loose ends, dead ends, multiple interpretations' (58). Even on the simplest matters, supposedly reliable eyewitnesses testify to the effect that Oswald's height is 5 feet nine, and ten, and eleven, his eye colour grey, and blue, and brown; and less simply, 'reality' is deliberately confused, with records lost and amended, signatures forged, objects mislabelled, and photographs modified with one person's head superimposed upon another's body.

That last confusion, or amalgamation of incompatible elements, might be taken as emblematic of identity more generally. For like Thomas Pynchon's Stencil and the other examples cited in our previous chapter, Oswald is portrayed by DeLillo as himself unable to assume a unified and coherent character: he represents once more, as Parrish describes, 'the postmodern fragmentation of self', 'a failed maker of narratives'.[19] It is not for nothing that his astrological sign is Libra, the Scales or the Balance, so that he can be described as 'a man who harbours contradictions . . . ready to be tilted either

---

[19] Parrish, *Civil War*, p. 29.

way' (319); he repeatedly changes his aliases, his jobs, his location, and his allegiances; and he is a man whose actions are impossible not only to predict but also retrospectively to contain and explain within a unitary and purposeful life story.

With his portrayal of these complexities in his central character, and the endless intricacies of his fluctuating relationships with others who are similarly complex, DeLillo succeeds brilliantly in demonstrating the impossibility of tying everything together, of making coherent sense of it all, or of providing anything like a definitive account of one pivotal episode in history – 'the seven seconds that broke the back of the American century' (181). Any sense that can be made – or that is permitted to be made – is made for a purpose; and DeLillo questions the 'official' version of events which insists, against the conspiracy theorists, that Oswald was acting alone. As Nicholas Branch – and DeLillo's readers – are forced to realise, the solidity of even Lee Harvey Oswald himself seems to dissipate the more closely he is observed: he is in the end shown to have been unlikely to have fired the fatal shot, but is revealed as self-deluding, 'a fictional character in his own life',[20] and ultimately a 'part of some exercise in the secret manipulation of history' (377). With the mysterious death of numerous potential witnesses, with his name forged on documents, and his photographs conveniently doctored, he has, amidst all the conflicting rumours and lies, been made 'a dupe of history' (418). And it is no wonder, then, that Branch's own history is to be classified as 'secret': unlikely ever to be made public, it is 'meant for CIA's own closed collection' (442), its function blatantly political.

As another work of historical fiction, then, *Libra* effectively challenges the supposed, and often claimed, ideological neutrality of history. The ideal of a single narrative written from a single perspective is shown in practice to be impossible of attainment. As in Pynchon's *V*, it is superseded by the reality of fragmentation which, as Parrish writes, 'inevitably leaves multiple narratives with conflicting and often hostile audiences (or communities) to fight over what is "true"'.[21] DeLillo succeeds, again through practical exemplification, in laying bare the political function of historical narratives – the motivations, machinations, and manipulations of history's constructors and controllers.

However much itself a work of fiction, therefore, *Libra* effectively encourages greater awareness of history's nature and underlying political purposes – and that indicates a further function for history itself: namely the exposing of

---

[20]   So DeLillo, 'The Fictional Man', a response to Courtwright's essay, in Carnes, (ed.), *Novel History*, p. 92.

[21]   Parrish, *Civil War*, p. 31.

its own construction and its own ideological underpinning. That is something to which we shall return in the following chapter, where we examine Daniel Mendelsohn's investigation into the 'lost' members of his own family. For by retrieving something of the past of those previously 'lost' to history, by restoring them into an historical narrative (however limited), Mendelsohn throws light on their previous exclusion, and so finally thwarts earlier attempts to impose a politically/ideologically motivated history in which they had no place.

Graham Swift, Waterland[22]

First, though, we turn again to Graham Swift's novel *Waterland* (1983), which, after the postmodern procedures of Thomas Pynchon and Don DeLillo, seems comparatively straightforward in its narrative technique. Yet it is no less concerned with historiography and with the *functions* of history – matters that it addresses quite explicitly. For, as we have seen, the central character and narrator is a non-conforming history teacher named Tom Crick – a man who deliberately refuses any promotion which would remove him from his teaching role, and who then pays the price when his Headmaster closes down the school's History Department. The unsympathetic Head believes that Crick has only been providing 'a rag-bag of pointless information' (23) anyway, though Crick himself claims to have done his best for thirty-two years 'to unravel the mysteries of the past' to his pupils (5). But in fact he has done more than either of those two descriptions indicate, presenting something altogether more 'equivocal' (126); for being obviously aware of some major issues in historical theory, he has left some awareness of those as a major part of his educational legacy – having, as we are told, 'in one sense, and of his own accord, ceased to teach history' as conventionally understood (5).

We have already, in Chapter 1, discussed some of Tom Crick's ideas about such matters as the relationship of history with fiction, the problematic nature of 'facts', causation, Providence, and teleological explanations. But we need here to return to his story in *Waterland* in relation to a number of further issues – and especially those concerning the possible uses and *functions* of history. And it is immediately noteworthy that Graham Swift's treatment exemplifies

---

[22] Graham Swift, *Waterland* [1983], London, Picador, 1992. Page references will be given in the text.

once again the way that issues of historical theory can be usefully presented in an accessible manner in what is essentially a work of fiction.

As a teacher, Tom Crick has inevitably been forced to confront questions concerning the practical point of his subject. He has one particularly provocative pupil, Price, who tells him unequivocally that he can 'stuff' his past (141), for 'what matters is the here and now. Not the past. The here and now – and the future' (6). That matter of the 'here and now' recurs throughout the book, and Crick himself readily concedes that history is indeed vulnerable from that perspective – providing, as it does, only 'a thin garment, easily punctured' in the face of its challenge (36). Yet he notes also that those words 'here and now' are themselves problematic: for 'what is this much-adduced Here and Now? What is this indefinable zone between what is past and what is to come; this free and airy present tense in which we are always longing to take flight into the boundless future?' It is of course, as he recognises, an elusive concept – even, perhaps, with its potential for surprise, more elusive than the past; for the past, as being past, at least can lay claim to some sort of fixity or completion (60).

That may be why we turn to the past in search of explanations, for explanations are what human beings seek. Indeed, Crick suggests that one might actually define man as 'the animal which demands an explanation, the animal which asks Why'. For, after all, it is an explanation that is being sought by pupils who ask questions about the purpose of history – questions that they are quite right to ask (as we read at the beginning of this chapter, 'All history classes should ask, What is the point of history? Why history?'). But their very question does of course itself provide an answer: 'your "Why?" gives the answer. Your demand for explanation provides an explanation.' For any explanation implies a search for causes, and so necessitates a chronological, historical investigation – a looking back from where we are in order to see what happened previously, and to try and ascertain how we got from there to here. The present effect derived from some past cause (or causes), and history is an enquiry specifically designed to 'uncover the mysteries of cause and effect. To show that for every action there is a reaction.' Therefore, 'so long as we have this itch for explanations', we seem destined always to 'carry round with us this cumbersome but precious bag of clues called History' (106–7).[23]

But causation in history is itself highly problematic, for in our attempts to trace that elusive causal chain, we are forced further and further back in time. For 'when we have gleaned that reason we will want to know, But why *that*

---

[23] A similar argument is made in very similar terms by the historical theorist Amy J. Elias in the opening paragraph of her essay 'Metahistorical Romance, the Historical Sublime, and Dialogic History', *Rethinking History* 9, 2005, pp. 159–60.

reason? Because . . . And when we have that further reason, But why again – ? Because . . . Why? . . . Because . . . Why?' Historians are trapped, then, in an infinite regress: the further they go back, the further still they need to go back, and they are confronted by 'that incessant question Whywhywhy' until it becomes 'like a siren wailing in our heads', announcing the impossibility of any final or complete explanation (107).

That remains a problem, and not one that is confined to historians: indeed, it is one confronted by Tom Crick in 'real life' (as portrayed in the novel), when his mentally ill wife steals a baby. The police in their subsequent enquiries need an explanation of what has occurred, so ask: 'Look, sir, shall we go back to the beginning?' That, for an investigating policeman, sounds a reasonable enough request, but, as Crick is aware, 'the more you try to dissect events, the more you lose hold of them' (139); and, as he responds (to himself): 'The beginning? But where's that? How far back is that?' (314) The need to go back *endlessly* in that way becomes intolerable: somewhere we have to call a halt. For the sake of our sanity, might it not actually be better 'if we could acquire the gift of amnesia?' (107–8).

It is, though, especially when things go wrong that our need for explanation becomes most insistent: it is then above all that we look back, in order to find the historical root of our troubles. 'History begins only at the point where things go wrong; history is born only with trouble, with perplexity, with regret' (106); 'people only explain when things are wrong' (167). And they hope, of course, by looking back, to see how and why it happened, and hope, too, to prevent similar mistakes in the future: that is 'the history master's hoary stand-by' – that we can learn from past mistakes in order to do better in the future (107).

But that is like bolting stable doors after the horse has escaped, and history is anyway far from ever proving straightforwardly progressive: 'Do not fall into the illusion that history is a well-disciplined and unflagging column marching unswervingly into the future' (135). On the contrary, it seems to go 'in two directions at once' – backwards as well as forwards, taking detours, and depriving us of any consoling master-narratives of progress (whether theological, scientific, technological, or whatever).

Those earlier consoling narratives provided a meaningful sense of direction through time. Without them, we seem to be lost in an existential chaos, and it his recognition of that condition that leads to Tom Crick's own interest in *stories*. These, he believes, as enabling humans to make sense of what would otherwise be chaotic, indicate the bedrock of what history is actually *for*; they are essentially what histories consist of. That is why, as we have already seen (in Chapter 1), humans, with their need for explanations, are considered by him to be best characterised as story-telling animals. And their stories are now, following the breakdown of any belief in past progressive narratives, more necessary than ever. For there are no longer any signposts along a meaningful trajectory on which to place ourselves, and 'no compasses for journeying in time. As far as our sense of direction in this unchartable dimension is concerned, we are like lost travellers in a desert.' While we may believe we are going forwards, 'towards the oasis of Utopia', we may be doing no more than going round in circles (135).

Recognition of that non-progressive circularity in our histories is hard to bear. In Tom Crick's nautical analogy, it is not enough for humans to look back at their own 'chaotic wake': they need, rather, to leave behind themselves 'the comforting marker-buoys and trail-signs of stories' (63). Their experience needs to be made meaningful through its inscription in a narrative, and that is just what history does – fulfilling thereby a vital *therapeutic* function. For children, as we are reminded, have always been told stories, 'in order to quell restless thoughts' (7); and it is not only children who suffer from such thoughts. Everyone needs stories: as another character in the novel, Helen Atkinson, explains, negative experiences cannot just be forgotten or erased from consciousness, but they can be made tolerable by being put into stories: narrative history becomes 'a way of bearing what won't go away, a way of making sense of madness' (225). As another novelist, E. L. Doctorow, wrote in 1983, 'history is a kind of fiction in which we live and *hope to survive*'.[24]

'All right', agrees Tom Crick, 'so it's all a struggle to preserve an artifice. It's all a struggle to make things not seem meaningless. All a fight against fear' (241). What he had himself originally wanted was history with a capital 'H' – 'the Grand Narrative, the filler of vacuums, the dispeller of fears of the dark' (62). But he (like Hayden White again, and Don DeLillo's Nicholas Branch) came to realise that that was a hopeless quest, in that the narratives presented in such histories are themselves only *imposed upon* data (upon historical evidence), and so are only ever made-up, *fictional*, incomplete. So although he might, like all historians, in theory wish to propound to his pupils 'the complete and final version' (7–8), in practice that is impossible. All that he can provide is a history that is 'fabrication', a 'diversion', nothing more than a '*reality-obscuring* drama' (40, my emphasis). Its function is to obscure the 'reality' that humans, as T. S. Eliot too observed, find hard to bear; for when we look back into what W. G. Sebald described as the 'abysm of time',

---

[24] E. L. Doctorow (1977), quoted by Barbara Foley, *Telling the Truth: The Theory and Practice of Documentary Fiction*, Ithaca and London, Cornell University Press, 1986, p. 9 (my emphasis).

'everything lies all jumbled up in it, and when you look down you feel dizzy and afraid'.[25]

Much vaunted 'historical method', then, in its search for explanations and for 'truth', comes to be seen as 'a way of coming up with just another story' (263) to help us through our emotional difficulties. Events of themselves lack meaning, but we look for meaning in them and ascribe meaning to them; and with freedom granted to all to interpret as they will, history becomes, as Crick concedes, nothing more than 'a lucky dip of meanings'. And the implication is not lost on his pupil: so, Price observes, 'we can find whatever meaning we like in history'; and we are hardly surprised to hear of him later as having 'suddenly announced in the middle of a class that history was a fairy-tale' (154). The confusion of history and fiction is once more confirmed, providing perhaps a further argument in favour of putting down 'this mountain of baggage called History, which we are obliged to lug with us' – an 'ever-frustrating weight' which gets increasingly heavy, and which may be actually impeding our ability to go forwards.

But in the analysis presented here by Graham Swift, that would be far from the appropriate outcome; for in addition to its therapeutic role in providing meaningful stories, history has another crucial intellectual and moral function. For, in what is a constantly recurring theme in *Waterland*, history can be seen in an important sense to resemble the Fens – the Fens which provide the atmospheric geographical (and highly symbolic) background to this whole novel. For like the fenlands, despite our best attempts, the past is never fully under our control, never finally conquered. The Fens, those low lying swamps brought into agricultural use by drainage, 'strictly speaking . . . are never reclaimed, only *being reclaimed*' (10, my emphasis); and nature can periodically achieve some reversals, with floods once more threatening the man-made order. And similarly with the past, history seeks to do what is ultimately unachievable – to give a definitive account of events about which the agents themselves lacked understanding. History, we are reminded, 'is that impossible thing: the attempt to give an account, with incomplete knowledge, of actions themselves undertaken with incomplete knowledge'. Historians may seem, like the drainers of the Fens, to have finally defeated the material with which they have for so long struggled – in their case, to have got the past under their control, to comprehend it, to have achieved a 'definitive' version of what 'actually happened'. But, like the newly discovered photograph, some fresh piece of evidence comes along which threatens that whole edifice of

[25] W. G. Sebald, *On the Natural History of Destruction*, London, Hamish Hamilton, 2003, p. 74.

understanding; so that, if not quite back to 'square one', considerable re-vision and re-construction is required. In the end, then, the best that history can do is to teach 'only the dogged and patient art of making do'. That may seem a singularly negative conclusion, but it actually highlights an extremely positive function for history – namely, 'that by forever attempting to explain, we may come, not to an Explanation, but to *a knowledge of the limits of our power to explain*' (108, my emphasis).

Conclusion

A knowledge of the limits of our power to explain seems to make a fitting con-clusion to a chapter devoted to the functions of history; and it chimes with the thought of those contemporary theorists who make a positive virtue of coming to terms with human limitations – and who, in some cases, see history as potentially helpful in provoking reassessment of our capabilities. For, as we have seen, historians have often claimed peculiar virtues for their subject: on the assumption that they have the ability to reach 'the truth' about the past, they have taken on a number of important roles – not least as advisers on the future, which is expected to resemble the past, and on personal and national identities, which are assumed to derive from that past. And their central importance in these matters is widely accepted by educators and politicians, who recognise the power of history and seek to harness it.

But there is of course a crucial problem here. For that power of history derives from its being seen as provider of a *truthful* account of what has hap-pened in the past – an account that is *factual*. Historians, that is, are assumed to live up to their claims of being 'objective' and 'detached' – of practising their subject with no ulterior purpose in mind, but only *'for its own sake'*. It is only by thus presenting themselves as properly uninvolved and 'scientific' that they retain their intellectual (and thence political) authority. But despite that (and now on the other hand), historians are expected to *utilise* their subject – to make it have some use in the wider world: they are required to provide those narratives – those trajectories from the past – that lead to whatever future is, for the time being, proposed. Like Claudia Hampton's teacher, their function is to show, for example, how England (or any other country) became great – whether in terms of imperial domination, economic power, intellectual and cultural achievements, or anything else – so that some foundation is there to underpin whatever is planned for the future. But that in turn implies *partiality* – a picture that is, once again, partial in both senses of that word; for it is inevitably relative to the perspective adopted – and therefore, as being composed or made up for a specific purpose, inevitably *fictive*.

It seems, then, that as soon as historians give up their pretensions to attain – or even to have any hope of attaining – a unitary truth, they are confronted by the problem of differentiating 'truth' from speculation, fact from fiction. As long as they remain as the privileged 'high-priests' of the past, who, through their own discipline and sacrifice of self, are enabled to attain direct contact with that past, and who can then act as mediums through whom their resultant, directly apprehended, knowledge can be transmitted, historians can repudiate 'fiction' as they repudiate 'myth', as something to be overcome and superseded by historical fact. But once that literally supernatural ability has been exposed as itself a long-lived (because highly convenient) myth, the floodgates of fictionality, like sluice-gates in the fens, are opened to reveal once more the limitations by which historians, as mere mortals, are constrained. Socrates, we are reminded through history, was accounted wise in that he recognised his own ignorance; the wisdom of historians may similarly lie in recognition of their own limited ability, not only to provide explanations, but even clearly to distinguish 'factual history' from 'fiction'.

Further reading

Benda, Julien, *The Great Betrayal*, trans. R. Aldington, London, Routledge, 1928.

DeLillo, Don, *Libra* [1988], London, Penguin, 1989.

Holton, Robert, *Jarring Witnesses: Modern Fiction and the Representation of History*, Hemel Hempstead, Harvester Wheatsheaf, 1994.

Parrish, Timothy, *From the Civil War to the Apocalypse: Postmodern History and American Fiction*, Amherst, University of Massachusetts Press, 2008.

Pynchon, Thomas, *V* [1963], London, Picador, 1975.

Southgate, Beverley, *What is History For?*, London, Routledge, 2005.

Swift, Graham, *Waterland* [1983], London, Picador, 1992.

Tosh, John, *Why History Matters*, Basingstoke, Palgrave Macmillan, 2008.

Chapter 8

Endings

In this chapter, we return to the more general issue of History and Fiction and consider, first, the impropriety of claiming bipolar distinctions between the two; second, the nature of any 'borderland' between them; and finally, the desirability of amending our definition of 'history', and reassessing our expectations of the subject, in the light of its relationship – if not identification – with fiction. As a concluding case study we take Daniel Mendelsohn's The Lost – *a work that, this time in the context of a practical historical investigation, raises once more the questions under discussion here relating to historical theory, and provides further illumination on the whole vexed relationship between history, fact and fiction.*

This book has been about meeting points between history and fiction, including especially the way that historians are liable to confront provocative representations of both themselves and their subject in works that are nominally 'fictional'. We have looked in particular at aspects of historical *theory* – including questions of memory and identity, ethics and some functions of history – with which novelists, perhaps with surprising frequency, have shown concern. But here we return to the more general discussion of history and fiction – and history as now involving actual *practice* – introduced in Chapters 1 and 2.

The complexity, as well as importance, of history's relationship with fiction is becoming ever more widely recognised as we confront, even in everyday experience, a hotchpotch of (in Bradley's words again) 'truth and tangled falsehood'. In practical terms, any disentanglement of the two, any clear distinguishing between history and fiction, has long been rendered problematic in such literary forms as 'historical fiction' and more 'speculative' histories. But more recently, there has been a profusion of 'reconstructions' (of both individual lives and historical events) and 'docudramas' (where imaginative dramatisation has overlaid or even supplanted documentary reportage) produced as entertainment for a 'popular' (as opposed to strictly academic) market; and these have served to obfuscate the boundaries yet further. And as some long accepted definitions are questioned and disciplinary frontiers are challenged or ignored, anxieties have grown about how *any* distinctions can be maintained between two subjects, each with its own approach to the past, which have traditionally been perceived as diametrically opposed. 'The dividing line between fiction and non-fiction is becoming increasingly hard to draw', as we read emphatically stated in a daily newspaper in January 2008.[1] And as if in confirmation, the thrust of a new book, its reviewer states a few months later, 'seems to be that . . . *fact has become a kind of fiction*'.[2]

That evident erosion of clarity is sometimes seen as a part of the more general decline of such Enlightenment ideals as 'rationality' and 'progress' – a decline that is manifested also in a more general 'mystical' turn, often derived from Eastern thought, in 'alternative' (or 'quack') medicine, in unsupported and a-historical claims about 'conspiracy theories', and – of particular relevance here – in the denial of historically confirmed events in the past. So there are, at least potentially, important *practical* implications that derive from this debate; and as we proceed, and by way of conclusion, I shall try to clarify my own position.

Bipolarities, boundaries, and borderlands

The binary opposition between fiction and fact is no longer relevant. (Paul de Man)[3]

The title of this book may seem to presuppose the existence of polar opposites, or at least two concepts that may, despite their frequent meetings, be considered as mutually exclusive – 'history' and 'fiction'. That 'binary opposition' has indeed been traditionally maintained. Claimed by its practitioners as 'factual', history, as we have seen, has often been defined by reference to its exclusion of the 'fictive'; it is not 'made up'; it derives from and is based upon

---

[1] Damian Thompson (editor of the *Catholic Herald*), essay in *The Daily Telegraph*, 12 January 2008, p. 26. See further his *Counterknowledge: How We Surrendered to Conspiracy Theories, Quack Medicine, Bogus Science and False History*, London, Atlantic Books, 2008.

[2] Theo Tait on Gordon Burn's *Born Yesterday: The News as a Novel* (2008), *London Review of Books*, 5 June 2008, p. 16 (my emphasis).

[3] Paul de Man, quoted by Linda Hutcheon, *The Poetics of Postmodernism: History, Theory, Fiction*, London, Routledge, 1988, p. 113.

'hard' empirical evidence, and it re-presents nothing fictional but the very 'truth' about the past. And fiction, conversely, has traditionally been considered as an imaginative construct that has no claimed relationship with any such 'reality' or truth; it derives from the author's brain rather than the 'real world'. Yet between these two antithetical concepts we have also seen confusing overlaps that serve to erode assumed polarities and to support Paul de Man's proposition, quoted above, concerning the irrelevance now of any previously assumed 'binary opposition between fiction and fact' – or, by implication, between fiction and 'factual' history.

The repudiation of such oppositional stances is particularly appropriate in cases where non-'natural' entities are in dispute – by which I mean, where discussion centres on something like 'history', which of itself lacks any *natural* essence but signifies, rather, a human construction that remains susceptible to adaptations and modifications through time. In such cases, there clearly needs to be some flexibility in our definitions and attributions, as the subject changes in the light of new circumstances and requirements – and of our own understanding of its possible characteristics and purposes. We cannot get by, in our universally shared role of communicators, without some definitions and categorisations, but these should be seen as contingent – appropriate or useful within specific contexts, but always susceptible to challenge and change.

So the historian John Demos has written of how 'the history/fiction boundary has never looked more interesting', and has indeed become not so much a boundary as 'a *borderland* of surprising width and variegated topography'. That determinedly positive appraisal was made in a concluding assessment to a diverse collection of essays on the theme of 'History, Fiction, and Historical Fiction', published in 2005. Professor Demos still presupposes a clear distinction between the strictly 'factual' and the merely 'fictional', and concludes that history and fiction, while sharing 'a capacious borderland', must retain their own distinctive characteristics; so that, although extending their brief beyond what has often been thought appropriate, historians would continue to differentiate clearly – perhaps by the use of different typefaces – whenever they changed register to include material for which they lacked empirical evidence. Veering towards more imaginative procedures, such as are currently the preserve of novelists, historians might well find ways 'to express the parts we "know" . . . notwithstanding the absence of full "proof"'; but they would somehow signify to their readers that they had strayed into less defensible territory.[4]

---

[4] John Demos, 'Afterword: Notes From, and About, the History/Fiction Borderland', *Rethinking History* 9, 2005, pp. 329–35.

The clear differentiation still implied there is, as we have been arguing, highly questionable, since once one goes beyond a statement of simple 'facts' about the past, the fictional nature of constructed narratives quickly becomes apparent; historical, no less than fictional, narratives are imaginative constructions imposed upon, rather than discovered within, the data. But in practical terms, we do still contrive to make distinctions – not so much between the strictly factual and 'merely' fictional, but on the basis of varying degrees of *probability*. Thus, in a law court we accept that one account or explanation of events is, on the basis of the limited evidence to which we have access, more persuasive than its competitors, or more likely to approximate to what happened. And to deny the feasibility of making any such assessments as to the relative validity of historical accounts in the same way does seem to present dangers – dangers and difficulties such as might arise in any community that lacks any conception of 'truth' (and thence trust). One of those dangers, which is of particular importance here, is that it might lead to a *theory*-based denial of events known all too well (sometimes through personal experience) to have taken place in *practice*.

That is not to deny the hypothetical, incomplete, constructed, corrigible nature of any narrative, but it is to assert some difference between what can and what cannot be defended in rational and empirical ways; and although reason and empiricism may be inadequate to embrace the whole of human experience, it is hard to identify alternative criteria for assessments with anything like comparable authority or persuasiveness. And while we contrive of necessity to live without absolute certainties, we do nonetheless seem to require at the least some sliding scale of *credibilities* by which to carry on our daily lives.

That does, in the case of history and fiction, leave us (as John Demos, again, has argued) not so much with a boundary, as with some sort of extensive 'borderland', where criteria of probability cannot be easily applied, or where the balance of relative probabilities may remain in dispute; and that uncertain territory has for long (but perhaps increasingly of late) been well occupied by representatives of both historical and literary forces. In the latter case, the variety and diversity of references, within fiction, to history and historical theory indicate what Amy Elias has identified as a virtual 'obsession' with related issues; and they further indicate the perceived importance of those subjects for everyday life, and for a 'general' (rather than just academically specialised) readership. Despite recurring allusions to an imminent 'end' of history, and despite occasional pleas (most recently by postmodernist critics) for the wholesale repudiation of history, with its unhelpful and even stultifying focus on the past, novelists persist in showing in their works – often in the context of memory and forgetfulness, but also with reference to the need for continuing (or innovating) dialogue – the continuing relevance of that past to the present and future.

In some cases, indeed, what is nominally presented as 'fiction' may be as close as it is possible to get to any 'truth' about the matter; for that truth may be expressive of a 'reality' that is not susceptible to the empirical procedures and validation that history strictly requires. That point (as we have seen) was long since recognised by Walter Scott and Thomas Carlyle, and has more recently been elaborated by authors such as Tim O'Brien (whose work we considered in Chapter 5): these three writers may be seen as colonists of the history/fiction borderland, and as having allegiances in both camps. Scott, as we saw in Chapter 1, started as an historian and extended his work beyond what was conventionally acceptable as history; Carlyle, as noted in Chapter 2, was sympathetic to that 'romantic' stream of thought which, as against the 'factual', mechanical approach of the Dryasdust/Gradgrind school, placed emphasis on imagination and the cultivation of 'wonder'; and Tim O'Brien, whose career indicates an aspiration to bear witness to the Vietnam War, has written both an 'historical' account of that and one that he claims as 'fictional'.

As an example of a writer thus (currently) occupying the history/fiction borderland, O'Brien is particularly interesting as acknowledging his own concern with *theory*. For as a 'theory man', he confesses in *In the Lake of the Woods* to being left with something less than certainty – indeed, 'with little more than supposition and possibility'. Despite his best attempts to be 'faithful to the evidence', and despite, we might add, his personal experience and research on some of the Vietnamese terrain in question, 'much of what might appear to be *fact* in this narrative . . . must ultimately be viewed as a diligent but still *imaginative* reconstruction of events'.[5] And none the worse for that, we might insert; for his 'factual' and 'fictional' works are complementary, together seeming to convey some 'authenticity' and 'truth' about the 'reality' of Vietnam. (How do we justify that impression? Not by claiming some one-to-one correspondence between the written description and what 'actually happened', nor by any assertion of 'accurate' or 'objective' re-presentation of the past; but by being persuaded of its coherence in the light of our whole previous experience. We may, of course, be utterly mistaken; quite possibly we have been naïvely taken for a ride by an author intent on deception, and/or by our own inadequate responses in and to the past. But while acknowledging the risks, we incline to trust our judgements, if only for the pragmatic purpose of enabling us to get around in the world. That is not the only possible world – we

---

[5] Tim O'Brien, *In the Lake of the Woods*, London, Penguin, 1995, p. 199, n. 88; p. 30, n. 21 (my emphases).

know that – nor is it the best of all possibilities of which we may conceive; but for the present, it is the one in which we are, and in which it is preferable to survive rather than not.)

But with his confessional clarification, Tim O'Brien is making just the sort of disclaimer that John Demos suggests should be made by historians when they cross from the strictly 'historical' into areas where they may be highly competent (as was clearly the case here), but where their assertions cannot be defended in terms of conventional disciplinary procedures. A number of historians have long been openly 'transgressing' in that way: Natalie Zemon Davis, in her meticulously researched and referenced study of the sixteenth-century French peasant Martin Guerre, wrote of offering what was '*in part my invention*, but held tightly in check by the voices of the past'; and the very title of Simon Schama's experimental work *Dead Certainties (Unwarranted Speculations)* reveals the ambiguities embedded in his text, including as that does biographical studies which, as he describes, on the one hand 'follow the documented record with some closeness', but on the other hand 'are *works of the imagination*'. In works such as these, history once more meets fiction, and it is historians who deliberately and openly colonise the 'borderlands'. And in the company of Scott, Carlyle, and O'Brien, they thereby challenge the very concept of what properly constitutes 'history'.[6]

The subject, it is implied, may need once more to be redefined in such a way as to include matters previously excluded – in such a way as to appeal not only to the intellect but to 'the whole human being'; for 'a successful story brings the body into agreement with the mind'.[7] Or, as Norman Mailer suggested, history may need to be supplemented by material that is conventionally assumed to lie outside the historian's competence – taking over, as he believed his own fiction did, at 'precisely that point where experience is sufficiently emotional, spiritual, psychical, moral, existential, or supernatural to expose the fact that the historian in pursuing the experience would be obliged to quit the clearly demarcated limits of historical inquiry'.[8] Those

[6] Natalie Zemon Davis, *The Return of Martin Guerre*, Harmondsworth, Penguin, 1985, p. 5 (my emphasis); Simon Schama, *Dead Certainties (Unwarranted Speculations)*, London, Granta, 1991, p. 320 (my emphasis).

[7] Tim O'Brien, 'The Whole Story' – a response to Bruce Franklin's 'Kicking the Denial Syndrome: Tim O'Brien's *In the Lake of the Woods*', in Mark C. Carnes (ed.), *Novel History: Historians and Novelists Confront America's Past (and Each Other)*, London, Simon & Schuster, 2001, pp. 344–5.

[8] Norman Mailer, *The Armies of the Night: History as a Novel, the Novel as History*, London, Weidenfeld and Nicolson, 1968, p. 255. In this 'non-fiction novel', Mailer gives 'historicised' and 'novelised' accounts of the Anti-Vietnam War March on the Pentagon (in which he participated) in October 1967.

clearly demarcated limits may, then, need to be extended, or removed. And as bipolarities are thus rendered inappropriate, as boundaries assume fluidity, as borderlands become indefinitely extended, Paul de Man appears vindicated in his appraisal of the irrelevance of any 'binary opposition between fiction and fact'.

History: closure or continuation?

'Closure' has long been seen as the ultimate goal in most cultural pursuits, including both history and fiction, where the virtue of a structure incorporating a beginning, middle, and end, has generally been taken as self-evident, and the attainment of some sort of finality or completion has been accepted as an aesthetic (and perhaps moral) end. The arts, like the sciences, consist in the imposition of some sort of order, however provisional, contingent, and temporary, upon the chaos of experience and/or natural phenomena. And on the whole, it seems that in a literary context readers like to know where they are – where characters, whether historical or fictional, have come from, what they have done, and where they are going; they like things tidy, tidied up – with historians and novelists imitating the vision of lives as presented by obituarists, who can (or must) within finite limits sort the muddle of lived lives into a narrative, with birth as a beginning, followed by a purposeful career (or some melodramatic equivalent), and with death serving as a convenient and aesthetically satisfactory ending. Like funerals or memorial services, obituaries provide closure: that is finally that. And their form is exemplary – a model of literary construction, with their subject given the appearance of being firmly enclosed within bounds, tidied up, and already disposable.

Even in the case of obituaries, though, narrative reconstructions of a life are of course inevitably partial and provisional: new pieces of evidence may emerge, new witnesses come forward, as a result of which perceptions of the subject may be radically changed. Human beings, like events, ultimately evade finality, full comprehensibility; they defy being 'tidied up' and thence 'tidied away'.

Interpretative or explanatory closure in such cases is precluded, then, in part by the object's (the other's) own complexity, but also, and perhaps above all, by the subject's (our own) inability ever to transcend the constraints of its (our) own finite selfhood. So although we may tell the bare 'facts' of a person's life, and even fashion them into a coherent story, we can never ever really lay claim to full or complete or final understanding; we can never ever (as Graham

Swift concluded in *Waterland*) hope to provide fully satisfactory explanations. Reverting in this context once more to Tim O'Brien, he notes how all of us are 'fascinated . . . by the implacable *otherness* of others': however much we try – by various means, scientific and imaginative – to penetrate to the core of that otherness, even in the case of those closest to us, it always proves elusive and remains beyond our reach.[9] So that we are always and necessarily left in uncertainty, unable ever finally to understand or explain what happens or what happened – and unable therefore ever to give a 'definitive' account, or re-presentation, of the past.

That inability, as O'Brien goes on to claim, is a two-edged sword which duly cuts both ways. For it slices off for us portions both of frustration and of fascination; so that we are at once exasperated with our failure, and provoked to make yet another attempt to succeed. And it is in the latter – the provocation – that we are to take heart; for, while 'craving to know what cannot be known', we nonetheless realise that, as the writer of fiction, now in Derridean mode, insists: 'Absolute knowledge is [or would be] absolute closure.'[10] Which would, in turn, portend the end – the end, not only of a novel or a history, but of all creativity, and so of life. That unlikely outcome is not imminent, but the negativity of closure – so often seen as a virtue and desirable – does bear re-emphasis. According to O'Brien, then, 'there is no end, happy or otherwise. Nothing is fixed. Nothing is solved . . . *There is no tidiness.*' So we soldier on, we continue. And, as we have seen in the case of his novel, we continue forever in uncertainty about what has actually transpired, and will.[11]

Thus, once again we have a novelist, a writer of what is avowedly *fiction*, expounding what is effectively a philosophy, and more particularly a philosophy with implications for *history*. For the points made in relation to fiction apply no less to history, where too there can be no fixity or tidy closures. There can never be any complete or definitive answer to that basic historical question we saw identified by Graham Swift, the question 'Why?' Rather, as the theorist Amy Elias has put it, there must be 'an ongoing negotiation with the chaos of history that continually *strives towards completion* and fulfilment, towards final knowledge, and is *continually thrown back*'.[12] There we see O'Brien's frustration linked with fascination: the search for the unattainable – for finality and certainty – is not simply given up; we continue, fascinated by its elusive

[9] O'Brien, *Lake*, p. 101 (my emphasis).

[10] O'Brien, *Lake*, p. 266, n. 117.

[11] O'Brien, *Lake*, pp. 295, 266, n. 117, 301, n. 133 (my emphasis).

[12] Amy J. Elias, 'Metahistorical Romance, the Historical Sublime, and Dialogic History', *Rethinking History* 9, 2005, p. 163 (my emphases). See also Elias's *Sublime Desire: History and Post-1960s Fiction*, Baltimore and London, Johns Hopkins, 2001.

charms, to strive towards it; but we know that the attempt to reach it must forever be frustrated, that we will be 'continually thrown back'.

Repeated returns to the past, then, are to be made not with any hope of closure, but in the interests of a 'creative openness', through which we may enjoy a 'dialogue with the voices we hear there' – a dialogue that may inform our own self-formation, and contribute to our own redefinition of 'reality'. And that, Elias believes, is an important reason for history to persist as a continuing subject of interest, despite all recent critiques. For people in postmodernity, as she writes further, having failed to find what they need in contemporary culture, seem 'desperately to scan the horizon of the past for some kind of orientation, some kind of value, some kind of self-validation' – a situation in which the past remains essential, as a sort of quarry, or touchstone, or point of reference.[13]

In that respect Elias may remind us of Nietzsche's analysis of his own contemporary 'dissatisfied modern culture', where he identifies a 'tremendous historical need' that he believes should be attributed specifically to a loss sustained in the past – 'the loss of myth'. For what he calls the 'Dionysian' side of humans – their imaginative, creative, aspirational, even 'mystical' side – has become dominated and tamed within an 'Apollonian' tradition, that is characterised by a secularised and 'scientific' approach manifested not least in historiography itself. For scientistic history is, as we have previously indicated, specifically 'directed towards the annihilation of myth', as being merely fictional; and historians did in fact succeed in reducing previously accepted myths 'into the narrow defile of [their own] alleged historical reality'. So that, enabled (or forced) to understand themselves 'historically', people felt free 'to smash to pieces the mythical bulwarks' that had previously surrounded and sustained them. But the result of that elimination of myth was far from wholly positive, for it left humans with a sense of lack and loss: it was myth, however 'fictional' in relation to scientific history, that provided the orientation, value, and self-validation to which Elias refers. So that, as Nietzsche concludes, 'now the man bereft of myth stands eternally starving among all the past ages and digs and rummages in search of roots'.[14]

It may not be too fanciful to analyse our own culture in similar terms. Once again we perceive dissatisfaction, and a malaise often taking the form of an 'historical need', shown once more in a frantic digging and rummaging into the past 'in search of roots'. Third generation immigrants revive and resuscitate the culture of their grandparents, striving to make connections with countries

[13] Elias, 'Metahistorical Romance', pp. 169, 161.
[14] Nietzsche, *The Birth of Tragedy*, trans. Douglas Smith, Oxford, Oxford University Press, 2000, pp. 123, 61.

of which they themselves have no direct experience; and, more generally, popular treatments of the past – often imaginatively romanticised and diverging from historical 'reality' – provide the myths, the foundation stories, however fictional, that purport to tell people where they came from and where they might be going.

That may depress those who, with very good reason, call for new beginnings – for emancipation from such pasts as have led to today's less than perfect situation, for the repudiation of histories that serve to underpin and perpetuate presents that cry out for change, and for the elimination of a conservative-inclining historical consciousness. But resort to the past need not be wholly negative: positive examples of people, practices and values, long since overlooked, forgotten and lost, may profitably be retrieved.

That potential use for history may again require some re-evaluation and redefinition of 'history' itself. It is both the subject matter of history and our ways of treating it that need re-examination – both history as the past and history as an attempted record of that past. The two are of course closely interconnected. For history purports to deal with matters fixed, as being past; and on the assumption of a fixed and real past, it has long been taken as a legitimate aim simply to re-present that static reality as accurately as possible. But that whole enterprise is based on a misunderstanding, or a refusal to accept the transitory and endlessly elusive nature of the past itself. For that past exists in the present only through our own perceptions of it, and those perceptions constantly shimmer and shift. It is, therefore, misguided to expect to capture it and tame it within our own conceptual nets. There cannot be a meaningful attempt at some 'definitive' account of past events, any more than there could be a definitive image for an artist, such as Monet, who painted numerous studies of the 'same' material object, in different lights and from different perspectives, and from whom it would be simply inappropriate or stupid to expect a final, singularly 'true' image of a haystack or cathedral.[15]

The endlessly elusive nature of external (as well as internal) reality does seem, though, to have been recognised more by imaginative artists than by historians; and the corresponding attempts to embrace complexity, through adaptations to form and technique, are more evident in the imaginative arts than in the more rigid discipline of history. So Ann Rigney has concluded that, in relation to both form and content, historians have been left in fiction's wake – 'running after novelists'.[16] That is in part to do with an unwillingness,

[15] Cf. Cézanne, who seems to have 'regarded himself as engaged in a permanent search': Hilary Lawson, *Closure: A Story of Everything*, London, Routledge, 2001, p. 352, n. 3.

[16] Ann Rigney, *Imperfect Histories: The Elusive Past and the Legacy of Romantic Historicism*, Ithaca and London, Cornell University Press, 2001, pp. 95, 98.

or inability, to think beyond the paradigms and parameters of disciplines as they currently exist; and a willingness and ability to do that is more likely to be seen in areas where practitioners do not fear, but rather pride themselves on, such matters. It is, in other words, the imaginative artists and writers (here representing 'fiction') who are likely to be better able to challenge those existing rules and procedures, by which practitioners in any subject are at any given time constrained; for they, unlike many historians, see such challenges as positively virtuous.

Still, history is, no more than fiction, *essentially* or *naturally* fixed: history is what we choose to make it; and historians working in, and for, the future may also need to be less diffident about challenging existing definitions and expectations. And they may need in particular openly to recognise and acknowledge their own interconnections with – and even inseparability from – writers of fiction. It may be hard to make that jump – and jump it is – over what has often been seen as an impassable chasm between fundamentally opposite approaches; for historians have a heavy investment – academic, institutional, and especially emotional – in maintaining their subject as, for the last two hundred years, it has been. But the discipline of history, like its content, is (if we so choose) malleable, and able to profit from re-visioning; it is a human construct rather than a 'given' once for all.

So the process of continuing, rather than attaining closure, can be a virtue in both sciences and arts – and therefore in history as well as in fiction. That point is well made by the central character in John Banville's recent novel *The Sea* (2005): 'We finish things, while for the real worker . . . there is no finishing a work, only the abandoning of it'; and, as illustration, he recalls how the painter Bonnard got a friend to divert the attention of the guard at the Musée du Luxembourg 'while he whips out his paint-box and reworks a patch of a picture of his own that had been hanging there for years'.[17]

In similar mode, and much earlier, R. G. Collingwood described in his *Autobiography* how, at an early age, he had discovered through watching the work of his father, mother, and other professional painters, that 'no "work of art" is ever finished'; work finishes on a painting or manuscript only because some external deadline has been reached, or one has got bored with the subject.[18] And no more is science, or by implication history, ever completed, or ever (in that overworked word of ultimate praise) 'definitive'.

It appears, then, that both the subject matter of history – the past – and our approaches to it – the very discipline of history – can never properly be

---

[17] John Banville, *The Sea*, London, Picador, 2005, p. 41.
[18] R. G. Collingwood, *An Autobiography* [1939], Harmondsworth, Penguin, 1944, p. 8.

closed, but stand in need of continuing reappraisal, revision, redefinition, and renewal.

History, fact and fiction in practice: Daniel Mendelsohn, The Lost: A Search for Six of Six Million

To conclude our discussion here (though not of course to end it), we shall briefly examine Daniel Mendelsohn's book *The Lost*.[19] Unlike the subjects of our other case studies, this is not itself a work of fiction, but rather the record of a practical historical investigation. As such, it too raises interesting questions of historiography, and not least the ones with which we have been particularly concerned here – including such matters as narrative, memory, ethics, identity, and indeed the whole problematic relationship between history and fiction.

Daniel Mendelsohn explains that he set out to investigate the deaths of six of his relatives who had been 'lost' in the war – these are the six of the subtitle, six of the estimated six million Jews killed in the Holocaust: his great-uncle Shmiel Jäger, his wife Ester, and their four daughters, Lorka, Frydka, Ruchele, and Bronia. They were described by his grandfather as having simply been '*killed by the Nazis*', an account so abbreviated as to come to seem totally inadequate. For, as Mendelsohn recalls, even from childhood he had felt the need to have explanatory stories of the past in order to comprehend his present; and so he set about filling what appeared to be a gaping lacuna in his family history – trying 'to learn whatever scraps of details about them [his relatives] might still be knowable, what they looked like, what their personalities were like, and yes, how they died, if anyone could still tell me that' (205). The resultant quest took him from New York to Europe, Israel, Scandinavia, Australia, and New Zealand; and his book is particularly moving for effectively providing illumination of the Holocaust in general, through the medium of his very specific family members. As he rightly observes, readers are better able 'to absorb the meaning of a vast historical event through the story of a single family' (18).

The account of his self-conscious construction of that story also, and incidentally, provides illumination for some of the issues which we have been considering in earlier chapters. In the first place, that *specificity* to which reference has just been made is something on which Mendelsohn concentrates throughout; and it is hard, with that in mind – hard, if not impossible – to avoid the

---

[19] Daniel Mendelsohn, *The Lost: A Search for Six of Six Million*, London, HarperCollins, 2007. Page references are given in the text.

intrusion into history of *ethics* and moral judgements, however dispassionately stated. There are parallels here with Tolstoy's *War and Peace*, when
for instance Mendelsohn insists that the concept of *mass* killings is all too
abstract: 'the Holocaust is so big, the scale of it is so gigantic, so enormous,
that it becomes easy to think of it as something mechanical. Anonymous.' But,
as in Tolstoy's account of the great battles of Napoleon's army in Russia, the
death of each person is specific, and responsibility for such deaths is shown
ultimately to devolve on specific individuals: 'everything that happened,
happened because someone made a decision. To pull a trigger, to flip a switch,
to close a cattle car door, to hide, to betray' (479).

In similar vein, it is all too easy, Mendelsohn concludes towards the end of
his book, 'to say that this or that *city* has been destroyed, when what you really
mean is that *all the people in the city* have been killed' (469, my emphases). So
that it is morally desirable to avoid abstract generalities in such contexts; and
it becomes his own task 'to rescue my relatives from generalities, symbols,
abbreviations, to restore to them their particularity and distinctiveness' (112).
'It's always the small things', as one of his witnesses recognises; it is those that
make it 'like life' (413) – while another who provides testimony provokes the
authorial comment that she gave 'this *generic* story a new *specificity*' (125, my
emphases).

Like many historians, then, Daniel Mendelsohn is concerned to tell
specific stories; but unlike some he comes to appreciate just how problematic
the attempt to do so is in relation to an assumed historical 'truth'. So we are
brought, next, to the question of narrative construction. The author started
with the aim that any writer has, of contriving 'to impose order on a chaos of
facts by assembling them into a story that has a beginning, a middle, and an
end' (38; cf. 436); for it seemed essential to place his relatives' lives within
some sort of narrative (indeed, within *any* sort of narrative), in order that their
deaths be endowed with some meaning: that, he believed, 'would make their
deaths be *about* something' (149). To be lost to history, as they were, or even
to be relegated to a minor role in someone else's story – that is to be 'truly dead'
(434). So he determined to write a *narrative* on their behalf – the story of
'people who had no story, anymore' (315).

The quest for their own specific stories, though, proved highly problematic; and far from immediately achieving the satisfaction of a single narrative
thread, Mendelsohn describes how he became ever more aware of the complexities by which he was assailed. For 'stories multiplied and gave birth to
other stories'; and although often interesting for what they revealed about the
people who told them, they failed to tell 'the *whole story*' that he sought (411).
Even towards the end of his travels, he confesses to being despondent, that

'when all was said and done I couldn't tell the whole story, couldn't rescue *that* for them, or for my grandfather, or for me' (437).

For one thing, some people were reluctant to reveal and contribute their memories: they were protective of their own stories; and, as the researcher came to see, that was not without good reason. Mrs Meg Grossbard, for example, was fearful that he would somehow appropriate the material for himself and thereby diminish it – that he 'would take the Frydka she had known and reduce her to a stick figure, a cipher' (199). He sympathised with that anxiety: 'I understood perfectly what she was afraid of, why she wouldn't let *her* tales enter *my* book. She knew that the minute she allowed me to start telling *her* stories, they would become *my* stories' (252, my emphases).

Quite apart from that reluctance, on the part of some, to entrust their stories with another, there are additional problems that inevitably arise in their telling. For all stories, as we have previously observed, contain their own inbuilt functions: there is always some reason for their telling; there is only ever history *for* some purpose; or as Mendelsohn concludes, 'nobody has ever told a story without having some kind of agenda' (128). And that agenda is often (usually, even) set (whether consciously or unconsciously) through our own self-centredness: 'We are each of us . . . myopic; always at the centre of our own stories' (147); and so we fail to do justice to others. And we are likely to become so concerned with the coherence and integrity of our own narratives, that we are tempted to bend the truth accordingly – or to modify our version of what seems to have happened, or to accept accounts, however intrinsically unreliable, on the ground of their consistency with our earlier conclusion. So we think a story (for instance, about Frydka's betrayal) is true, or accept it as such,

> [b]ecause somebody else, somebody who hadn't been there either when it happened, somebody who had hidden successfully and who'd also only heard about what happened to Frydka after the war was over, had heard it from somebody else, who'd heard it from someone else; and because a certain detail from that thirdhand story now dovetailed with a detail that Malcia had heard from someone who'd heard it from someone else. (328–9)

It seems, in short, that '[c]ertain kinds of manipulation of the truth are irresistible if what one wants to create is a story with a satisfying shape' (446). Aesthetics, as Hayden White has long since argued, is no doubt a major (if not determining) factor in the construction of historical narratives; and we are thus explicitly confronted once more by the problematic relationship between historical truth and fiction.

Memories, too – and here we reach another of our themes – memories, too, that provide the vital primary source material for historians, are liable to similar distortions. For '[i]n the end, we see what we want to see and the rest falls away' (72–3); and that provides the flimsy basis for our memories. So *'What is memory?'*, asks the thoughtful witness Ilana Adler; 'What is *memory?* Memory is what you remember'; and of course 'you change the story, you "remember"'. So that 'there is the memory, there is the truth'; but they are different, and what is the relationship between the two? Her honest conclusion takes us back once more to our earlier discussion, for it is, that 'you don't know, never' (388).

It is no wonder, then, that Mendelsohn himself at one point concludes that, 'the more I talked to people, the more I was aware of how much simply can't be known'. That is partly because some events were never witnessed by anyone who still survives; but it is also 'partly because memory itself, of those things that were witnessed, can play tricks, can elide what is too painful or be trimmed to fit a pattern that we happen to like' (205). Acute historiographical problems arise from the fact that 'the mind . . . *misremembers* even fresh information, because of the need to make certain random scraps of data into part of the stories we have been brought up to tell ourselves about the world, and which for that reason we cherish' (223, my emphasis). It seems that, further problematising the relationship of history and fiction, our memories conspire to aid in the construction of narratives that are not so much 'true', as aesthetically and emotionally pleasing.

So nothing can be taken at face value: there is no direct route to any historical 'truth' – or even to the truth of any historical event. Whether dealing with oral testimony or with written texts, the complexities seem overwhelming. In relation to the former, witnesses have their own perspectives on the events they experienced – their own highly (and necessarily) selective memories, their own interests and agendas; and that is before we in turn have to endeavour to interpret what they say, where mistakes can be made at the most basic level. The thread of one such mistake runs through the book. Mendelsohn was told by his grandfather that his great-uncle Shmiel with his daughter Frydka were betrayed after hiding in a 'Kassel' or what sounded like that, a 'castle', of which, strangely, the local people had no recollection. That mystery was finally solved when the author was shown his relatives' actual hiding place – a small subterranean hole beneath a trapdoor in the floor, a space appropriately described as a 'box', or (in Yiddish) a 'kestl'.

Such simple (but vitally important) mistakes that occur in oral evidence are multiplied in the case of written records, where it seems that all historians (as well as others) share an 'impulse to manoeuvre the text so that it tells us what we want it to say' (121). Quite apart from the 'innocent mistakes' that are easily made by 'the eye that travels down to the wrong line when transcribing from an entry from a faded piece of paper' (223), historians are guilty of less innocent manipulations: for 'Who does not find ways to make the texts we deal with mean what we want them to mean?' (105). So Mendelsohn describes how he was forced to consider the possibility of mistakes, however seemingly insignificant, that might 'lurk in the stories and, even more, in the texts on which we so often blindly rely for the "facts" ' (223). And to give but one example, Jewish records in Israel provide – or seem to provide – the bare 'facts' about Shmiel's daughter Lorka; but after his own research, he is able to confirm that 'in fact, not a single element of this entry in the Yad Vashem database is accurate' (224). So, he writes, in his historical enquiries he became 'used to the discrepancies between the facts and the "record" ' (225); and that was another factor in persuading him of 'how fragile each story I heard really was' (303).

One result, then, of Daniel Mandelsohn's researches was his realisation of the huge complexity of the issues in any historical enquiry. Trying to work out and to imagine what actually occurred, he came to appreciate 'how limited my resources are' (204). As we try to grasp, to comprehend, even to relive, what happened, we often find ourselves supplying images and sounds at second- or third-hand, as it were – from films, perhaps, or television documentaries, which have themselves been 'produced by people who have been paid to reconstruct, to the best of *their* ability – based on whatever reading, visiting, and looking they have done, extrapolated from whatever experiences they may have had – what such events might have looked or sounded like, although that, too, is just an approximation, ultimately' (205).

For in the end, we can never ever come to understand, or fully 'empathise with', people who lived through a past, the nature of which is infinitely remote from our own experience. 'Whatever we see in museums, the artefacts and the evidence, can give us only the dimmest comprehension of what the event itself was like' (237); and 'it is important to avoid the temptation to ventriloquise, to "imagine" and then "describe" something for which there is simply no parallel in our experience of life . . . there is simply no way of reconstructing . . . subjective experiences' (226). Eyewitness reports do, admittedly, 'permit us to construct a mental picture – a blurry one to be sure – of certain things that were *done to them*, or rather were *likely* done to them' and so 'arrive at a likely version of what probably happened . . . but of course I will never know' (226). For even if, as an historian, he succeeds in getting 'some idea of what happened [to his cousin] . . . there is no way to reconstruct what she herself went through' (206). As he concludes:

> We can never be other than ourselves, imprisoned by our time and place and circumstances. However much we want to learn, to know, we can only ever see things with our own eyes and hear with our own ears, and how we interpret what we see and hear depends, ultimately, on who we are and what we already think we know, or want to know. (482)

So he is periodically left asking the sort of question, which recurs throughout his book, to which the only possible answer is: '*Impossible to know*' (383, my emphases).

That may sound a negative conclusion, and it is clear that, as a result of his practical research, Daniel Mendelsohn does end up as something of an historiographical sceptic; which is to say that he is left sceptical about the historian's ability ever to reach the 'truth' of what happened in the past – and especially the 'subjective truth' of other people's feelings. There are, as we have seen, altogether too many complexities in relation to evidence, whether oral or written, and our own apprehensions of that evidence, to enable any single story to be told that could justify a claim to have actually reached 'the truth'. The fragments of the past which we do, or might, manage to unearth can never, as he concludes, 'quite come together to make a whole picture' (435). Indeed, when presented with an account in which all the details 'fit too neatly', we are liable for that very reason to mistrust it. Or we should mistrust it; for we should be aware that 'only in stories does every small detail fit neatly into place'. It is more likely that the narratives we tell 'are the image of what we wish had happened, the unconscious justifications for the lives we've ended up living' (347). We mould the past to chime with our own self-constructed and self-centred autobiographies.

That conclusion sits ill with the orthodox mainstream of twenty-first-century historiography. And so too does Mendlesohn's unapologetic emotional involvement in the object of his study, and the emphasis he puts on feelings: the approach he describes presents an image of something other than the scientifically 'detached' historian, so often presented as the disciplinary ideal.[20] Acknowledging his brother Matt's example, he records how, on showing some photographs to a potential witness, he 'took care to ask him about the *feelings* they evoked in him' (415, my emphasis). And the affirmation of his own emotions as he encounters evidence for the story of his relatives' last days

---

[20] Even in the week that I drafted this, I read of the continuing 'broad consensus . . . among professional historians as to how history should be written: in particular, it should in some sense be "scientific"'. Chris Given-Wilson, 'Past Times for All', *Times Literary Supplement*, 15 February, 2008, p. 14 (my emphasis).

and hours makes for some of the most moving passages in the book – when, for instance he describes how, on finally getting reliable confirmation of their end, 'something snapped in me at that moment. I simply sank down and squatted there in the dust of the street and started to cry.'[21] Previously, he explains, he had heard versions only from people who had got their information at second hand. But '[n]ow I was talking to a Ukrainian, not a Jew, which is to say, someone who was there when it happened. Suddenly, it seemed less like a story than a fact. I had hit bedrock' (477); and through that personal testimony from someone actually there at the time, he felt confidence in 'a story that accounted for all the bits and pieces that [previously] . . . hadn't quite been able to gel into a coherent narrative, a story with a beginning and a middle and an end' (499). Unsurprisingly, he was emotionally moved by that.

The final encounter with that claimed 'bedrock' does serve to provide a more positive ending, which we might profitably use as a provisional conclusion to our own discussion of history and fiction. For it does indicate that something – even if only a higher degree of probability, or a higher level of satisfaction – might be gained through the process of historical enquiry. Indeed, the complexities inherent in, and revealed by, such enquiries need not (as Mendlesohn was advised by a friend), and even should not, be seen as a problem, but rather as themselves some sort of 'solution'; and similarly, an 'aporia', or what seems a 'hopeless impasse', can be construed, more positively, as 'a passageway' (283) – a route to greater understanding.

In support of that, the author does, as he admits, become aware of a certain irony – 'that in the end, we'd learned far more about what we hadn't been looking for than about what we'd set out to find' (436). Which in itself provides illumination, indicating not least that, 'if you look for things, if you search, you will, by the very act of searching, make something happen that would not otherwise have happened, *you will find something*'. The search is what is important, and brings its own, often unexpected, rewards. For in history, there is on the one hand 'always a vast series of random potentialities . . . and on the other hand, intersecting with this unimaginable and infinite universe of factors and possibilities, there is the irrevocable fact of individual personality and individual will'; and the attempts to disentangle those two – and here we are reminded again of Tolstoy's agenda for a history that would investigate the limits of free will within an apparently deterministic universe – are what history is (or can be) about. 'There is', as Daniel Mendelsohn concludes, 'only looking, and finally seeing, what was always there' (485–6).

---

[21] See also his protestation in the yard where Shmiel and Friydka were actually killed: 'I can't deal with this now' (480).

So his 'ending', like mine, shows, not so much how close we've got to anything, but 'how far we'd always be' (450). As with 'negative theology', virtue
lies, not in gaining (or in claiming to have gained) new knowledge about
the past (or God), but in losing the illusion that we can ever attain such knowledge. So Mendelsohn claims to *'have finally come to see . . . an extremely
accurate picture of the way that people behave in unimaginably extreme conditions'*; but he then goes on to describe that accurate picture as *'a picture of a
blur, an image of something that remains, in the end, totally unknowable and
completely mysterious'*. All he can say is *'that some people simply choose to do evil
and some choose to do good'* (493).[22]

But we are still left with a moral message, for although 'There is so much
that will always be *impossible to know*', one lesson has been learnt about his six
relatives, and by implication the six million others who were similarly 'lost':
'that they were, once, themselves, *specific*, the subjects of their own lives and
deaths, and not simply puppets to be manipulated for the purposes of a good
story' (502); or, we might add, puppets not only to be exterminated bodily but
also to be removed from any possibility of memory, as if they had never ever
lived. Despite all the complexities, and the inextricably interconnected
threads of history and fiction, then, there remains some virtue in the very
process of endeavouring to disentangle them and retain some (however tenu-
ous) distinction between the two. For the attempt to do so may enlarge our
own capacities, and provide some light about what it is to be human.

So *The Lost* is a work of historical exploration – or, perhaps more accurately, of historical archaeology, as indicating sedimentary layers of memories
and descriptions of the past, and slowly uncovering, revealing, what lies
beneath. As such, it is inevitably concerned with our theme of 'History meeting Fiction', where the former stands for the search for some kind of truth
about the past, while the latter has to do with such claims, descriptions, explanations, as are found to be, in the end, and for whatever reasons, not (in that
'historical' sense) true at all. In the course of Mendelsohn's own investigations, a whole hierarchy of narratives was revealed – of which the last seemed
(for reasons that we have seen) to be the most accurate or truthful, or in
accordance with what actually happened.

But what was revealed, too, is that 'fictions' can very easily intrude into our
supposedly true historical narratives: the names of characters get muddled
and obscured and lost, not least through simple changes in spelling (from
Jäger to Jaeger to Yager etc.); maps are shown to be indeterminate and unreliable, as streets and towns and whole countries change their boundaries; words

---

[22] The quoted passages in this paragraph are italicised in the original.

are misheard or mistranslated; pregnancies are assigned to the wrong girl; external physical characteristics are misremembered, misdescribed; and about internal emotional states, there can only ever be, at best, speculation.

The difficulties are so numerous as to be ultimately, from a theoretical standpoint, insurmountable; we shall never reach certainty or historical 'truth'. But in terms of practice, there is still some virtue in the search – by which I mean some moral point to it – and in that respect history, as I shall hope to clarify in my concluding section, once again encounters fiction.

Conclusion

For as a report of 'factual' research, Daniel Mendelsohn's *The Lost* points to a function for history that had already been made explicit in another context by a number of African-American women writers of 'fiction': namely, that individuals who have become, or are in danger of becoming, 'lost' should be retrieved – both for their own sakes and for the sake of their descendants. As Robert Holton (to whom I am here once more indebted) shows, such writers as Gayl Jones, Paule Marshall, and Toni Morrison have likewise been concerned to consolidate remembrance of past individuals and events that may be in danger of otherwise being forgotten or deliberately erased from memory. For them too there is a sense in which the dead, whose death has not been adequately accounted for and fitted into some sort of narrative, continue to haunt the living as not yet properly 'laid to rest'.[23]

We have seen that Daniel Mendelsohn embarked on his research through dissatisfaction with the obviously superficial account of his own relations' ends. The 'Nazi' exterminators of the Jews had done their best to cover their own tracks and eliminate any records of what had happened; so what, as an historian, Mendelsohn succeeded in doing was finally to get the better of them – by (re-)opening up those aspects of the past which they would have preferred to keep finally closed, erased, forgotten, and lost. And with slavery there is similar work to do, for there too obvious attempts were made to eliminate pasts – both individual pasts, as when the original names of slaves were replaced with those assigned by their new masters, and more generally with the whole institution and practice of slavery, where, as we hear from a character in Gayl Jones' novel *Corregidora* (1975), 'they burned all the slavery papers so it

---

[23] As Lyotard claims, 'The dead are not dead so long as the living have not recorded their death in narrative', quoted by Robert Holton, *Jarring Witnesses: Modern Fiction and the Representation of History*, Hemel Hempstead, Harvester Wheatsheaf, 1994, p. 214.

would be like they never had it'.[24] If only for that very reason – the attempted destruction of historical evidence – slaves themselves became determined that their past *should and would* be remembered: 'history' would not then be restricted to the narratives of dominant whites, but would be extended to include (or on occasion be replaced by) the stories of those who had suffered and died.

In that retrieval and maintenance of an otherwise lost story, oral transmission would play an important part – an oral transmission 'from generation to generation so we'd never forget . . . Even though they'd burned everything to play like it didn't never happen', the fact that it did happen would thus be remembered; and there was a *duty* on each generation to hand the story on – to preserve the memory of people who, as Daniel Mendelsohn put it about his relatives, otherwise 'had no story, anymore' and would therefore be 'truly dead'. Again there is a defiant aspiration to deny the persecutors the privilege of having the last word: 'They didn't want to leave no evidence of what they done – so it couldn't be held against them. *And I'm leaving evidence.* And you got to leave evidence too. And your children got to leave evidence.'[25]

In that way, again, the oppressors (and would-be suppressors of evidence) would in the end be defeated. For with that evidence, and in that remembrance of the past, lie hopes for regeneration in the future. 'Only that historian will have the gift of fanning the spark of hope in the past who is firmly convinced that *even the dead* will not be safe from the enemy if he wins', wrote Walter Benjamin; and much African-American fiction, Robert Holton insists, is to do with saving the dead from the enemy – with restoring a voice to the hitherto voiceless, and so attempting 'to fan a spark of hope in the past by safeguarding or defending the dead'.[26] In that way, as Paule Marshall wrote in 1974, the previously oppressed can finally 'overcome their oppressors and take control of their lives'; they can go on to construct their future – but only after first exploring their past, and contriving '*to use their history creatively*'.[27]

That theme is reiterated in the 'fictional' work of Toni Morrison. In her prize-winning novel *Beloved* (1988), 'Beloved' is at the end a single word on a gravestone; but as her Dedication indicates, it memorialises all 'Sixty Million and more' slaves whose names and testimonies have not been recorded. Such memorialising and attempts to use history creatively do not imply any obsessive attachment to the past: as we have already considered above in Chapter 4,

---

[24] Gayl Jones, quoted by Horton, *Jarring Witnesses*, p. 187.

[25] Gayl Jones, quoted by Holton, *Jarring Witnesses*, pp. 187–8 (my emphasis).

[26] Holton, *Jarring Witnesses*, p. 164.

[27] Paule Marshall, quoted by Holton, *Jarring Witnesses*, p. 184 (my emphasis).

such backward-looking negativity can result in an inability to act at all in the present. So while recognising that there must always be some tension between repressing a traumatic past and 'working through' it, there does decidedly remain, as Robert Holton insists, a need 'to possess the past rather than being possessed by it'.[28] With that in mind, the 'fictional' work of Toni Morrison does provide an interesting parallel with that of Daniel Mendelsohn's 'factual' record of his search for six individuals who similarly stand as representatives of millions more. Both these works (as well as the others just mentioned) once again show positive ways in which history and fiction meet.

They have also caused me to make belated adjustments to my own position, as I shall now try to explain in a brief Postscript.

Further reading

Demos, John, 'Afterword: Notes From, and About, the History/Fiction Borderland', *Rethinking History* 9, 2005, 329–35.

Elias, Amy J., 'Metahistorical Romance, the Historical Sublime, and Dialogic History', *Rethinking History* 9, 2005, pp. 159–72.

Elias, Amy J., *Sublime Desire: History and Post-1960s Fiction*, Baltimore and London, Johns Hopkins, 2001.

Evans, Richard J., *Telling Lies About Hitler: The Holocaust, History and the David Irving Trial*, London, Verso, 2002.

Holton, Robert, *Jarring Witnesses: Modern Fiction and the Representation of History*, Hemel Hempstead, Harvester Wheatsheaf, 1994.

Lawson, Hilary, *Closure: A Story of Everything*, London, Routledge, 2001.

Mendelsohn, Daniel, *The Lost: A Search for Six of Six Million*, London, HarperCollins, 2007.

Morrison, Toni, *Beloved*, New York, Plume, 1988.

---

[28] Holton, *Jarring Witnesses*, p. 194. On 'working through', see Dominick LaCapra in e.g. *History and Memory after Auschwitz*, Ithaca and London, Cornell University Press, 1998; *History in Transit: Experience, Identity, Critical Theory*, Ithaca and London, Cornell University Press, 2004.

Postscript

Like servicemen in the war, writers often do not know where they're going until they're there: the act of writing forces one to reassess, and seek to clarify, one's own position. And, to be personal, the study of history's relationship with fiction has at once opened up more avenues than I could possibly explore, and forced me – as I hope it will also encourage my readers – to persist with, and periodically modify, my own thinking. But despite all the intellectual objections there may be to 'closure', texts must at least have a physical end, and (in the interest of communication) provide some semblance of order. So in the previous chapter, Daniel Mendelsohn's *The Lost* satisfactorily tied together a number of knots (relating to representation, memory, ethics, identity, and the functions of history) that had hopefully been disentangled (by which I mean separated out for analysis) in previous chapters. It did, though, in my case, tend not so much to finalise as to unsettle; and rather than claiming to *conclude* now, I shall simply offer a personal 'postscript'. This will recapitulate on five main points.

First, we have seen that there has been a long tradition of defining 'history' in such a way as to distinguish it clearly – indeed, emphatically to *contrast* it – with 'fiction'. Thus, so far as the past is concerned, 'history' has been what enables us to replace 'myth', or fictional accounts of that past, with *fact* – with true representations of what 'actually happened'. As such, history has been assigned a central role in education and in culture more generally, being seen as a solid foundation on which current identities are, or can be, built. From that position, fiction is sometimes viewed as an inferior genre – and certainly historical fiction has been viewed askance by historical 'professionals' – and sometimes seen, more sympathetically, as complementary, with its ability to fill in certain gaps left by conventional histories; in that latter view, fiction arises, as the nineteenth-century German Romantic poet Novalis put it, 'out of the *shortcomings* of history', or as Michel de Certeau later maintained, 'fiction is the *repressed other* of historical discourse'.[1] Those shortcomings – and that repressed other – have often been seen as applying especially to an absence, or underestimation of the importance, of *feelings* – a deficiency that derives as a necessary consequence of assuming a 'scientific' methodology based on professional detachment at the expense of subjective involvement.

Whether on equal terms or not, history and fiction proceeded along ways that were separate except for the occasional, but increasingly insistent, invasions by novelists on to historiographical terrain. So we have seen in particular how, for their various reasons, Dickens, Tolstoy, Gide, Wyndham Lewis, Penelope Lively, and Graham Swift all, in their fictional writings, provide cogent critiques of history as practised and theorised at their respective times of writing.

Those literary-based critiques – and here we reach my second point – have been confirmed and amplified by postmodernist theorists. Working within a long tradition of sceptical philosophy, these have presented arguments in relation to history and fiction that seem to me simply irrefutable. That is to say, the essential distinction between history and fiction, as long maintained, has been rendered untenable: it is now clear that all history is fictional, in the sense that it is a literary (rhetorical, aesthetic) construction based on evidence that is itself of *inevitably* questionable reliability. If, as a literary discourse, it bears any relationship to the 'facts' of what actually happened, we can never know what that relationship is; for we can never *know* – have certain knowledge of – the past by which to test the validity of any descriptions of, or assertions about, it. We can, in short, never re-present that past (as history) in any way of which it makes sense to talk of 'truth' or 'certainty', or in any way that is finally and irrefutably distinct from fiction.

That conclusion does of course run directly counter to claims often made by historians themselves. But even the eminent practitioner Patrick Collinson has recently conceded that, 'it is possible for competent historians to come to radically different conclusions on the basis of the same evidence. Because, of course, 99 per cent of the evidence, above all unrecorded speech, is not available to us.'[2] Collinson is far from being a 'postmodernist', but this gives some indication of the extent to which postmodern scepticism, or anti-dogmatic

---

[1] Novalis quoted by Richard Slotkin, 'Fiction for the Purposes of History', *Rethinking History* 9, 2005, p. 221 (my emphasis). De Certeau is quoted by Hayden White in the same issue: 'Introduction: Historical Fiction, Fictional History, and Historical Reality', p. 147.

[2] Patrick Collinson in *London Review of Books*, 29 November 2007, p. 33.

diffidence, has encroached upon the historical profession; and it reveals the increased blurring of the history/fiction divide.

That blurring, it may be argued, has always been accepted: history has never been a claimant to certainty; historians have always been aware of the *hypothetical* nature of their works. And for some that may be so. But for others it patently is not – as can readily be seen in the 'popular' attitudes displayed in reviews of books, variously described as 'definitive', or 'balanced', or in some way 'flawed'; where all those adjectives depend for their meaning on a conception of an absolutely truthful model, which exists and is somehow (at least theoretically) attainable, and against which it is then possible to assess and grade various attempted reconstructions. 'Definitive' implies that some perfect match has finally been attained between the historical account and what actually happened; there is no further room for improvement,[3] so to ascribe that adjective to a work is highly complimentary (and, surprisingly, not all that uncommon: even as I revise this draft, I find the adjective applied to Richard Evans' 'narrative of Nazi Germany and the Second World War' – subjects about which it might seem difficult to have the last word – in a publication of one of Britain's most prestigious academic institutions[4]). 'Balance' similarly assumes an ideal, here of perfect 'objectivity', in the sense that no particular standpoint is adopted in relation to what is being observed and described, and that somehow it is possible to view any matter (including the past) simultaneously from every conceivable standpoint, and take all equally into account; or alternatively, a perfect 'even-handedness' has been maintained between extremes. Continuing belief in the possibility (and desirability) of 'balance' may be deduced from the not infrequent complaints about its lack, whether applied to the BBC or Al Jazeera. 'Flawed', conversely, is a word of disapproval often used by critics, and especially about works of history. It assumes some falling short of perfection, some reprehensible omission or imbalance, or some discrepancy between the history as written and the past it purports to represent. (More cynically, we might think it represents disagreement with the reviewer's own beliefs.)

All such words – 'definitive', 'balanced', 'flawed' – presuppose a Platonic-style conception of an idealised external world or 'past', to which access can, by the favoured few, be gained; and that presupposition still underpins popular (and sometimes professional) attitudes to both current news reporting and historical treatments of the past. But 'balance', or 'bias', or 'reliability', or 'distortion', are themselves all ascribed in relation to a 'message' that it is wished

---

[3] *Oxford English Dictionary* defines as 'having the function of *finally deciding*: determinative, *final*' (my emphases).

[4] *LSE Events*, 22 September–11 December 2008, p. 26.

or hoped to convey; and the conception of an ideal absolute, which transcends such concerns, and in terms of which it is then meaningful to speak of 'truth', is simply no longer credible.

The question then arises – and this constitutes my third point here – as to whether all this matters: does it actually *matter* that we seem unable to make a clear distinction between history and fiction?

And now I surprise myself by having come to believe (especially after reading *The Lost*) that yes, it does, and that, despite the strength of all the arguments against it, we do still need to make distinctions between differing and sometimes conflicting accounts of what happened in the past; there does seem to me to be a need to acknowledge some sort of authenticity or 'truth', however ultimately unattainable, by reference to which, however tentatively, to make those distinctions.

For otherwise, why do we feel differently towards even a physical object – a painting, say, or piece of pottery – when we ascertain that it is not, after all, genuine, or properly attributed to the person or period as previously claimed, but just a fake? We look, as we say, with different eyes, or with different emotions, upon an authenticated Rembrandt portrait or Ming Dynasty vase, even though a copy may (to all but the most expert) be virtually indistinguishable from the original. And similarly with writing, we react differently to a memoir composed by an author who has personally experienced what he recounts, from the way we react to one who has not actually lived through the events he describes but has imaginatively made them up – an example here being the genuine accounts of Auschwitz left, as a former prisoner, by Primo Levi, and the concocted memoirs of another (as he claimed) Holocaust survivor, Binjamin Wilkomirski. (The latter were published as an 'unselfconscious and powerful' report which would enable the reader to 'experience love, terror, friendship and above all survival', but they were later revealed as fictitious. In such cases, do not readers feel 'taken in', defrauded, intellectually and emotionally *abused*?) Inability in such cases to discriminate between the genuine author – by which I mean here someone who does not claim to be other than he is or believes himself to be – and the pretender, who claims truth for what is fictitious, can lead, at its extreme, to universal mistrust and so to the denial of reported events (such as those of the Holocaust or more recently of 9/11), the facticity of which it is (for practical reasons relating to the future) important to acknowledge.

That brings me to my fourth observation, which has to do with relating theory to practice. For having concluded in our theories that certainty in history, as in many (or in any) other fields, is an elusive goal that lies forever out of reach, we have to find a way of going on – of living positively with uncertainty.

And that is a challenge at once intellectual and emotional. For we all know from personal experience of cases (including claims about the past) where we can never be sure, or where any possibility of approaching certainty has to be (at least for the time being) deferred. So that we find ourselves moving back once more to the approach, formally adopted in seventeenth-century theology and science, and almost universally assumed today in practice: a pragmatic approach based on varying degrees of probability.

Probability translates in historical terms to credibility. So that highly credible evidence enables us to feel reasonably *certain* about the date on which the British Prime Minister announced the commencement of what came to be known as the Second World War; slightly lower down the scale of certainty, there is evidence, sufficient for practical purposes, to convince most, but evidently not quite all, of the existence of an attempted genocide perpetrated by Nazi Germany; and, further down the scale and so approaching speculation, there is conflicting evidence concerning, for example, the effect of bombing on civilian morale. So we approach different parts of histories with different expectations and differing degrees of belief.

And that of course is how we proceed more generally in everyday life: in courts of law, or in our own personal lives, we rarely, if ever, act on the basis of absolute certainty – but we do the best we can to make tentative judgements on the basis of whatever limited evidence is currently available; and we then act accordingly. For however racked with indecision, we do for practical purposes have to make up our minds – even if we are later compelled to admit to having been mistaken. In history, then, the best we can do is to adopt a similar approach.

That points, fifthly, to a reconsideration of our *definition* of 'history'. Perhaps (and this is only to repeat what others have periodically proposed) it is more than time to broaden the limits of history's concerns and procedures. For it is, surely, difficult to assess whether, in terms of 'history', the account of the 'professional' historian who makes supposedly logical inferences from archival 'data' (that is meant to be, but clearly never is, just 'given') is better than, or for whatever reason preferable to, that of the 'amateur' who deliberately and openly provides imaginative embellishments. To persist with bipolarities, does the Rankean or the Romantic provide us with a closer approximation to the 'truth' of life in the past? And does not our inability decisively to answer that question suggest that 'history' should be defined in such a way as to include them both, as complementary?

Some such extension of history's definition might embrace further suggestions, and here it has to be said that historians themselves have sometimes led the way – without, however, often being followed. Fernand Braudel, for example, wrote over half a century ago of his 'desire and need [as an historian] to see on a grand scale'. History, he insisted, 'can do more than study walled gardens'.[5] Many 'walled gardens' have subsequently been meticulously cultivated; but Braudel himself went on, more expansively, to write of a 'study of *humanity*' – a theme that has been more recently re-echoed by John Demos, who suggests that real-life historians might be emboldened by the fictitious model presented by Wallace Stegner in *Angle of Repose*, to take a larger view of their own efforts – and once again following the lead of a novelist, get beyond the particulars (with which their subject is meant to be concerned) and embrace the truly generic – that which is quintessentially '*human*'.[6] And that that is a practical possibility is shown, as we have just seen above, by Daniel Mendelsohn's successful embrace of the generic – the human – through the specific, in *The Lost*.

Such aspirations for history, though, depend upon recognition of an infinite number of potential specifics – and the enlargement of history to include some (ideally all) of those hitherto excluded. That has of late been widely recognised within a historical profession that has collectively sought to retrieve, and reinstate in memory, many of the previously 'lost'. But the point is worth re-emphasising, and that can be done with the help of two novelists whose humour makes a serious case. Thus, Penelope Lively's Claudia Hampton implicitly challenges the 'univocality' of histories that are supposedly 'objective', as she speculates about telling her history 'from the point of view of the soup, maybe'.[7] And Julian Barnes, in the first chapter of his *A History of the World in 10 1/2 Chapters*, makes his narrator a woodworm which had stowed away on Noah's Ark.[8] The success of the woodworm in smuggling itself into the Ark, and its subsequent infiltration into history, may be emblematic of a subject more expansively defined.

That chimes finally, and perhaps appropriately, with Hayden White's plea, made long ago but with characteristic perspicuity and humanitarian concern, for 'the assimilation of history to a higher kind of intellectual inquiry', which could therapeutically lead 'a sick society back to the path of enlightenment and

---

[5] Fernand Braudel, *The Mediterranean and the Mediterranean World in the Age of Philip II* [1949], 2 vols; London, Fontana, 1975, vol. 1, p. 22.

[6] John Demos in Mark C. Carnes (ed.), *Novel History: Historians and Novelists Confront America's Past (and Each Other)*, London, Simon & Schuster, 2001, p. 143.

[7] Penelope Lively, *Moon Tiger*, London, Penguin, 1988, p. 3.

[8] That anthropomorphising is continued in a later chapter, when woodworms in the Middle Ages are arraigned for their responsibility for weakening a bishop's throne and the cathedral roof timbers. Julian Barnes, *A History of the World in 10 1/2 Chapters*, London, Picador, 1990, pp. 1–30.

progress'.[9] For far too long history has been a 'burden' (as indicated by the title of White's essay) from which we need relief, a 'prison-house', as Martin Davies has described it, from which we would do well to escape, or, in the terminology of James Joyce's fictional Stephen Daedalus, a 'nightmare' from which we need to be awakened. And although we cannot, it seems to me (for reasons I have tried to indicate), simply disburden ourselves, extract ourselves from all constraints – just jettison the past and forget it – we can surely encourage preferable dreams through a history that incorporates some aspects of experience that have hitherto been relegated to the domain of fiction. In that higher and wider kind of intellectual inquiry, 'truth' would no doubt remain in the company of 'tangled falsehood', but such redefined 'history' might serve a therapeutic function for a sick society, imaginatively exposing and proposing alternative and preferable futures.

[9]   Hayden White, 'The Burden of History' (1966), in *Tropics of Discourse: Essays in Cultural Criticism*, Baltimore and London, Johns Hopkins, 1978, pp. 29–30.

Bibliography

Abelove, Henry et al. (eds), *Visions of History*, Manchester, Manchester University Press, 1983.

Acton, Lord, Review of Mandell Creighton, *A History of the Papacy*, in *The English Historical Review* 2, 1887, pp. 571–81.

Amis, Kingsley, *Lucky Jim* [1954], London, Penguin, 1961.

Ankersmit, Frank, 'Manifesto for an Analytical Political History', in Keith Jenkins, Sue Morgan and Alun Munslow (eds), *Manifestos for History*, London, Routledge, 2007, pp. 179–96.

Ankersmit, Frank, *Sublime Historical Experience*, Stanford, Stanford University Press, 2005.

Augustine, *Confessions*, trans. R. S. Pine-Coffin, Harmondsworth, Penguin, 1961.

Baker, Herschel, *The Race of Time*, [Toronto], University of Toronto, 1967.

Banville, John, *The Sea*, London, Picador, 2005.

Barnes, Julian, *A History of the World in 10 1/2 Chapters*, London, Picador, 1990.

Bellow, Saul, *Mr Sammler's Planet*, Harmondsworth, Penguin, 1977.

Benda, Julien, *The Great Betrayal*, trans. R. Aldington, London, Routledge, 1928.

Bentley, Michael, *Modern Historiography: An Introduction*, London, Routledge, 1999.

Berlin, Isaiah, *The Hedgehog and the Fox: An Essay on Tolstoy's View of History* [1953], London, Weidenfeld and Nicolson, 1967.

Bolingbroke, Lord Henry St. John, *Letters on the Study and Use of History* [1752], London, Alexander Murray, 1870.

Bourke, Joanna, *An Intimate History of Killing*, London, Granta, 2000.

Bradley, F. H., *The Presuppositions of Critical History* [1874], ed. Lionel Rubinoff, Chicago, Quadrangle Books, 1968.

Braudel, Fernand, *The Mediterranean and the Mediterranean World in the Age of Philip II* [1949], 2 vols; London, Fontana, 1975.

Braudy, Leo, *Narrative Form in History and Fiction*, Princeton, Princeton University Press, 1970.

Braw, Daniel, 'Vision as Revision: Ranke and the Beginning of Modern History', *History and Theory* 46, 2007, pp. 45–60.

Briggs, Julia, *Virginia Woolf: An Inner Life*, London, Harcourt, 2005.

Brittain, Vera, *Testament of Youth: An Autobiographical Study of the Years 1900–1925* [1933], London, Virago, 1978.

Britton, Ronald, *Belief and Imagination: Explorations in Psychoanalysis*, London, Routledge, 1998.

Brogan, Hugh, *Alexis de Tocqueville: A Biography*, London, Profile Books, 2006.

Burns, Robert M. and Rayment-Pickard, Hugh (eds), *Philosophies of History: From Enlightenment to Postmodernity*, Oxford, Blackwell, 2000.

Butterfield, Herbert, *The Historical Novel: An Essay*, Cambridge, Cambridge University Press, 1924.

Byatt, A. S. and Harvey Wood, Harriet (eds), *Memory: An Anthology*, London, Chatto & Windus, 2008.

Capote, Truman, *In Cold Blood*, London, Penguin, 1967.

Carlyle, Thomas, *English and Other Critical Essays*, London, J. M. Dent, 1915.

Carlyle, Thomas, *The Letters and Speeches of Oliver Cromwell*, ed. S. C. Lomas, 3 vols; London, Methuen, 1904.

Carlyle, Thomas, *Past and Present*, [1843], London, Ward, Lock, n.d.

Carlyle, Thomas, *Sartor Resartus* [1836], London, Ward, Lock, n.d.

Carnes, Mark C. (ed.), *Novel History: Historians and Novelists Confront America's Past (and Each Other)*, London, Simon & Schuster, 2001.

Carr, David, 'The Reality of History', in Jörn Rüsen (ed.), *Meaning and Representation in History*, Oxford, Berghahn, 2006, pp. 123–36.

Carr, David, *Time, Narrative, and History*, Bloomington, Indiana University Press, 1986.

Chakrabarty, Dipesh, 'History and the Politics of Recognition', in Keith Jenkins, Sue Morgan and Alun Munslow (eds), *Manifestos for History*, London, Routledge, 2007, pp. 77–87.

Cicero, *Treatise on the Laws*, in *The Political Works of Marcus Tullius Cicero*, trans. Francis Barham, 2 vols; London, Edmund Spettique, 1841.

Collingwood, R. G., *An Autobiography* [1939], Harmondsworth, Penguin, 1944.

Collingwood, R. G., *The Idea of History* [1946], Oxford, Oxford University Press, 1961.

Courtwright, David T., 'Why Oswald Missed: Don DeLillo's *Libra*', in Mark C. Carnes (ed.), *Novel History: Historians and Novelists Confront America's Past (and Each Other)*, London, Simon & Schuster, 2001, pp. 77–91.

Crosby, Christina, *The Ends of History: Victorians and 'The Woman Question'*, London, Routledge, 1991.

Curthoys, Ann and Docker, John, *Is History Fiction?*, Sydney, University of New South Wales, 2006.

Danto, Arthur C., *The Transfiguration of the Commonplace: A Philosophy of Art*, Cambridge, Mass., Harvard University Press, 1981.

Davies, Martin L., *Historics: Why History Dominates Contemporary Society*, London, Routledge, 2006.

Davies, Martin L., *The Prison-House of History*, New York, Routledge, 2009.

Davis, Natalie Zemon, *The Return of Martin Guerre*, Harmondsworth, Penguin, 1985.

DeLillo, Don, 'The Fictional Man', in Mark C. Carnes (ed.), *Novel History: Historians and Novelists Confront America's Past (and Each Other)*, London, Simon & Schuster, 2001, pp. 91–2.

DeLillo, Don, *Libra* [1988], London, Penguin, 1989.

Demos, John, 'Afterword: Notes From, and About, the History/Fiction Borderland', *Rethinking History* 9, 2005, pp. 329–35.

Demos, John, 'Real Lives and Other Fictions: Reconsidering Wallace Stegner's *Angle of Repose*', in Mark C. Carnes (ed.), *Novel History: Historians and Novelists Confront America's Past (and Each Other)*, London, Simon & Schuster, 2001, pp. 132–45.

Dening, Greg, 'Performing Cross-culturally', in Keith Jenkins, Sue Morgan and Alun Munslow (eds), *Manifestos for History*, London, Routledge, 2007, pp. 98–107.

Dickens, Charles, *Hard Times* [1854], ed. David Craig, Harmondsworth, Penguin, 1969.

Dostoevsky, Fyodor, *Crime and Punishment* [1866], trans. David Magarshack, Harmondsworth, Penguin, 1951.

Du Maurier, Daphne, *Rebecca*, London, Victor Gollancz, 1938.

Dunant, Sarah, *In the Company of the Courtesan*, London, Virago, 2007.

Eksteins, Modris, *Walking Since Daybreak: A Story of Eastern Europe, World War II, and the Heart of the Twentieth Century* [1999], London, Macmillan, 2000.

Elam, Diane, *Romancing the Postmodern*, London, Routledge, 1992.

Elias, Amy J., 'Metahistorical Romance, the Historical Sublime, and Dialogic History', *Rethinking History* 9, 2005, pp. 159–72.

Elias, Amy J., *Sublime Desire: History and Post-1960s Fiction*, Baltimore and London, Johns Hopkins, 2001.

Eliot, George, *Daniel Deronda* [1876], ed. Terence Cave, London, Penguin, 1995.

Eliot, George, *Middlemarch* [1871–2], London, Oxford University Press, 1947.

Eliot, T. S., *The Cocktail Party* [1950], London, Faber and Faber, 1958.

Eliot, T. S., 'The Hollow Men', in *Collected Poems, 1909–1962*, London, Faber and Faber, 1963.

Etulain, Richard W., 'Western Fiction and History: A Reconsideration', in Arthur Anthony (ed.), *Critical Essays on Wallace Stegner*, Boston, G. K. Hall, 1982, pp. 146–63.

Evans, Richard J., *In Defence of History*, London, Granta, 1997.

Evans, Richard J., *Telling Lies About Hitler: The Holocaust, History and the David Irving Trial*, London, Verso, 2002.

Foley, Barbara, *Telling the Truth: The Theory and Practice of Documentary Fiction*, Ithaca and London, Cornell University Press, 1986.

Franklin, Bruce, 'Kicking the Denial Syndrome: Tim O'Brien's *In the Lake of the Woods*', in Mark C. Carnes (ed.), *Novel History: Historians and Novelists Confront America's Past (and Each Other)*, London, Simon & Schuster, 2001, pp. 332–43.

Gaskell, Elizabeth, *North and South* [1855], London, Collins, n.d.

Gay, Peter, *Style in History*, London, Jonathan Cape, 1974.

Geoffrey of Monmouth, *The History of the Kings of Britain*, ed. Lewis Thorpe, Harmondsworth, Penguin, 1966.

Gide, André, *The Immoralist* [1902], trans. Dorothy Bussy, Harmondsworth, Penguin, 1960.

Hale J. R. (ed.), *The Evolution of British Historiography*, London, Macmillan, 1967.

Hanning, Robert W., *The Vision of History in Early Britain*, New York and London, Columbia University Press, 1966.

Harlan, David, *The Degradation of American History*, Chicago and London, University of Chicago Press, 1997.

Harlan, David, 'Historical Fiction and Academic History', in Keith Jenkins, Sue Morgan and Alun Munslow (eds), *Manifestos for History*, London, Routledge, 2007, pp. 108–30.

Hattaway, Michael, 'The Shakespearean History Play', in Michael Hattaway (ed.), *The Cambridge Companion to Shakespeare's History Plays*, Cambridge, Cambridge University Press, 2002, pp. 3–24.

Hayward, Rhodri, *Resisting History: Religious Transcendence and the Invention of the Unconscious*, Manchester, Manchester University Press, 2007.

Hegel, G. W. F., *Reason in History: A General Introduction to the Philosophy of History* [1837], trans. Robert S. Hartman, New York, Bobbs-Merrill, 1953.

Hobsbawm, Eric, *Interesting Times: A Twentieth-Century Life*, London, Abacus, 2003.

Holderness, Graham, *Shakespeare: The Histories*, Basingstoke, Macmillan, 2000.

Holton, Robert, *Jarring Witnesses: Modern Fiction and the Representation of History*, Hemel Hempstead, Harvester Wheatsheaf, 1994.

Huizinga, Johan, 'The Task of Cultural History' (1926), in *Men and Ideas: History, the Middle Ages, the Renaissance*, Princeton, Princeton University Press, 1959.

Hutcheon, Linda, *A Poetics of Postmodernism: History, Theory, Fiction*, London, Routledge, 1988.

Huxley, T. H., *Collected Essays*, 9 vols; London, Macmillan, 1893–4.

Ibbett, John, 'The Significance of a Past', in T. Bela and Z. Mazur (eds), *The Legacy of History: English and American Studies and the Significance of the Past*, Krakow, Jagiellonian University Press, 2003, vol. 1, pp. 33–50.

Ibsen, Henrik, *Hedda Gabler* [1890], in *Three Plays*, trans. Una Ellis-Fermor, Harmondsworth, Penguin, 1950.

James, Henry, 'The Art of Fiction', in *The Art of Fiction and Other Essays*, ed. M. Roberts, New York, Oxford University Press, 1948.

Jenkins, Keith, *On 'What is History?': From Carr and Elton to Rorty and White*, London, Routledge, 1995.

Jenkins, Keith, *Refiguring History*, London, Routledge, 2003.

Jenkins, Keith, *Why History? Ethics and Postmodernity*, London, Routledge, 1999.

Jenkins, Keith, Morgan, Sue, and Munslow, Alun (eds), *Manifestos for History*, London, Routledge, 2007.

Kansteiner, Wulf, 'Alternate Worlds and Invented Communities: History and Historical Consciousness in the Age of Interactive Media', in Keith Jenkins, Sue Morgan and Alun Munslow (eds), *Manifestos for History*, London, Routledge, 2007, pp. 131–48.

Kelley, Donald (ed.), *Versions of History from Antiquity to the Enlightenment*, New Haven and London, Yale University Press, 1991.

Kerr, James, *Fiction against History: Scott as Storyteller*, Cambridge, Cambridge University Press, 1989.

Kingsley, Charles, *The Water Babies* [1863], London and Glasgow, Blackie, n.d.

Klein, Kerwin Lee, 'On the Emergence of Memory in Historical Discourse', *Representations* 69, 2000, 127–50.

Kuhn, T. S., *The Structure of Scientific Revolutions*, Chicago and London, University of Chicago, 1962.

LaCapra, Dominick, *History and Memory after Auschwitz*, Ithaca and London, Cornell University Press, 1998.

LaCapra, Dominick, *History in Transit: Experience, Identity, Critical Theory*, Ithaca and London, Cornell University Press, 2004.

LaCapra, Dominick, *History, Politics, and the Novel*, Ithaca and London, Cornell University Press, 1987.

LaCapra, Dominick, 'Resisting Apocalypse and Rethinking History', in Keith Jenkins, Sue Morgan and Alun Munslow (eds), *Manifestos for History*, London, Routledge, 2007, pp. 160–78.

Lawson, Hilary, *Closure: A Story of Everything*, London, Routledge, 2001.

Leavis, F. R., *The Great Tradition*, Harmondsworth, Penguin, 1972.

Le Goff, Jacques, *History and Memory*, trans. Steven Rendall and Elizabeth Claman, New York, Columbia University Press, 1992.

Lepenies, Wolf, *Between Literature and Science: The Rise of Sociology*, Cambridge, Cambridge University Press, 1988.

Lerner, Laurence (ed.), *The Victorians*, London, Methuen, 1978.

Lewis, Wyndham, *Rude Assignment*, London, Hutchinson, 1928.

Lewis, Wyndham, *Self Condemned* [1954], Santa Barbara, Black Sparrow Press, 1983.

Lewis, Wyndham, *Time and Western Man*, London, Chatto & Windus, 1927.

Lewis, Wyndham, *The Writer and the Absolute*, London, Methuen, 1952.

Lindquist, Sven, *A History of Bombing*, trans. Linda Haverty Rugg, London, Granta, 2001.

Lively, Penelope, *According to Mark*, Harmondsworth, Penguin, 1985.

Lively, Penelope, *City of the Mind*, London, Penguin, 1992.

Lively, Penelope, *Cleopatra's Sister*, London, Quality Paperbacks Direct, 1993.

Lively, Penelope, *Moon Tiger*, London, Penguin, 1988.

Lively, Penelope, *Perfect Happiness*, London, Penguin, 1985.

Lively, Penelope, *The Photograph*, London, Penguin, 2004.

Lively, Penelope, *The Road to Lichfield* [1977], Harmondsworth, Penguin, 1983.

Lodge, David, *Author, Author*, London, Penguin, 2005.

Lucian of Samosata, *The Works*, trans. H. W. Fowler and F. G. Fowler, 4 vols; Oxford, Clarendon Press, 1905.

Lukács, Geörg, *The Historical Novel* [1937], trans. Hannah and Stanley Mitchell, Harmondsworth, Penguin, 1969.

Macaulay, Thomas Babington, Review of Hallam's *Constitutional History of England* in *The Edinburgh Review*, 1828; in *Critical and Historical Essays*, ed. A. J. Grieve, 2 vols; London, Dent, 1907.

McHale, Brian, *Postmodernist Fiction*, New York and London, Methuen, 1987.

MacMullen, Ramsay, *Feelings in History*, Claremont, Regina Books, 2003.

McNeill, William H., *The Pursuit of Truth: A Historian's Memoir*, Lexington, University Press of Kentucky, 2005.

Mailer, Norman, *The Armies of the Night: History as a Novel, the Novel as History*, London, Weidenfeld and Nicolson, 1968.

Margalit, Avishai, *Ethics of Memory*, Cambridge, Mass. and London, Harvard University Press, 2002.

Marwick, Arthur, *The New Nature of History: Knowledge, Evidence, Language*, Basingstoke, Palgrave, 2001.

Mendelsohn, Daniel, *The Lost: A Search for Six of Six Million*, London, HarperCollins, 2007.

Mill, John Stuart, *Autobiography* [1873], London, Oxford University Press, 1924.

Mill, John Stuart, 'Carlyle's French Revolution', in *Mill's Essays on Literature and Society*, ed. J. B. Schneewind, London, Collier-Macmillan, 1965.

Mink, Louis O., 'History and Fiction as Modes of Comprehension', in Brian Fay, Eugene O. Golob, and Richard T. Vann (eds), *Historical Understanding*, Ithaca and London, Cornell University Press, 1987, pp. 42–60.

Morrison, Toni, *Beloved*, New York, Plume, 1988.

Munslow, Alun, *Deconstructing History*, London, Routledge, 1997.

Munslow, Alun, *Narrative and History*, Basingstoke, Palgrave Macmillan, 2007.

Nietzsche, Friedrich, *The Birth of Tragedy*, trans. Douglas Smith, Oxford, Oxford University Press, 2000.

Nietzsche, Friedrich, *Ecce Homo*, trans. R. J. Hollingdale, London, Penguin, 1979.

Nietzsche, Friedrich, *Thus Spake Zarathustra*, trans. Walter Kaufmann, Harmondsworth, Penguin, 1978.

Nietzsche, Friedrich, *Untimely Meditations*, ed. Daniel Breazeale, Cambridge, Cambridge University Press, 1997.

Novick, Peter, *The Holocaust and Collective Memory*, London, Bloomsbury, 2000.

Novick, Peter, *That Noble Dream: The 'Objectivity Question' and the American Historical Profession*, Cambridge, Cambridge University Press, 1988.

Nuttall, A. D., *Dead from the Waist Down: Scholars and Scholarship in Literature and the Popular Imagination*, New Haven and London, Yale University Press, 2003.

O'Brien, Tim, *If I Die in a Combat Zone* [1973], London, Flamingo, 1995.

O'Brien, Tim, *In the Lake of the Woods*, London, Penguin, 1995.

O'Brien, Tim, *The Things They Carried* [1990], New York, Broadway Books, 1998.

Orwell, George, *Nineteen Eighty-Four* [1949], Harmondsworth, Penguin, 1954.

Parrish, Timothy, *From the Civil War to the Apocalypse: Postmodern History and American Fiction*, Amherst, University of Massachusetts Press, 2008.

Plutarch, Essay on 'Tranquillity and Contentment', in *Plutarch's Moral Essays*, trans. Philemon Holland, ed. E. H. Blakeney, London, J. M. Dent, c.1911.

Proust, Marcel, *Remembrance of Things Past* [1920–27], trans. C. K. Scott Moncrieff and Terence Kilmartin, 3 vols; London, Penguin, 1983.

Pynchon, Thomas, *V* [1963], London, Picador, 1975.

Rigney, Ann, 'Being an Improper Historian', in Keith Jenkins, Sue Morgan and Alun Munslow (eds), *Manifestos for History*, London, Routledge, 2007, pp. 149–59.

Rigney, Ann, *Imperfect Histories: The Elusive Past and the Legacy of Romantic Historicism*, Ithaca and London, Cornell University Press, 2001.

Roth, Michael S., *The Ironist's Cage: Memory, Trauma, and the Construction of History*, New York, Columbia University Press, 1995.

Rousseau, Jean-Jacques, *Discourse on the Sciences and Arts*, in *The Collected Writings of Rousseau*, ed. Roger D. Masters and Christopher Kelly, Hanover and London, University Press of New England, 1992.

Rousseau, Jean-Jacques, *Émile* [1762], trans. Barbara Foxley, London, J. M. Dent, 1911.

Sampson, R. V., *Tolstoy: The Discovery of Peace*, London, Heinemann, 1973.

Schama, Simon, *Dead Certainties (Unwarranted Speculations)*, London, Granta, 1991.

Scholes, Robert, 'A Talk with Kurt Vonnegut, Jr.', in Jerome Klinkowitz and John Somer (eds), *The Vonnegut Statement*, St Albans, Panther, 1975, pp. 94–119.

Scott, Walter, *Ivanhoe. A Romance, with the Author's Last Notes and Additions*, Paris, Baudry's Foreign Library, 1831.

Sebald, W. G., *On the Natural History of Destruction*, London, Hamish Hamilton, 2003.

Sharpless, F. Parvin, *The Literary Criticism of John Stuart Mill*, The Hague and Paris, Mouton, 1967.

Shaw, Harry E., *Narrating Reality: Austen, Scott, Eliot*, Ithaca, Cornell University Press, 1999.

Sidney, Sir Philip, *An Apologie for Poetrie* [1595], ed. Evelyn S. Shuckburgh, Cambridge, Cambridge University Press, 1891.

Slotkin, Richard, 'Fiction for the Purposes of History', *Rethinking History* 9, 2005, pp. 221–36.

Southgate, Beverley, *What is History For?*, London, Routledge, 2005.

Spencer, Herbert, *Education*, London, Williams & Norgate, 1910.

Stegner, Wallace, *Angle of Repose* [1971], New York, Fawcett Crest, 1972.

Stegner, Wallace and Etulain, Richard W., *Conversations with Wallace Stegner on Western History and Literature*, Salt Lake City, University of Utah, 1983.

Stendhal, *The Charterhouse of Parma* [1839], trans. Margaret R. B. Shaw, Harmondsworth, Penguin, 1958.

Stern, Fritz (ed.), The *Varieties of History from Voltaire to the Present*, New York, Meridian Books, 1956.

Strachey, Lytton, *Eminent Victorians* [1918], London, Chatto & Windus, 1928.

Strachey, Lytton, *Portraits in Miniature and Other Essays*, London, Chatto & Windus, 1933.

Swift, Graham, *Waterland* [1983], London, Picador, 1992.

Taylor, Charles, *Sources of the Self: The Making of Modern Identity*, Cambridge, Cambridge University Press, 1989.

Thompson, Damian, *Counterknowledge: How We Surrendered to Conspiracy Theories, Quack Medicine, Bogus Science and False History*, London, Atlantic Books, 2008.

Thucydides, *History of the Peloponnesian War*, trans. R. Crawley, London, J. M. Dent and Sons, 1910.

Tillotson, Geoffrey, *Thackeray the Novelist* [1954], London, Methuen, 1974.

Tóibín, Colm, *The Master*, London, Picador, 2005.

Tolstoy, Leo, *Anna Karenina* [1877], trans. Louise and Aylmer Maude, Oxford, Oxford University Press, 1995.

Tolstoy, Leo, *The Raid and Other Stories* [1852], trans. Louise and Aylmer Maude, Introduction by P. N. Furbank, Oxford, Oxford University Press, 1982.

Tolstoy, Leo, *War and Peace* [1868, 1869], trans. Louise and Aylmer Maude, London, Oxford University Press, 1941.

Tosh, John, *Why History Matters*, Basingstoke, Palgrave Macmillan, 2008.

Waddington, C. H., *The Scientific Attitude* [1941], London, Hutchinson, 1968.

Walsh, Mary Ellen, '*Angle of Repose* and the Writings of Mary Hallock Foote: A Source Study', in Arthur Anthony (ed.), *Critical Essays on Wallace Stegner*, Boston, G. K. Hall, 1982, pp. 184–209.

White, Hayden, 'Introduction: Historical Fiction, Fictional History, and Historical Reality', *Rethinking History* 9, 2005, pp. 147–57.

White, Hayden, *Metahistory: The Historical Imagination in Nineteenth-Century Europe*, Baltimore, Johns Hopkins, 1973.

White, Hayden, *Tropics of Discourse: Essays in Cultural Criticism*, Baltimore and London, Johns Hopkins, 1978.

White, Hayden, '*War and Peace*: Against Historical Realism', in Q. Edward Wang and Franz L. Fillafer (eds), *The Many Faces of Clio: Cross-cultural Approaches to*

Historiography, Essays in Honor of Georg G. Iggers, New York and Oxford, Berghahn, 2007, pp. 42–58.

Wilkomirski, Binjamin, *Fragments: Memories of a Childhood, 1939–1948*, London, Picador, 1996.

Williams, Raymond, *Culture and Society, 1780–1950*, Harmondsworth, Penguin, 1961.

Wilson, A. N., *Tolstoy*, London, Penguin, 1989.

Woolf, Virginia, *Between the Acts* [1941], London, Granada, 1978.

Woolf, Virginia, *Jacob's Room* [1922], London, Panther, 1976.

Woolf, Virginia, 'The Mark on the Wall', in *A Haunted House* [1944], London, Grafton, 1982.

Woolf, Virginia, *The Waves* [1931], Harmondsworth, Penguin, 1951.

Zaehner, R. C., *Mysticism, Sacred and Profane*, Oxford, Clarendon Press, 1957.

Index